SARAH MELLAND

BUCKET LIST

OVER 10,000 IDEAS TO LIVE LIFE FABULOUSLY

CONTENTS

INTRODUCTION

Have you ever wanted a bucket list but have no idea where to start? It's cumbersome and time-consuming. Well, here is the most conclusive bucket list out there with all the World Heritage Sites listed, all the Michelin-rated restaurants to eat at, over 1,300 movies to view, over 1,000 books to read, random things to do, classes to take.

I have broken it down into easy categories. If for some reason you don't want to do something, just X it off your list or black it out. I don't like beer but I didn't want you to not have that pleasure.

There are things I have missed while doing this bucket list, so I have also left room in each section for you to write down whatever else I may have missed.

Another note is that some things may be repeated throughout as you may want to do ziplining but you don't necessarily get to it when you are traveling to Costa Rica. Another is not being able to try foods in their native land but at least trying it somewhere.

This is also just a checklist, no pictures, no descriptions, just a simple, easy checklist.

TRAVEL

- ☐ Stay in a Real Igloo
- ☐ See a Spectacular Fountain
- ☐ Sleep in a Capsule Hotel
- ☐ Sleep in a Haunted House
- ☐ Sleep on a Houseboat
- ☐ Sleep in a Treehouse
- ☐ Sleep in an Ice Hotel
- ☐ Sleep in an Overnight Train
- ☐ Stay at a Bed & Breakfast
- ☐ Stay at a Dude Ranch
- ☐ Stay in an Underwater Hotel
- ☐ Step Foot in all 7 Continents
- ☐ Take a Train Cross Country
- ☐ Take a Trip with your Parents
- ☐ Throw a Dart at a Map and Go
- ☐ Touch a Pyramid
- ☐ Tour a Factory
- ☐ Tour a Mission
- ☐ Tour a Vineyard
- ☐ Tour a Working Farm
- ☐ Travel Internationally
- ☐ Vacation Solo
- ☐ Vacation with a Stranger
- ☐ Visit a Butterfly Sanctuary
- ☐ Visit a Castle and/or Sleep in One
- ☐ Visit a Ghost Town
- ☐ Visit a Temple
- ☐ Celebrate a Holiday in a Different Country
- ☐ Climb to the Top of a Lighthouse
- ☐ Explore a Rain Forest
- ☐ Go on a Spontaneous Road Trip
- ☐ Go to an Aquarium
- ☐ Couch surf
- ☐ Camp in the middle of nowhere
- ☐ Sleep in the rainforest
- ☐ Spend a day on a deserted island
- ☐ Fly first class
- ☐ Fly on a private jet
- ☐ See the Northern Light (Aurora Borealis)
- ☐ Go north of the Arctic Circle
- ☐ Go to the airport and pick a random flight
- ☐ Go on a cruise
- ☐ Stay in a 5-Star Hotel
- ☐ Stay in a Hostel

- ☐ Experience a Beautiful Sunset
- ☐ Sleep in a Teepee
- ☐ Swim in Every Ocean in the World
  - ☐ Pacific
  - ☐ Atlantic
  - ☐ Indian
  - ☐ Arctic
  - ☐ Black Sea
  - ☐ Caspian
  - ☐ Baltic Sea
  - ☐ Mediterranean Sea
  - ☐ North Sea
  - ☐ Persian Gulf
  - ☐ Red Sea
  - ☐ Bay of Bengal
- ☐ Go on a Backpacking Trip
- ☐ Stay in a Ryokan
- ☐ Stay in a Capsule Hotel
- ☐ Stay in a Zoo Hotel
- ☐ Trek on an Ice Glacier
- ☐ Get Face-to-Face with Molten Lava
- ☐ Go on a Cross-Country Motorcycle Trip
- ☐ Stay in a Space Hotel
- ☐ Fly in Etihad Airways Residence Suite
- ☐ Travel on Virgin Galactic
- ☐ Fill up a Passport of Stamps
- ☐ Live Permanently in at least One Different Country
- ☐ Live Abroad for at least One Year
- ☐ Fly Emirates
- ☐ Time Travel to Experience New Year's Eve Twice
- ☐ See a Blowhole
- ☐ Ride a "360 Boat"
- ☐ Ride through the Desert in a Dune Buggy
- ☐ Surf a Sand Dune
- ☐ Shower in a Waterfall
- ☐ Stay in a Floating Pool Bed
- ☐ Sleep at a Jjimjilbang
- ☐ Walk on a Nude Beach
- ☐ Live on a Boat
- ☐ Travel the USA in an RV
- ☐ Ride on a Major Ski Lift in the Alps
- ☐ Take a Trip on a Glass Bottom Boat
- ☐ Celebrate Christmas in a Warm Climate
- ☐ Be a Tourist in Your Own Town
- ☐ Sit in an Outdoor Hot Tub in Winter
- ☐ Air Boat Across an Alligator Infested Swamp
- ☐ Arrive by Seaplane
- ☐ Walk a Suspension Bridge
- ☐ Sleep in a Stable in a Haystack
- ☐ Sleep in a Yurt
- ☐ Swim in the Ocean
- ☐ Swim in an Aquarium

- ☐ Swim with a School of Fish
- ☐ Swim with Sea Turtles
- ☐ Walk on a Black Sand Beach
- ☐ Visit Your Childhood Home
- ☐ Attend a Wedding in a Different Country
- ☐ Sit Front Row at a Fashion Show
- ☐ Order Room Service
- ☐ Stay at an All-Inclusive Resort
- ☐ Experience Amish Country
- ☐ Smoke a Hookah at a Hookah Bar
- ☐ _____
- ☐ _____
- ☐ _____
- ☐ _____
- ☐ _____
- ☐ _____
- ☐ _____
- ☐ _____
- ☐ _____
- ☐ _____
- ☐ _____
- ☐ _____
- ☐ _____
- ☐ _____

- ☐ _____
- ☐ _____
- ☐ _____
- ☐ _____
- ☐ _____
- ☐ _____
- ☐ _____
- ☐ _____
- ☐ _____
- ☐ _____
- ☐ _____
- ☐ _____
- ☐ _____
- ☐ _____
- ☐ _____
- ☐ _____
- ☐ _____
- ☐ _____
- ☐ _____
- ☐ _____
- ☐ _____

AFRICA BUCKET LIST

- ☐ Scuba dive in the Red Sea | Africa/Asia
- ☐ Safari
- ☐ Sail the Nile
- ☐ Dance with an African tribe

- ☐ **ALGERIA**
  - ☐ WORLD HERITAGE LIST
    - ☐ Al Qal'a of Beni Hammad
    - ☐ Djémila
    - ☐ M'Zab Valley
    - ☐ Tassili n'Ajjer
    - ☐ Timgad
    - ☐ Tipasa
    - ☐ Kasbah of Algiers
- ☐ **ANGOLA**
  - ☐ WORLD HERITAGE LIST
    - ☐ Mbanza Kongo, Vestiges of the Capital of the former Kingdom of Kongo
- ☐ **BENIN**
  - ☐ WORLD HERITAGE LIST
    - ☐ Royal Palaces of Abomey
    - ☐ W-Arly-Pendjari Complex
- ☐ **BOTSWANA**
  - ☐ WORLD HERITAGE LIST
    - ☐ Tsodilo
    - ☐ Okavango Delta
- ☐ **BURKINA FASO**
  - ☐ WORLD HERITAGE LIST
    - ☐ W-Arly-Pendjari Complex
    - ☐ Ruins of Loropéni
    - ☐ Ancient Ferrous Metallurgy Sites of Burkina Faso
- ☐ **BURUNDI**

- ☐ **CAMEROON**
  - ☐ WORLD HERITAGE LIST
    - ☐ Dja Faunal Reserve
    - ☐ Sangha Trinational
- ☐ **CAPE VERDE**
  - ☐ WORLD HERITAGE LIST
    - ☐ Cidade Velha, Historic Centre of Ribeira Grande
- ☐ **CENTRAL AFRICA REPUBLIC**
  - ☐ WORLD HERITAGE LIST
    - ☐ Manovo-Gounda St Floris National Park
    - ☐ Sangha Trinational
- ☐ **CHAD**
  - ☐ WORLD HERITAGE LIST
    - ☐ Lakes of Ounianga
    - ☐ Ennedi Massif: Natural and Cultural Landscape
- ☐ **COMOROS**
- ☐ **CÔTE D'IVOIRE**
    - ☐ Mount Nimba Strict Nature Reserve
    - ☐ Taï National Park
    - ☐ Comoé National Park
    - ☐ Historic Town of Grand-Bassam
    - ☐ Sudanese style mosques in northern Côte d'Ivoire
- ☐ **DJIBOUTI**
- ☐ **DEMOCRATIC REPUBLIC OF THE CONGO**
  - ☐ WORLD HERITAGE LIST
    - ☐ Virunga National Park
    - ☐ Kahuzi-Biega National Park
    - ☐ Garamba National Park
    - ☐ Salonga National Park
    - ☐ Okapi Wildlife Reserve
- ☐ **EGYPT**
    - ☐ The Great Pyramids
    - ☐ Catacombs of Kom el Shoqafa | Alexandria
    - ☐ Cairo Citadel
    - ☐ The Valley of the Kings
    - ☐ The Great Sphinx
    - ☐ White Desert National Park
    - ☐ Amun Temple Enclosure
    - ☐ Temple of Horus

☐ Great Temple of Ramses II
☐ MUSUEMS
  ☐ Royal Jewelry Museum | Alexandria
  ☐ The Egyptian Museum | Cairo
  ☐ Luxor Museum | Luxor
☐ FOOD/DRINK
  ☐ Eat Molokhia
☐ WORLD HERITAGE LIST
  ☐ Abu Mena
  ☐ Ancient Thebes with its Necropolis
  ☐ Historic Cairo
  ☐ Memphis and its Necropolis – the Pyramid Fields from Giza to Dahshur
  ☐ Nubian Monuments from Abu Simbel to Philae
  ☐ Saint Catherine Area
  ☐ Wadi Al-Hitan (Whale Valley)

☐ **EQUATORIAL GUINEA**
☐ **ERITREA**
  ☐ WORLD HERITAGE LIST
    ☐ Asmara: A Modernist African City
☐ **ESWATINI**
☐ **ETHIOPIA**
  ☐ HIKES
    ☐ Simien Mountain National Park, Ethiopia
  ☐ MUSEUMS
    ☐ National Museum of Ethiopia (Addis Ababa, Ethiopia)
  ☐ FOOD/DRINK
    ☐ Eat Ethiopian food with your hand
  ☐ WORLD HERITAGE LIST
    ☐ Rock-Hewn Churches, Lalibela
    ☐ Simien National Park
    ☐ Fasil Ghebbi, Gondar Region
    ☐ Aksum
    ☐ Lower Valley of the Awash
    ☐ Lower Valley of the Omo
    ☐ Tiya
    ☐ Harar Jugol, the Fortified Historic Town
    ☐ Konso Cultural Landscape

- ☐ **GABON**
  - ☐ WORLD HERITAGE LIST
    - ☐ Ecosystem and Relict Cultural Landscape of Lopé-Okanda
    - ☐ Ivindo National Park
- ☐ **GAMBIA**
  - ☐ WORLD HERITAGE LIST
    - ☐ Kunta Kinteh Island and Related Sites .
    - ☐ Stone Circles of Senegambia
- ☐ **GHANA**
  - ☐ WORLD HERITAGE LIST
    - ☐ Forts and Castles, Volta, Greater Accra, Central and Western Regions
    - ☐ Asante Traditional Buildings
- ☐ **GUINEA**
  - ☐ WORLD HERITAGE LIST
    - ☐ Mount Nimba Strict Nature Reserve
- ☐ **GUINEA BISSAU**
- ☐ **IVORY COAST**
- ☐ **KENYA**
  - ☐ Live with the Maasai
  - ☐ Climb Mount Kilimanjaro | Best in March, Kenya/Tanzania
  - ☐ Serengeti Safari during the Great Wildebeest Migration | Kenya/Tanzania
  - ☐ Giraffe Manor
  - ☐ MUSEUMS
    - ☐ Nairobi National Museum | Nairobi
  - ☐ WORLD HERITAGE LIST
    - ☐ Lake Turkana National Parks
    - ☐ Mount Kenya National Park/Natural Forest
    - ☐ Lamu Old Town
    - ☐ Sacred Mijikenda Kaya Forests
    - ☐ Fort Jesus, Mombasa
    - ☐ Kenya Lake System in the Great Rift Valley
    - ☐ Thimlich Ohinga Archaeological Site
- ☐ **LESOTHO**
  - ☐ WORLD HERITAGE LIST
    - ☐ Maloti-Drakensberg Park
- ☐ **LIBERIA**

- ☐ **LIBYA**
  - ☐ MUSEUMS
    - ☐ Red Castle Museum | Tripoli
  - ☐ WORLD HERITAGE LIST
    - ☐ Archaeological Site of Cyrene
    - ☐ Archaeological Site of Leptis Magna
    - ☐ Archaeological Site of Sabratha
    - ☐ Rock-Art Sites of Tadrart Acacus
    - ☐ Old Town of Ghadamès
- ☐ **MADAGASCAR**
  - ☐ Walk the Avenue of Baobabs
  - ☐ FUNNY NAMES TO VISIT
    - ☐ Gogogogo
  - ☐ WORLD HERITAGE LIST
    - ☐ Tsingy de Bemaraha Strict Nature Reserve
    - ☐ Royal Hill of Ambohimanga
    - ☐ Rainforests of the Atsinanana
- ☐ **MALAWI**
  - ☐ WORLD HERITAGE LIST
    - ☐ Lake Malawi National Park
    - ☐ Chongoni Rock-Art Area
- ☐ **MALI**
  - ☐ Hike Pays Dogon, Mali
  - ☐ WORLD HERITAGE LIST
    - ☐ Old Towns of Djenné
    - ☐ Timbuktu
    - ☐ Cliff of Bandiagara (Land of the Dogons)
    - ☐ Tomb of Askia
- ☐ **MAURITANIA**
  - ☐ WORLD HERITAGE LIST
    - ☐ Banc d'Arguin National Park
    - ☐ Ancient *Ksour* of Ouadane, Chinguetti, Tichitt and Oualata
- ☐ **MAURITIUS**
  - ☐ The Seven Colored Earths
  - ☐ MUSEUMS
    - ☐ Blue Penny Museum | Port Louis
  - ☐ WORLD HERITAGE LIST
    - ☐ Aapravasi Ghat
    - ☐ Le Morne Cultural Landscape

9

- ☐ **MAYOTTE**
- ☐ **MOROCCO**
    - ☐ GARDENS
        - ☐ Jardin Majorelle, Marrakech garden
    - ☐ MUSEUMS
        - ☐ Photography Museum of Marrakech (Marrakech, Morocco)
    - ☐ WORLD HERITAGE LIST
        - ☐ Medina of Fez
        - ☐ Medina of Marrakesh
        - ☐ Ksar of Ait-Ben-Haddou
        - ☐ Historic City of Meknes
        - ☐ Archaeological Site of Volubilis
        - ☐ Medina of Tétouan (formerly known as Titawin)
        - ☐ Medina of Essaouira (formerly Mogador)
        - ☐ Portuguese City of Mazagan (El Jadida)
        - ☐ Rabat, Modern Capital and Historic City: a Shared Heritage
- ☐ **MOZAMBIQUE**
    - ☐ WORLD HERITAGE LIST
        - ☐ Island of Mozambique
- ☐ **NAMIBIA**
    - ☐ See the Wind Cathedral
    - ☐ WORLD HERITAGE LIST
        - ☐ Twyfelfontein or /Ui-//aes
        - ☐ Namib Sand Sea
- ☐ **NIGER**
    - ☐ WORLD HERITAGE LIST
        - ☐ Air and Ténéré Natural Reserves
        - ☐ W-Arly-Pendjari Complex
        - ☐ Historic Centre of Agadez
- ☐ **NIGERIA**
    - ☐ WORLD HERITAGE LIST
        - ☐ Sukur Cultural Landscape
        - ☐ Osun-Osogbo Sacred Grove
- ☐ **REPUBLIC OF THE CONGO**
- ☐ **REUNION**
- ☐ **RWANDA**
- ☐ **SAINT HELENA**
- ☐ **SAO TOME AND PRINCIPE**

☐ **SENEGAL**
    ☐ Take a bath in the pink Lake Retba
  ☐ MUSEUMS
    ☐ House of Slaves | Dakar
  ☐ WORLD HERITAGE SITES
    ☐ Island of Gorée
    ☐ Niokolo-Koba National Park
    ☐ Djoudj National Bird Sanctuary
    ☐ Island of Saint-Louis
    ☐ Stone Circles of Senegambia
    ☐ Saloum Delta
    ☐ Bassari Country: Bassari, Fula and Bedik Cultural Landscapes

☐ **SEYCHELLES**
  ☐ WORLD HERITAGE LIST
    ☐ Aldabra Atoll
    ☐ Vallée de Mai Nature Reserve

☐ **SIERRA LEONE**

☐ **SOMALIA**

☐ **SOUTH AFRICA**
    ☐ Cape Town
    ☐ Jacarandas in Cullinan
    ☐ Kirstenbosch National Botanical Garden, Cape Town
  ☐ HIKES
    ☐ Table Mountain
    ☐ North Drakensberg Traverse, South Africa
    ☐ Otter Trail, South Africa
  ☐ MUSEUMS
    ☐ Apartheid Museum | Johannesburg
    ☐ Origins Centre Museum | Johannesburg
    ☐ Iziko South African Museum | Cape Town
    ☐ Robben Island Museum | Cape Town
  ☐ FOOD/DRINK
    ☐ Biltong
  ☐ WORLD HERITAGE LIST
    ☐ Fossil Hominid Sites of South Africa
    ☐ iSimangaliso Wetland Park
    ☐ Robben Island
    ☐ Maloti-Drakensberg Park

- ☐ Mapungubwe Cultural Landscape
- ☐ Cape Floral Region Protected Areas
- ☐ Vredefort Dome
- ☐ Richtersveld Cultural and Botanical Landscape
- ☐ ‡Khomani Cultural Landscape
- ☐ Barberton Makhonjwa Mountains

☐ **SOUTH SUDAN**

☐ **SUDAN**
- ☐ WORLD HERITAGE LIST
  - ☐ Gebel Barkal and the Sites of the Napatan Region
  - ☐ Archaeological Sites of the Island of Meroe
  - ☐ Sanganeb Marine National Park and Dungonab Bay – Mukkawar Island Marine National Park

☐ **TANZANIA**
- ☐ Stay at the Four Seasons Safari Lodge Serengeti
- ☐ Ngorongoro Crater
- ☐ WORLD HERITAGE LIST
  - ☐ Ngorongoro Conservation Area
  - ☐ Ruins of Kilwa Kisiwani and Ruins of Songo Mnara
  - ☐ Serengeti National Park
  - ☐ Selous Game Reserve
  - ☐ Kilimanjaro National Park
  - ☐ Stone Town of Zanzibar
  - ☐ Kondoa Rock-Art Sites

☐ **TOGO**
- ☐ WORLD HERITAGE LIST
  - ☐ Koutammakou, the Land of the Batammariba

☐ **TUNISIA**
- ☐ WORLD HERITAGE LIST
  - ☐ Amphitheatre of El Jem
  - ☐ Archaeological Site of Carthage
  - ☐ Medina of Tunis
  - ☐ Ichkeul National Park
  - ☐ Punic Town of Kerkuane and its Necropolis
  - ☐ Kairouan
  - ☐ Medina of Sousse
  - ☐ Dougga / Thugga

☐ **UGANDA**
  ☐ WORLD HERITAGE LIST
    ☐ Bwindi Impenetrable National Park
    ☐ Rwenzori Mountains National Park
    ☐ Tombs of Buganda Kings at Kasubi
☐ **WESTERN SAHARA**
☐ **ZAMBIA**
    ☐ Victoria Falls and or shower in Victoria Falls | Zambia/Zimbabwe
    ☐ Swim in Devil's Pool in Victoria Falls | Zambia/Zimbabwe
  ☐ WORLD HERITAGE LIST
    ☐ Mosi-oa-Tunya / Victoria Falls
☐ **ZIMBABWE**
  ☐ WORLD HERITAGE LIST
    ☐ Mana Pools National Park, Sapi and Chewore Safari Areas
    ☐ Great Zimbabwe National Monument
    ☐ Khami Ruins National Monument
    ☐ Mosi-oa-Tunya / Victoria Falls
    ☐ Matobo Hills

☐ _____
☐ _____
☐ _____
☐ _____
☐ _____
☐ _____
☐ _____
☐ _____
☐ _____

ANTARCTICA BUCKET LIST

- ☐ Take a zodiac ride among the icebergs and swim in the Southern Ocean
- ☐ Interact with Penguins
- ☐ Explore the icy waters in a Kayak
- ☐ Swim at Deception Bay
- ☐ Learn the history of Whaling and Science at Deception Island
- ☐ Whale Watching
- ☐ Stop at the bar at Vernadsky Research Base
- ☐ Visit the British Research Station Museum – Post Office
- ☐ Cross the Drake Passage
- ☐ Climb Mount Vinson
- ☐ Trek to the South Pole

☐ EVENTS/FESTIVALS
  - ☐ Polar Plunge

☐ _____

☐ _____

☐ _____

☐ _____

☐ _____

☐ _____

☐ _____

☐ _____

☐ _____

ASIA BUCKET LIST

☐ Swim from Asia to Europe over the Bosporus strait

☐ **AFGHANISTAN**
    ☐ WORLD HERITAGE SITES
        ☐ Minaret and Archaeological Remains of Jam
        ☐ Cultural Landscape and Archaeological Remains of the Bamiyan Valley

☐ **ARMENIA**
    ☐ WORLD HERITAGE SITES
        ☐ Monasteries of Haghpat and Sanahin
        ☐ Cathedral and Churches of Echmiatsin and the Archaeological Site of Zvartnots
        ☐ Monastery of Geghard and the Upper Azat Valley

☐ **AZERBAIJAN**
    ☐ WORLD HERITAGE SITES
        ☐ Walled City of Baku with the Shirvanshah's Palace and Maiden Tower
        ☐ Gobustan Rock Art Cultural Landscape
        ☐ Historic Centre of Sheki with the Khan's Palace

☐ **BAHRAIN**
    ☐ WORLD HERITAGE SITES
        ☐ Qal'at al-Bahrain – Ancient Harbour and Capital of Dilmun
        ☐ Pearling, Testimony of an Island Economy
        ☐ Dilmun Burial Mounds

☐ **BANGLADESH**
    ☐ WORLD HERITAGE SITES
        ☐ Historic Mosque City of Bagerhat
        ☐ Ruins of the Buddhist Vihara at Paharpur
        ☐ The Sundarbans

☐ **BHUTAN**
☐ **BRUNEL**

☐ **CAMBODIA**
- ☐ Angkor Wat
- ☐ Sail up the Mekong River
- ☐ MUSEUMS
  - ☐ Tuol Sleng Genocide Museum | Phnom Penh
- ☐ FOOD/DRINKS
  - ☐ Eat prahok & amok
- ☐ WORLD HERITAGE LIST
  - ☐ Angkor
  - ☐ Temple of Preah Vihear
  - ☐ Temple Zone of Sambor Prei Kuk, Archaeological Site of Ancient Ishanapura

☐ **CHINA**
- ☐ Climb "The heavenly Stairs" | Mount Hua
- ☐ See the Pudong skyline and the Oriental Pearl Tower | Shanghai
- ☐ Porcelain Tower of Nanjing
- ☐ Forbidden City
- ☐ Rice Field Terraces
- ☐ Hallelujah Avatar Mountain | Zhangjiajie National Park
- ☐ Terra Cotta Warriors | Xi'an
- ☐ Hanging Temple in Mount Hengshan
- ☐ Walk of Faith, Tianmen Mountain AKA Heaven's Gate
- ☐ Yangtze River
- ☐ Humble Administrator's Garden
- ☐ MUSEUMS
  - ☐ The Forbidden City Museum | Beijing
  - ☐ The National Museum of China | Beijing
  - ☐ UCCA Center for Contemporary Art
  - ☐ The Museum of Qin Terra-Cotta Warriors | Xi'an
  - ☐ The Shanghai Museum | Shanghai
  - ☐ West Bund Museum | Shanghai
  - ☐ Nanjing Massacre Memorial Hall | Nanjing
- ☐ FESTIVALS/CELEBRATIONS
  - ☐ Celebrate the Chinese New Year in China, around the end of January during the new moon

16

☐ Attend the Harbin Ice & Snow Festival, from late December to February

☐ FOOD/DRINK

- ☐ Xiaolongbao
- ☐ candied crabapples
- ☐ Peking Duck in Beijing
- ☐ Lychee
- ☐ Kumquats Durian

☐ RESTAURANTS

- ☐ Dine at Sanyou Cave Hanging Cliff Restaurant | Fangweng

☐ WORLD HERITAGE LIST

- ☐ Imperial Palaces of the Ming and Qing Dynasties in Beijing and Shenyang
- ☐ Mausoleum of the First Qin Emperor
- ☐ Mogao Caves
- ☐ Mount Taishan
- ☐ Peking Man Site at Zhoukoudian
- ☐ The Great Wall
- ☐ Mount Huangshan
- ☐ Huanglong Scenic and Historic Interest Area
- ☐ Jiuzhaigou Valley Scenic and Historic Interest Area
- ☐ Wulingyuan Scenic and Historic Interest Area
- ☐ Ancient Building Complex in the Wudang Mountains
- ☐ Historic Ensemble of the Potala Palace, Lhasa
- ☐ Mountain Resort and its Outlying Temples, Chengde
- ☐ Temple and Cemetery of Confucius and the Kong Family Mansion in Qufu
- ☐ Lushan National Park
- ☐ Mount Emei Scenic Area, including Leshan Giant Buddha Scenic Area
- ☐ Ancient City of Ping Yao
- ☐ Classical Gardens of Suzhou
- ☐ Old Town of Lijiang
- ☐ Summer Palace, an Imperial Garden in Beijing
- ☐ Temple of Heaven: an Imperial Sacrificial Altar in Beijing

- ☐ Dazu Rock Carvings
- ☐ Mount Wuyi
- ☐ Ancient Villages in Southern Anhui – Xidi and Hongcun
- ☐ Imperial Tombs of the Ming and Qing Dynasties
- ☐ Longmen Grottoes
- ☐ Mount Qingcheng and the Dujiangyan Irrigation System
- ☐ Yungang Grottoes
- ☐ Three Parallel Rivers of Yunnan Protected Areas
- ☐ Capital Cities and Tombs of the Ancient Koguryo Kingdom
- ☐ Historic Centre of Macao
- ☐ Sichuan Giant Panda Sanctuaries - Wolong, Mt Siguniang and Jiajin Mountains
- ☐ Yin Xu
- ☐ Kaiping Diaolou and Villages
- ☐ South China Karst
- ☐ Fujian *Tulou*
- ☐ Mount Sanqingshan National Park
- ☐ Mount Wutai
- ☐ China Danxia
- ☐ Historic Monuments of Dengfeng in "The Centre of Heaven and Earth"
- ☐ West Lake Cultural Landscape of Hangzhou
- ☐ Chengjiang Fossil Site
- ☐ Site of Xanadu
- ☐ Cultural Landscape of Honghe Hani Rice Terraces
- ☐ Xinjiang Tianshan
- ☐ Silk Roads: the Routes Network of Chang'an-Tianshan Corridor *
- ☐ The Grand Canal
- ☐ Tusi Sites
- ☐ Hubei Shennongjia
- ☐ Zuojiang Huashan Rock Art Cultural Landscape
- ☐ Kulangsu, a Historic International Settlement
- ☐ Qinghai Hoh Xil
- ☐ Fanjingshan
- ☐ Archaeological Ruins of Liangzhu City

- ☐ Migratory Bird Sanctuaries along the Coast of Yellow Sea-Bohai Gulf of China (Phase I)
- ☐ Quanzhou: Emporium of the World in Song-Yuan China

☐ **CYPRUS**
- ☐ WORLD HERITAGE SITES
  - ☐ Paphos
  - ☐ Painted Churches in the Troodos Region
  - ☐ Choirokoitia

☐ **GEORGIA**
- ☐ WORLD HERITAGE SITES
  - ☐ Gelati Monastery
  - ☐ Historical Monuments of Mtskheta
  - ☐ Upper Svaneti
  - ☐ Colchic Rainforests and Wetlands

☐ **HONG KONG**
  - ☐ Sail on a junk boat in the Hong Kong harbor
  - ☐ See and/or climb the Tin Tian, Big Buddha
  - ☐ Experience the symphony of lights on the Star Ferry
- ☐ MUSEUMS
  - ☐ The Hong Kong Museum of History
  - ☐ Hong Kong Museum of Art
- ☐ FOOD
  - ☐ Smelly tofu

☐ **INDIA**
  - ☐ Travel through India by train
  - ☐ Drive a Rickshaw (perhaps participate in the Rickshaw Run)
  - ☐ Get a Henna tattoo
- ☐ MUSEUMS
  - ☐ National Museum of India | New Delhi
  - ☐ Sulabh International Museum of Toilets | New Delhi
  - ☐ The Indian Museum | Calcutta
  - ☐ Salar Jung Museum | Hyderabad
  - ☐ Chhatrapati Shivaji Maharaj Vastu Sangrahalaya | Mumbai

- ☐ FESTIVALS
    - ☐ Take part in the Holi Festival, in the spring time around march
    - ☐ Elephant Festival (Same time as Holi festival)
- ☐ FOOD
    - ☐ Tandoori Chicken
    - ☐ curry & Tikka Masala
    - ☐ Jackfruit
- ☐ WORLD HERITAGE LIST
    - ☐ Agra Fort
    - ☐ Ajanta Caves
    - ☐ Ellora Caves
    - ☐ Taj Mahal
    - ☐ Group of Monuments at Mahabalipuram
    - ☐ Sun Temple, Konârak
    - ☐ Kaziranga National Park
    - ☐ Keoladeo National Park
    - ☐ Manas Wildlife Sanctuary
    - ☐ Churches and Convents of Goa
    - ☐ Fatehpur Sikri
    - ☐ Group of Monuments at Hampi
    - ☐ Khajuraho Group of Monuments
    - ☐ Elephanta Caves
    - ☐ Great Living Chola Temples
    - ☐ Group of Monuments at Pattadakal
    - ☐ Sundarbans National Park
    - ☐ Nanda Devi and Valley of Flowers National Parks
    - ☐ Buddhist Monuments at Sanchi
    - ☐ Humayun's Tomb, Delhi
    - ☐ Qutb Minar and its Monuments, Delhi
    - ☐ Mountain Railways of India
    - ☐ Mahabodhi Temple Complex at Bodh Gaya
    - ☐ Rock Shelters of Bhimbetka
    - ☐ Champaner-Pavagadh Archaeological Park
    - ☐ Chhatrapati Shivaji Terminus (formerly Victoria Terminus)
    - ☐ Red Fort Complex
    - ☐ The Jantar Mantar, Jaipur
    - ☐ Western Ghats

- ☐ Hill Forts of Rajasthan
- ☐ Great Himalayan National Park Conservation Area
- ☐ Rani-ki-Vav (the Queen's Stepwell) at Patan, Gujarat
- ☐ Archaeological Site of Nalanda Mahavihara at Nalanda, Bihar
- ☐ Khangchendzonga National Park
- ☐ The Architectural Work of Le Corbusier, an Outstanding Contribution to the Modern Movement
- ☐ Historic City of Ahmadabad
- ☐ Victorian Gothic and Art Deco Ensembles of Mumbai
- ☐ Jaipur City, Rajasthan
- ☐ Dholavira: a Harappan City
- ☐ Kakatiya Rudreshwara (Ramappa) Temple | Telangana

☐ **INDONESIA**

- ☐ Cultural Landscape of Bali
- ☐ Taman Ayun Temple
- ☐ Walk through a Rice Terrace

☐ MUSEUMS

- ☐ Ullen Sentalu Museum | Yogyakarta

☐ FOOD/DRINKS

- ☐ Kopi Luwak Coffee
- ☐ Starfruit

☐ WORLD HERITAGE LIST

- ☐ Borobudur Temple Compounds
- ☐ Komodo National Park
- ☐ Prambanan Temple Compounds
- ☐ Ujung Kulon National Park
- ☐ Sangiran Early Man Site
- ☐ Lorentz National Park
- ☐ Tropical Rainforest Heritage of Sumatra
- ☐ Cultural Landscape of Bali Province: the *Subak* System as a Manifestation of the *Tri Hita Karana* Philosophy
- ☐ Ombilin Coal Mining Heritage of Sawahlunto

- ☐ **IRAN**
  - ☐ MUSEUMS
    - ☐ Astan Quds Razavi Central Museum | Mashhad
  - ☐ WORLD HERITAGE LIST
    - ☐ Meidan Emam, Esfahan
    - ☐ Persepolis
    - ☐ Tchogha Zanbil
    - ☐ Takht-e Soleyman
    - ☐ Bam and its Cultural Landscape
    - ☐ Pasargadae
    - ☐ Soltaniyeh
    - ☐ Bisotun
    - ☐ Armenian Monastic Ensembles of Iran
    - ☐ Shushtar Historical Hydraulic System
    - ☐ Sheikh Safi al-din Khānegāh and Shrine Ensemble in Ardabil
    - ☐ Tabriz Historic Bazaar Complex
    - ☐ The Persian Garden
    - ☐ Gonbad-e Qābus
    - ☐ Masjed-e Jāmé of Isfahan
    - ☐ Golestan Palace
    - ☐ Shahr-i Sokhta
    - ☐ Cultural Landscape of Maymand
    - ☐ Susa
    - ☐ Lut Desert
    - ☐ The Persian Qanat
    - ☐ Historic City of Yazd
    - ☐ Sassanid Archaeological Landscape of Fars Region
    - ☐ Hyrcanian Forests
    - ☐ Cultural Landscape of Hawraman/Uramanat
    - ☐ Trans-Iranian Railway
- ☐ **IRAQ**
  - ☐ WORLD HERITAGE LIST
    - ☐ Hatra
    - ☐ Ashur (Qal'at Sherqat)
    - ☐ Samarra Archaeological City
    - ☐ Erbil Citadel

22

- ☐ The Ahwar of Southern Iraq: Refuge of Biodiversity and the Relict Landscape of the Mesopotamian Cities
- ☐ Babylon

☐ ISRAEL

- ☐ Tour the Holy Sites
- ☐ Float in the Dead Sea | Israel/Jordan

☐ HIKES

- ☐ Israel National Trail, Israel

☐ MUSEUM

- ☐ Israel Museum | Jerusalem
- ☐ Yad Vashem Holocaust Memorial & Museum | Jerusalem

☐ WORLD HERITAGE LIST

- ☐ Masada
- ☐ Old City of Acre
- ☐ White City of Tel-Aviv – the Modern Movement
- ☐ Biblical Tels - Megiddo, Hazor, Beer Sheba
- ☐ Incense Route - Desert Cities in the Negev
- ☐ Bahá'i Holy Places in Haifa and the Western Galilee
- ☐ Sites of Human Evolution at Mount Carmel: The Nahal Me'arot / Wadi el-Mughara Caves
- ☐ Caves of Maresha and Bet-Guvrin in the Judean Lowlands as a Microcosm of the Land of the Caves
- ☐ Necropolis of Bet She'arim: A Landmark of Jewish Renewal
- ☐ Old City of Jerusalem and its Walls

☐ JAPAN

- ☐ Tokyo Tower
- ☐ Win at Pachinko
- ☐ Climb Mount Fuji
- ☐ Sensoji (Asakusa Kannon Temple) | Tokyo
- ☐ Take pictures in a Japanese/Korean photo booth | Japan/South Korea
- ☐ Cross the famous Shibuya-intersection
- ☐ Osaka
- ☐ Jigokudani Monkey Park
- ☐ Watch a Geisha dance and/or dress up as one

- ☐ Sing Karaoke
- ☐ Wear an authentic kimono
- ☐ Attend a traditional tea ceremony
- ☐ Do a Japanese spa/bath
- ☐ See a Sumo Wrestling match
- ☐ Stroll Through Sagano Bamboo Forest
- ☐ Walk around in a crowded area wearing a "Where's Waldo" costume (e.g., Shibuya, Japan)
- ☐ Tour the Japanese Gardens in Kyoto
- ☐ Walk Through the Wisteria Tunnel at Kawachi Fuji Gardens, in Kitakyushu
- ☐ See the 144-Year-Old Wisteria tree
- ☐ Kenroku-en, Kanasawa gardens
- ☐ MUSEUMS
  - ☐ Nagasaki Atomic Bomb Museum | Nagasaki
  - ☐ Dejima Open-Air Museum | Nagasaki
  - ☐ Hiroshima Peace Memorial Museum | Hiroshima
  - ☐ Momofuku Ando Instant Ramen Museum | Ikeda
  - ☐ Tokugawa Art Museum | Nagoya
  - ☐ Ghibli Museum | Tokyo
  - ☐ Tokyo National Museum | Tokyo
  - ☐ Edo-Tokyo Museum | Tokyo
  - ☐ Ramen Museum | Yokohama
- ☐ FESTIVALS
  - ☐ The Sapporo Snow Festival, Beginning of February
  - ☐ Obon Festival
- ☐ FOOD/DRINKS
  - ☐ Ikura
  - ☐ kobe beef in Kobe
  - ☐ ramen, sushi and katsudon
  - ☐ Horse sashimi
  - ☐ Sea urchin
  - ☐ Sake
  - ☐ Japanese Mochi
- ☐ RESTAURANTS
  - ☐ See the Robot Restaurant Show
- ☐ WORLD HERITAGE LIST
  - ☐ Buddhist Monuments in the Horyu-ji Area
  - ☐ Himeji-jo

- [ ] Shirakami-Sanchi
- [ ] Yakushima
- [ ] Historic Monuments of Ancient Kyoto (Kyoto, Uji and Otsu Cities)
- [ ] Historic Villages of Shirakawa-go and Gokayama
- [ ] Hiroshima Peace Memorial (Genbaku Dome)
- [ ] Itsukushima Shinto Shrine
- [ ] Historic Monuments of Ancient Nara
- [ ] Shrines and Temples of Nikko
- [ ] Gusuku Sites and Related Properties of the Kingdom of Ryukyu
- [ ] Sacred Sites and Pilgrimage Routes in the Kii Mountain Range
- [ ] Shiretoko
- [ ] Iwami Ginzan Silver Mine and its Cultural Landscape
- [ ] Hiraizumi – Temples, Gardens and Archaeological Sites Representing the Buddhist Pure Land
- [ ] Ogasawara Islands
- [ ] Fujisan, sacred place and source of artistic inspiration
- [ ] Tomioka Silk Mill and Related Sites
- [ ] Sites of Japan's Meiji Industrial Revolution: Iron and Steel, Shipbuilding and Coal Mining
- [ ] The Architectural Work of Le Corbusier, an Outstanding Contribution to the Modern Movement
- [ ] Sacred Island of Okinoshima and Associated Sites in the Munakata Region
- [ ] Hidden Christian Sites in the Nagasaki Region
- [ ] Mozu-Furuichi Kofun Group: Mounded Tombs of Ancient Japan
- [ ] Amami-Oshima Island, Tokunoshima Island, Northern part of Okinawa Island, and Iriomote Island
- [ ] Jomon Prehistoric Sites in Northern Japan

- [ ] **JORDAN**

- [ ] Hike Desert Trek to Petra, Jordan

- ☐ WORLD HERITAGE LIST
    - ☐ Petra
    - ☐ Quseir Amra
    - ☐ Um er-Rasas (Kastrom Mefa'a)
    - ☐ Wadi Rum Protected Area
    - ☐ Baptism Site "Bethany Beyond the Jordan" (Al-Maghtas)
    - ☐ As-Salt - The Place of Tolerance and Urban Hospitality
- ☐ **KAZAKHSTAN**
    - ☐ WORLD HERITAGE LIST
        - ☐ Mausoleum of Khoja Ahmed Yasawi
        - ☐ Petroglyphs of the Archaeological Landscape of Tanbaly
        - ☐ Saryarka – Steppe and Lakes of Northern Kazakhstan
        - ☐ Silk Roads: the Routes Network of Chang'an-Tianshan Corridor
        - ☐ Western Tien-Shan
- ☐ **KUWAIT**
- ☐ **KYRGYZSTAN**
    - ☐ WORLD HERITAGE LIST
        - ☐ Sulaiman-Too Sacred Mountain
        - ☐ Silk Roads: the Routes Network of Chang'an-Tianshan Corridor
        - ☐ Western Tien-Shan
- ☐ **LAOS**
    - ☐ Float Down Mekong River
    - ☐ Explore Tam Ting Caves
    - ☐ WORLD HERITAGE LIST
        - ☐ Town of Luang Prabang
        - ☐ Vat Phou and Associated Ancient Settlements within the Champasak Cultural Landscape
        - ☐ Megalithic Jar Sites in Xiengkhuang – Plain of Jars
- ☐ **LEBANON**
    - ☐ WORLD HERITAGE LIST
        - ☐ Anjar
        - ☐ Baalbek
        - ☐ Byblos

☐ Tyre
☐ Ouadi Qadisha (the Holy Valley) and the Forest of the Cedars of God (Horsh Arz el-Rab)

☐ **MACAU**

☐ Ruins of Saint Paul's Church
☐ Gamble and win in Macau

☐ **MALAYSIA**

☐ Petronas Tower | Kuala Lumpur

☐ FOOD/DRINKS

☐ Rambutan

☐ WORLD HERITAGE LIST

☐ Gunung Mulu National Park
☐ Kinabalu Park
☐ Melaka and George Town, Historic Cities of the Straits of Malacca
☐ Archaeological Heritage of the Lenggong Valley

☐ **MALDIVES**

☐ Sea of Stars | Vaadhoo Island

☐ RESTAURANT

☐ Eat at the Undersea Restaurant | Ithaa

☐ HOTEL

☐ Stay at the Boat Hotel in Cocoa Island

☐ **MONGOLIA**

☐ WORLD HERITAGE LIST

☐ Uvs Nuur Basin
☐ Orkhon Valley Cultural Landscape
☐ Petroglyphic Complexes of the Mongolian Altai
☐ Great Burkhan Khaldun Mountain and its surrounding sacred landscape
☐ Landscapes of Dauria

☐ **MYANMAR**

☐ The Golden Rock aka Kyaiktiyo Pagoda

☐ WORLD HERITAGE LIST

☐ Pyu Ancient Cities
☐ Bagan

☐ **NEPAL**

☐ Climb the Mount Everest (basecamp)

☐ WORLD HERITAGE LIST

☐ Kathmandu Valley
☐ Sagarmatha National Park

☐ Chitwan National Park
☐ Lumbini, the Birthplace of the Lord Buddha

☐ **NORTH KOREA**
  ☐ WORLD HERITAGE LIST
    ☐ Complex of Koguryo Tombs
    ☐ Historic Monuments and Sites in Kaesong

☐ **OMAN**
  ☐ WORLD HERITAGE LIST
    ☐ Bahla Fort
    ☐ Archaeological Sites of Bat, Al-Khutm and Al-Ayn
    ☐ Land of Frankincense
    ☐ *Aflaj* Irrigation Systems of Oman
    ☐ Ancient City of Qalhat

☐ **PAKISTAN**
    ☐ Hike Baltoro Glacier and K2
  ☐ WORLD HERITAGE LIST
    ☐ Archaeological Ruins at Moenjodaro
    ☐ Buddhist Ruins of Takht-i-Bahi and Neighbouring City Remains at Sahr-i-Bahlol
    ☐ Taxila
    ☐ Fort and Shalamar Gardens in Lahore
    ☐ Historical Monuments at Makli, Thatta
    ☐ Rohtas Fort

☐ **PALESTINE STATE**
  ☐ WORLD HERITAGE SITES
    ☐ Birthplace of Jesus: Church of the Nativity and the Pilgrimage Route, Bethlehem
    ☐ Palestine: Land of Olives and Vines – Cultural Landscape of Southern Jerusalem, Battir
    ☐ Hebron/Al-Khalil Old Town

☐ **PHILIPPINES**
    ☐ Boracay
    ☐ Taal Lake – a lake on an island in a lake on an island
    ☐ Canyoneering the Kawasan Falls
  ☐ WORLD HERITAGE SITES
    ☐ Baroque Churches of the Philippines
    ☐ Tubbataha Reefs Natural Park
    ☐ Rice Terraces of the Philippine Cordilleras

- ☐ Historic City of Vigan
- ☐ Puerto-Princesa Subterranean River National Park
- ☐ Mount Hamiguitan Range Wildlife Sanctuary

☐ **QATAR**
- ☐ MUSEUMS
    - ☐ Museum of Islamic Art | Doha
- ☐ WORLD HERITAGE SITES
    - ☐ Al Zubarah Archaeological Site

☐ **SAUDI ARABIA**
- ☐ FOOD/DRINKS
    - ☐ Eat Kabsa in Saudi Arabia/Middle East
- ☐ WORLD HERITAGE LIST
    - ☐ Hegra Archaeological Site (al-Hijr / Madā᾿in Ṣāliḥ)
    - ☐ At-Turaif District in ad-Dir'iyah
    - ☐ Historic Jeddah, the Gate to Makkah
    - ☐ Rock Art in the Hail Region of Saudi Arabia
    - ☐ Al-Ahsa Oasis, an Evolving Cultural Landscape
    - ☐ Ḥimā Cultural Area

☐ **SINGAPORE**
- ☐ Go to Marina Bay Sands
- ☐ GARDENS
    - ☐ Sky Gardens
    - ☐ Gardens by the Bay
- ☐ MUSEUMS
    - ☐ Asian Civilisations Museum
- ☐ HOTELS
    - ☐ Stay at the Marina Bay Sands.
- ☐ WORLD HERITAGE LIST
    - ☐ Singapore Botanic Gardens

☐ **SOUTH KOREA**
- ☐ Dance Gangnam style in Gangnam | Seoul
- ☐ MUSEUMS
    - ☐ The National Museum of Korea | Seoul
    - ☐ The National Folk Museum of Korea | Seoul
    - ☐ Gyeongju National Museum
- ☐ FOOD/DRINKS
    - ☐ Hongeo (rotten skate that smells and tastes like ammonia...)

29

- ☐ Live octopus
- ☐ Silk worms (Beondegi)
- ☐ Kimchi
- ☐ Bibimbap
- ☐ Banchan
- ☐ WORLD HERITAGE LIST
  - ☐ Haeinsa Temple Janggyeong Panjeon, the Depositories for the *Tripitaka Koreana* Woodblocks
  - ☐ Jongmyo Shrine
  - ☐ Seokguram Grotto and Bulguksa Temple
  - ☐ Changdeokgung Palace Complex
  - ☐ Hwaseong Fortress
  - ☐ Gochang, Hwasun and Ganghwa Dolmen Sites
  - ☐ Gyeongju Historic Areas
  - ☐ Jeju Volcanic Island and Lava Tubes
  - ☐ Royal Tombs of the Joseon Dynasty
  - ☐ Historic Villages of Korea: Hahoe and Yangdong
  - ☐ Namhansanseong
  - ☐ Baekje Historic Areas
  - ☐ Sansa, Buddhist Mountain Monasteries in Korea
  - ☐ Seowon, Korean Neo-Confucian Academies
  - ☐ Getbol, Korean Tidal Flats
- ☐ **SRI LANKA**
  - ☐ Climb to the Peak of Sigiriya Rock
  - ☐ WORLD HERITAGE LIST
    - ☐ Ancient City of Polonnaruwa
    - ☐ Ancient City of Sigiriya
    - ☐ Sacred City of Anuradhapura
    - ☐ Old Town of Galle and its Fortifications
    - ☐ Sacred City of Kandy
    - ☐ Sinharaja Forest Reserve
    - ☐ Rangiri Dambulla Cave Temple
    - ☐ Central Highlands of Sri Lanka
- ☐ **SYRIA**
  - ☐ WORLD HERITAGE LIST
    - ☐ Ancient City of Damascus
    - ☐ Ancient City of Bosra
    - ☐ Site of Palmyra
    - ☐ Ancient City of Aleppo

☐ Crac des Chevaliers and Qal'at Salah El-Din
☐ Ancient Villages of Northern Syria

☐ **TAIWAN**
    ☐ MUSEUMS
        ☐ The National Palace Museum | Taipei
    ☐ FESTIVALS
        ☐ Pingxi Lantern Festival, sometime in early February

☐ **TAJIKISTAN**
    ☐ WORLD HERITAGE LIST
        ☐ Proto-urban Site of Sarazm
        ☐ Tajik National Park (Mountains of the Pamirs)

☐ **THAILAND**
    ☐ Chiang Mai
    ☐ Volunteer at an Elephant Rescue
    ☐ Walking Street in Pattaya
    ☐ Karen (Kayan) Long Neck villages
    ☐ James Bond Island
    ☐ Explore Vietnam or Thailand on a scooter
    ☐ Visit Phuket and Ko Phi Phi
    ☐ Get a Thai massage
    ☐ Be hung over at the "lebua at State Tower" — from the Hangover 2 | Bangkok
    ☐ See a ping-pong show
    ☐ See a Ladyboy show
    ☐ GARDENS
        ☐ Nong Nooch Tropical Botanical Garden, Pattaya
    ☐ MUSEUMS
        ☐ The Bangkok National Museum
    ☐ FESTIVALS
        ☐ Let Go of a Floating Lantern at Yi Peng Festival
        ☐ Songkran Water Festival
    ☐ WORLD HERITAGE LIST
        ☐ Historic City of Ayutthaya
        ☐ Historic Town of Sukhothai and Associated Historic Towns
        ☐ Thungyai-Huai Kha Khaeng Wildlife Sanctuaries
        ☐ Ban Chiang Archaeological Site
        ☐ Dong Phayayen-Khao Yai Forest Complex

☐ Kaeng Krachan Forest Complex

☐ **TIBET**

☐ Meet the Dalai Lama or a monk at the Potala Palace.

☐ **TIMOR-LESTE**
☐ **TURKEY**

☐ See the Stone Mirror | Istanbul
☐ Hagia Sophia | Istanbul
☐ Balloon Over Cappadocia's Fairy Chimneys
☐ Hear the Call to Prayer at the Blue Mosque
☐ See the Whirling Dervishes
☐ Soak in Pamukkale Hot Springs
☐ Kayak in the Blue Lagoon
☐ Get scrubbed at a Hammam

☐ MUSEUMS

☐ Topkapı Palace Museum | Istanbul
☐ Zeugma Mosaic Museum | Gaziantep

☐ FUNNY NAMES TO VISIT

☐ Batman

☐ EVENTS/FESTIVALS

☐ Cappadocia Balloon Festival

☐ FOOD/DRINKS

☐ Eat kebab

☐ WORLD HERITAGE LIST

☐ Göreme National Park and the Rock Sites of Cappadocia
☐ Great Mosque and Hospital of Divriği
☐ Historic Areas of Istanbul
☐ Hattusha: the Hittite Capital
☐ Nemrut Dağ
☐ Hierapolis-Pamukkale
☐ Xanthos-Letoon
☐ City of Safranbolu
☐ Archaeological Site of Troy
☐ Selimiye Mosque and its Social Complex
☐ Neolithic Site of Çatalhöyük
☐ Bursa and Cumalıkızık: the Birth of the Ottoman Empire
☐ Pergamon and its Multi-Layered Cultural Landscape

- ☐ Diyarbakır Fortress and Hevsel Gardens Cultural Landscape
- ☐ Ephesus
- ☐ Archaeological Site of Ani
- ☐ Aphrodisias
- ☐ Göbekli Tepe
- ☐ Arslantepe Mound

☐ **TURKMENISTAN**
- ☐ WORLD HERITAGE LIST
  - ☐ State Historical and Cultural Park "Ancient Merv"
  - ☐ Kunya-Urgench
  - ☐ Parthian Fortresses of Nisa

☐ **UNITED ARAB EMIRATES**
- ☐ Dubai
- ☐ Ride a camel in Abu Dhabi
- ☐ Dress up as a sheikh in Abu Dhabi
- ☐ Ride the elevator to the top of Dubai's Burj Khalifa
- ☐ See "The Palm Jumeirah" | Dubai
- ☐ MUSEUMS
  - ☐ Sharjah Museum of Islamic Civilization (Sharjah, UAE)
- ☐ WORLD'S DANGEROUS WATERSLIDES
  - ☐ Tantrum Alley
- ☐ FOOD
  - ☐ Shawarma
- ☐ WORLD HERITAGE LIST
  - ☐ Cultural Sites of Al Ain (Hafit, Hili, Bidaa Bint Saud and Oases Areas)

☐ **UZBEKISTAN**
- ☐ WORLD HERITAGE LIST
  - ☐ Itchan Kala
  - ☐ Historic Centre of Bukhara
  - ☐ Historic Centre of Shakhrisyabz
  - ☐ Samarkand – Crossroad of Cultures
  - ☐ Western Tien-Shan

☐ **VIETNAM**
- ☐ Halong Bay
- ☐ Da Nang

- ☐ Hoi An
- ☐ See the Cu Chi Tunnels in Ho Chi Minh
- ☐ Shop at the Floating Market
- ☐ The Hang Son Doong Cave
- ☐ Cycle the rice fields
- ☐ MUSEUMS
  - ☐ War Remnants Museum | Ho Chi Minh City
- ☐ FESTIVAL
  - ☐ Attend a lantern festival
- ☐ FOOD/DRINK
  - ☐ Pho
  - ☐ Snake Wine
- ☐ WORLD HERITAGE LIST
  - ☐ Complex of Hué Monuments
  - ☐ Ha Long Bay
  - ☐ Hoi An Ancient Town
  - ☐ My Son Sanctuary
  - ☐ Phong Nha-Ke Bang National Park
  - ☐ Central Sector of the Imperial Citadel of Thang Long - Hanoi
  - ☐ Citadel of the Ho Dynasty
  - ☐ Trang An Landscape Complex

☐ **YEMEN**

- ☐ Dragon's Blood Trees
- ☐ WORLD HERITAGE LIST
  - ☐ Old Walled City of Shibam
  - ☐ Old City of Sana'a
  - ☐ Historic Town of Zabid
  - ☐ Socotra Archipelago

- ☐ _____
- ☐ _____
- ☐ _____
- ☐ _____
- ☐ _____
- ☐ _____

EUROPE BUCKET LIST

- [ ] Backpack through Europe
- [ ] Shop at the European Christmas Markets

- [ ] **ALBANIA**
    - [ ] WOLRD HERITAGE SITES
        - [ ] Natural and Cultural Heritage of the Ohrid region
        - [ ] Butrint
        - [ ] Historic Centres of Berat and Gjirokastra
        - [ ] Ancient and Primeval Beech Forests of the Carpathians and Other Regions of Europe
- [ ] **ANDORRA**
    - [ ] WORLD HERITAGE SITES
        - [ ] Madriu-Perafita-Claror Valley
- [ ] **AUSTRIA**
        - [ ] Hike Zillertal Alps
        - [ ] Kunsthistorisches Museum | Vienna
    - [ ] FESTIVALS
        - [ ] Snowbombing Music Festival: Happens in early April or Spring
    - [ ] WORLD'S DANGEROUS WATERSLIDES
        - [ ] L2
    - [ ] FOOD
        - [ ] Eat Wiener Schnitzel
    - [ ] FUNNY NAMES TO VISIT
        - [ ] Fucking
    - [ ] WORLD HERITAGE SITES
        - [ ] Historic Centre of the City of Salzburg
        - [ ] Palace and Gardens of Schönbrunn
        - [ ] Hallstatt-Dachstein / Salzkammergut Cultural Landscape
        - [ ] Semmering Railway

- ☐ City of Graz – Historic Centre and Schloss Eggenberg
- ☐ Wachau Cultural Landscape
- ☐ Historic Centre of Vienna
- ☐ Fertö / Neusiedlersee Cultural Landscape
- ☐ Ancient and Primeval Beech Forests of the Carpathians and Other Regions of Europe
- ☐ Prehistoric Pile Dwellings around the Alps
- ☐ Frontiers of the Roman Empire – The Danube Limes (Western Segment)
- ☐ The Great Spa Towns of Europe

☐ **BELARUS**
- ☐ WORLD HERITAGE SITES
  - ☐ Białowieża Forest
  - ☐ Mir Castle Complex
  - ☐ Architectural, Residential and Cultural Complex of the Radziwill Family at Nesvizh
  - ☐ Struve Geodetic Arc

☐ **BELGIUM**
- ☐ Le Grand-Place in Brussels
- ☐ The Royal Museums of Fine Arts of Belgium (Brussels, Belgium)
- ☐ FOOD
  - ☐ Belgium waffle
- ☐ RESTAURANTS
  - ☐ Atomium | Brussels
- ☐ WORLD HERITAGE SITES
  - ☐ Flemish Béguinages
  - ☐ La Grand-Place, Brussels
  - ☐ The Four Lifts on the Canal du Centre and their Environs, La Louvière and Le Roeulx (Hainaut)
  - ☐ Belfries of Belgium and France
  - ☐ Historic Centre of Brugge
  - ☐ Major Town Houses of the Architect Victor Horta (Brussels)
  - ☐ Neolithic Flint Mines at Spiennes (Mons)
  - ☐ Notre-Dame Cathedral in Tournai
  - ☐ Plantin-Moretus House-Workshops-Museum Complex

- ☐ Ancient and Primeval Beech Forests of the Carpathians and Other Regions of Europe
- ☐ Stoclet House
- ☐ Major Mining Sites of Wallonia
- ☐ The Architectural Work of Le Corbusier, an Outstanding Contribution to the Modern Movement
- ☐ Colonies of Benevolence
- ☐ The Great Spa Towns of Europe

☐ BOSNIA AND HERZEGOVINA

- ☐ Mostar
- ☐ WORLD HERITAGE SITES
  - ☐ Old Bridge Area of the Old City of Mostar
  - ☐ Ancient and Primeval Beech Forests of the Carpathians and Other Regions of Europe
  - ☐ Mehmed Paša Sokolović Bridge in Višegrad
  - ☐ Stećci Medieval Tombstone Graveyards

☐ BULGARIA

- ☐ WORLD HERITAGE SITES
  - ☐ Boyana Church
  - ☐ Madara Rider
  - ☐ Rock-Hewn Churches of Ivanovo
  - ☐ Thracian Tomb of Kazanlak
  - ☐ Ancient City of Nessebar
  - ☐ Pirin National Park
  - ☐ Rila Monastery
  - ☐ Srebarna Nature Reserve
  - ☐ Thracian Tomb of Sveshtari
  - ☐ Ancient and Primeval Beech Forests of the Carpathians and Other Regions of Europe

☐ CHANNEL ISLANDS

☐ CROATIA

- ☐ Yacht Week
- ☐ Listen to the sea organ in Zadar
- ☐ MUSEUMS
  - ☐ Museum of Broken Relationships | Zagreb
- ☐ WORLD HERITAGE SITES
  - ☐ Historical Complex of Split with the Palace of Diocletian
  - ☐ Old City of Dubrovnik

- [ ] Plitvice Lakes National Park
- [ ] Episcopal Complex of the Euphrasian Basilica in the Historic Centre of Poreč
- [ ] Historic City of Trogir
- [ ] The Cathedral of St James in Šibenik
- [ ] Ancient and Primeval Beech Forests of the Carpathians and Other Regions of Europe
- [ ] Stari Grad Plain
- [ ] Stećci Medieval Tombstone Graveyards
- [ ] Venetian Works of Defence between the 16th and 17th Centuries: *Stato da Terra –* Western *Stato da Mar*

- [ ] **CZECH REPUBLIC**
  - [ ] FOOD/DRINKS
    - [ ] Drink a pilsner (a Pilsner Urquell) in Plzeň
  - [ ] EVENTS/FESTIVALS
    - [ ] Do the Mongol Rally | Europe/Asia
  - [ ] WORLD HERITAGE SITES
    - [ ] Historic Centre of Český Krumlov
    - [ ] Historic Centre of Prague
    - [ ] Historic Centre of Telč
    - [ ] Pilgrimage Church of St John of Nepomuk at Zelená Hora
    - [ ] Kutná Hora: Historical Town Centre with the Church of St Barbara and the Cathedral of Our Lady at Sedlec
    - [ ] Lednice-Valtice Cultural Landscape
    - [ ] Gardens and Castle at Kroměříž
    - [ ] Holašovice Historic Village
    - [ ] Litomyšl Castle
    - [ ] Holy Trinity Column in Olomouc
    - [ ] Tugendhat Villa in Brno
    - [ ] Jewish Quarter and St Procopius' Basilica in Třebíč
    - [ ] Ancient and Primeval Beech Forests of the Carpathians and Other Regions of Europe
    - [ ] Erzgebirge/Krušnohoří Mining Region
    - [ ] Landscape for Breeding and Training of Ceremonial Carriage Horses at Kladruby nad Labem

- [ ] The Great Spa Towns of Europe

- [ ] **DENMARK**
  - [ ] See the Little Mermaid | Copenhagen
  - [ ] Walk the Nyhavn Waterfront | Copenhagen
  - [ ] Gasadalur | Faeroe Islands
  - [ ] Nationalmuseet | Copenhagen
  - [ ] Sail through the canals in Copenhagen on our own picnic boat
  - [ ] FOOD/DRINKS
    - [ ] Danish hotdog
  - [ ] WORLD HERITAGE SITES
    - [ ] Jelling Mounds, Runic Stones and Church
    - [ ] Roskilde Cathedral
    - [ ] Kronborg Castle
    - [ ] Ilulissat Icefjord
    - [ ] Wadden Sea
    - [ ] Stevns Klint
    - [ ] Christiansfeld, a Moravian Church Settlement
    - [ ] The par force hunting landscape in North Zealand
    - [ ] Kujataa Greenland: Norse and Inuit Farming at the Edge of the Ice Cap
    - [ ] Aasivissuit – Nipisat. Inuit Hunting Ground between Ice and Sea

- [ ] **ESTONIA**
  - [ ] Visit Tallinn and walk on the TV Tower
  - [ ] WORLD HERITAGE SITES
    - [ ] Historic Centre (Old Town) of Tallinn
    - [ ] Struve Geodetic Arc

- [ ] **FINLAND**
  - [ ] Go in a Finnish sauna
  - [ ] HOTELS
    - [ ] Stay in a Glass Igloo
  - [ ] WORLD HERITAGE SITES
    - [ ] Fortress of Suomenlinna
    - [ ] Old Rauma
    - [ ] Petäjävesi Old Church
    - [ ] Verla Groundwood and Board Mill
    - [ ] Bronze Age Burial Site of Sammallahdenmäki
    - [ ] High Coast / Kvarken Archipelago

☐ Struve Geodetic Arc

☐ **FRANCE**

- ☐ Go on top of the Eiffel Tower
- ☐ See the Eiffel Tower Glitter at Night
- ☐ Cluny Abbey
- ☐ Arc de Triomphe
- ☐ Attend Mass at Notre Dame Cathedral in Paris
- ☐ Put a Love Lock on Pont des Arts Bridge
- ☐ Sunbathe Topless on the French Riviera
- ☐ Walk Through the Lavender Fields in Provence
- ☐ Travel to Bora Bora and stay in an overwater bungalow
- ☐ Chateau de Villandry

☐ HIKES

- ☐ The Haute Route, France & Switzerland
- ☐ Tour Du Mont Blanc, France/Italy/Switzerland
- ☐ GR20, France

☐ MUSEUMS

- ☐ **See the Mona Lisa at the Louvre | Paris**
- ☐ Musée D'Orsay | Paris
- ☐ Centre Georges Pompidou | Paris
- ☐ Musée Du Quai Branly | Paris
- ☐ The Versailles Museums | Versailles
- ☐ Museum of European Mediterranean Civilisations | Marseille
- ☐ Musée National Du Moyen Âge | Paris
- ☐ Louis Vuitton Foundation | Paris
- ☐ Petit Palais | Paris
- ☐ Bourse de commerce | Paris

☐ EVENTS/FESTIVALS

- ☐ Tour de France
- ☐ Cannes Film Festival

☐ FOOD/DRINKS

- ☐ Drink chianti in Chianti,
- ☐ Bordeaux in Bourdeaux,
- ☐ Champagne in Champagne
- ☐ Cognac in Cognac

☐ WORLD HERITAGE SITES
 ☐ Chartres Cathedral
 ☐ Mont-Saint-Michel and its Bay
 ☐ Palace and Gardens of Versailles
 ☐ Prehistoric Sites and Decorated Caves of the Vézère Valley
 ☐ Vézelay, Church and Hill
 ☐ Amiens Cathedral
 ☐ Arles, Roman and Romanesque Monuments
 ☐ Cistercian Abbey of Fontenay
 ☐ Palace and Park of Fontainebleau
 ☐ Roman Theatre and its Surroundings and the "Triumphal Arch" of Orange
 ☐ From the Great Saltworks of Salins-les-Bains to the Royal Saltworks of Arc-et-Senans, the Production of Open-pan Salt
 ☐ Abbey Church of Saint-Savin sur Gartempe
 ☐ Gulf of Porto: Calanche of Piana, Gulf of Girolata, Scandola Reserve
 ☐ Place Stanislas, Place de la Carrière and Place d'Alliance in Nancy
 ☐ Pont du Gard (Roman Aqueduct)
 ☐ Strasbourg, Grande-Île and *Neustadt*
 ☐ Cathedral of Notre-Dame, Former Abbey of Saint-Rémi and Palace of Tau, Reims
 ☐ Paris, Banks of the Seine
 ☐ Bourges Cathedral
 ☐ Historic Centre of Avignon: Papal Palace, Episcopal Ensemble and Avignon Bridge
 ☐ Canal du Midi
 ☐ Historic Fortified City of Carcassonne
 ☐ Pyrénées - Mont Perdu
 ☐ Historic Site of Lyon
 ☐ Routes of Santiago de Compostela in France
 ☐ Belfries of Belgium and France
 ☐ Jurisdiction of Saint-Emilion
 ☐ The Loire Valley between Sully-sur-Loire and Chalonnes

41

- ☐ Provins, Town of Medieval Fairs
- ☐ Le Havre, the City Rebuilt by Auguste Perret
- ☐ Ancient and Primeval Beech Forests of the Carpathians and Other Regions of Europe
- ☐ Bordeaux, Port of the Moon
- ☐ Fortifications of Vauban
- ☐ Lagoons of New Caledonia: Reef Diversity and Associated Ecosystems
- ☐ Episcopal City of Albi
- ☐ Pitons, cirques and remparts of Reunion Island
- ☐ Prehistoric Pile Dwellings around the Alps
- ☐ The Causses and the Cévennes, Mediterranean agro-pastoral Cultural Landscape
- ☐ Nord-Pas de Calais Mining Basin
- ☐ Decorated Cave of Pont d'Arc, known as Grotte Chauvet-Pont d'Arc, Ardèche
- ☐ Champagne Hillsides, Houses and Cellars
- ☐ The Climats, terroirs of Burgundy
- ☐ The Architectural Work of Le Corbusier, an Outstanding Contribution to the Modern Movement
- ☐ Taputapuātea
- ☐ Chaîne des Puys - Limagne fault tectonic arena
- ☐ French Austral Lands and Seas
- ☐ Cordouan Lighthouse
- ☐ Nice, Winter Resort Town of the Riviera
- ☐ The Great Spa Towns of Europe

☐ **GERMANY**

- ☐ Drive the whole lap on Nürburgring (with a race car)
- ☐ Brandenburg Gate
- ☐ Berlin Wall
- ☐ Neuschwanstein Castle
- ☐ Munich and Frankfurt
- ☐ Berlin
- ☐ Rothenberg
- ☐ Blooming Cherry Trees in Bonn
- ☐ Hike Berliner *Höhenweg*

☐ Museums

- ☐ The Romano-Germanic Museum | Cologne

- ☐ Mercedes-Benz Museum | Stuttgart
- ☐ Vitra Design Museum | Weil Am Rhein
- ☐ Pergamon Museum | Berlin
- ☐ Jewish Museum | Berlin
- ☐ Topography of Terror | Berlin
- ☐ Humboldt Forum | Berlin

☐ RESTAURANTS/BARS
- ☐ Have a beer at the top of Zugspitze

☐ FOOD/DRINKS
- ☐ Drink Das Boot
- ☐ Drink Kölsch Beer in Cologne

☐ EVENTS/FESTIVALS
- ☐ Oktoberfest
- ☐ Participate in a Rubber duck race | Baden-Wurttemberg
- ☐ Attend the Windjammer Parade

☐ WORLD HERITAGE SITES
- ☐ Aachen Cathedral
- ☐ Speyer Cathedral
- ☐ Würzburg Residence with the Court Gardens and Residence Square
- ☐ Pilgrimage Church of Wies
- ☐ Castles of Augustusburg and Falkenlust at Brühl
- ☐ St Mary's Cathedral and St Michael's Church at Hildesheim
- ☐ Roman Monuments, Cathedral of St Peter and Church of Our Lady in Trier
- ☐ Frontiers of the Roman Empire
- ☐ Hanseatic City of Lübeck
- ☐ Palaces and Parks of Potsdam and Berlin
- ☐ Abbey and Altenmünster of Lorsch
- ☐ Mines of Rammelsberg, Historic Town of Goslar and Upper Harz Water Management System
- ☐ Maulbronn Monastery Complex
- ☐ Town of Bamberg
- ☐ Collegiate Church, Castle and Old Town of Quedlinburg
- ☐ Völklingen Ironworks
- ☐ Messel Pit Fossil Site

- ☐ Bauhaus and its Sites in Weimar, Dessau and Bernau
- ☐ Cologne Cathedral
- ☐ Luther Memorials in Eisleben and Wittenberg
- ☐ Classical Weimar
- ☐ Museumsinsel (Museum Island), Berlin
- ☐ Wartburg Castle
- ☐ Garden Kingdom of Dessau-Wörlitz
- ☐ Monastic Island of Reichenau
- ☐ Zollverein Coal Mine Industrial Complex in Essen
- ☐ Historic Centres of Stralsund and Wismar
- ☐ Upper Middle Rhine Valley
- ☐ Muskauer Park / Park Mużakowski
- ☐ Town Hall and Roland on the Marketplace of Bremen
- ☐ Old town of Regensburg with Stadtamhof
- ☐ Ancient and Primeval Beech Forests of the Carpathians and Other Regions of Europe
- ☐ Berlin Modernism Housing Estates
- ☐ Wadden Sea
- ☐ Fagus Factory in Alfeld
- ☐ Prehistoric Pile Dwellings around the Alps
- ☐ Margravial Opera House Bayreuth
- ☐ Bergpark Wilhelmshöhe
- ☐ Carolingian Westwork and Civitas Corvey
- ☐ Speicherstadt and Kontorhaus District with Chilehaus
- ☐ The Architectural Work of Le Corbusier, an Outstanding Contribution to the Modern Movement
- ☐ Caves and Ice Age Art in the Swabian Jura
- ☐ Archaeological Border complex of Hedeby and the Danevirke
- ☐ Naumburg Cathedral
- ☐ Erzgebirge/Krušnohoří Mining Region
- ☐ Water Management System of Augsburg
- ☐ Frontiers of the Roman Empire – The Danube Limes (Western Segment)

- ☐ Frontiers of the Roman Empire – The Lower German Limes
- ☐ Mathildenhöhe Darmstadt
- ☐ ShUM Sites of Speyer, Worms and Mainz
- ☐ The Great Spa Towns of Europe

☐ **GREECE**

- ☐ The Parthenon | Athens
- ☐ The Anastenaria Firewalking Ceremony
- ☐ Watch the Sunset in Santorini
- ☐ Meteora Monasteries
- ☐ Go island hopping
- ☐ Mount Olympus
- ☐ Corinth Canal

☐ MUSEUMS

- ☐ The Acropolis Museum | Athens
- ☐ The National Archaeological Museum | Athens

☐ FOOD/DRINKS

- ☐ Olives

☐ WORLD HERITAGE SITES

- ☐ Temple of Apollo Epicurius at Bassae
- ☐ Acropolis, Athens
- ☐ Archaeological Site of Delphi
- ☐ Medieval City of Rhodes
- ☐ Meteora
- ☐ Mount Athos
- ☐ Paleochristian and Byzantine Monuments of Thessalonika
- ☐ Sanctuary of Asklepios at Epidaurus
- ☐ Archaeological Site of Mystras
- ☐ Archaeological Site of Olympia
- ☐ Delos
- ☐ Monasteries of Daphni, Hosios Loukas and Nea Moni of Chios
- ☐ Pythagoreion and Heraion of Samos
- ☐ Archaeological Site of Aigai (modern name Vergina)
- ☐ Archaeological Sites of Mycenae and Tiryns
- ☐ The Historic Centre (Chorá) with the Monastery of Saint-John the Theologian and the Cave of the Apocalypse on the Island of Pátmos

- ☐ Old Town of Corfu
- ☐ Archaeological Site of Philippi
- ☐ **HOLY SEE**
  - ☐ WORLD HERITAGE SITES
    - ☐ Historic Centre of Rome, the Properties of the Holy See in that City Enjoying Extraterritorial Rights and San Paolo Fuori le Mura
    - ☐ Vatican City
- ☐ **HUNGARY**
  - ☐ FOOD/DRINKS
    - ☐ Goulash
  - ☐ WORLD HERITAGE SITES
    - ☐ Budapest, including the Banks of the Danube, the Buda Castle Quarter and Andrássy Avenue
    - ☐ Old Village of Hollókő and its Surroundings
    - ☐ Caves of Aggtelek Karst and Slovak Karst
    - ☐ Millenary Benedictine Abbey of Pannonhalma and its Natural Environment
    - ☐ Hortobágy National Park - the *Puszta*
    - ☐ Early Christian Necropolis of Pécs (Sopianae)
    - ☐ Fertö / Neusiedlersee Cultural Landscape
    - ☐ Tokaj Wine Region Historic Cultural Landscape
- ☐ **ICELAND**
  - ☐ Swim in the Blue Lagoon
  - ☐ Geysir and Strokkur
  - ☐ Gullfoss, Skagafoss & Vatnajökull
  - ☐ Check out the animals on Puffin Island
  - ☐ Icelandic Phallological Museum | Reykjavik
  - ☐ FOOD/DRINKS
    - ☐ Hákar
  - ☐ WORLD HERITAGE SITES
    - ☐ Þingvellir National Park
    - ☐ Surtsey
    - ☐ Vatnajökull National Park - Dynamic Nature of Fire and Ice
- ☐ **IRELAND**
  - ☐ Kiss the Blarney Stone
  - ☐ Drive through the Dark Hedges
  - ☐ See the Giant's Causeway and Causeway's Coast
  - ☐ Sleep in an Irish Castle

- ☐ Geek out at Trinity College
- ☐ The Dark Hedges
- ☐ Hike Croagh Patrick
- ☐ National Museum of Ireland | Dublin
- ☐ Guinness Storehouse | Dublin
- ☐ Titanic Belfast
- ☐ EVENTS/FESTIVALS
  - ☐ Celebrate St. Patrick's Day
- ☐ RESTAURANTS
  - ☐ Drink at the Guinness Brewery
- ☐ FUNNY NAMES TO VISIT
  - ☐ Blue Ball
- ☐ WORLD HERITAGE SITES – Some may be under United Kingdom.
  - ☐ Brú na Bóinne - Archaeological Ensemble of the Bend of the Boyne
  - ☐ Sceilg Mhichíl

☐ **ITALY**

- ☐ Mount Vesuvius
- ☐ Make a wish in the Trevi Fountain
- ☐ Roman Forum, Spanish Steps & Pantheon | Rome
- ☐ Yell "are you not entertained" at the Colosseum, Rome
- ☐ Castle Nuovo | Naples
- ☐ Duomo di Milano | Milan
- ☐ Take that "pushing/holding" photo in front of Pisa
- ☐ Do the gondolas, and don a mask, in Venice
- ☐ Visit Florence and the Santa Marie del Fiero
- ☐ Michelangelo's David | Florence
- ☐ Ponte Vecchio | Florence
- ☐ Hear Andrea Bocelli sing opera in Milan
- ☐ Watch an opera at the World-Famous Teatro alla Scala
- ☐ Ride a Vespa in Tuscany
- ☐ Stomp Grapes in Tuscany
- ☐ Sleep in a Tuscan Villa
- ☐ Swim in the Blue Grotto
- ☐ Walk Across the Tibetan Bridge in Claviere

- ☐ Burano
- ☐ Drive the Amalfi Coast
- ☐ La Traviata, the original opera with ballet
- ☐ Tour Lake Como by boat
- ☐ Sistine Chapel ceiling | The Vatican
- ☐ St. Peter's Basilica, climb to the top | The Vatican
- ☐ Hear the Pope Speak | The Vatican
- ☐ Giardini Botanici Villa Taranto, Piedmont

☐ HIKES
- ☐ Cinque Terre
- ☐ Dolomites
- ☐ Cities of Cinque Terre

☐ MUSEUMS
- ☐ The Vatican Museums | Vatican City
- ☐ Museo Egizio | Turin
- ☐ The Uffizi Gallery | Florence
- ☐ Galleria Dell'accademia | Florence
- ☐ Capitoline Museums | Rome
- ☐ Museo Nazionale Di Castel Sant'angelo | Rome
- ☐ Messner Mountain Museum South Tyrol & Veneto

☐ EVENTS/FESTIVALS
- ☐ Attend the Palio Horse Race in Siena
- ☐ Participate in the Battle of the Oranges
- ☐ Carnival of Venice

☐ FOOD/DRINKS
- ☐ Learn to Make Pasta from Scratch
- ☐ Gelato in Rome
- ☐ Cannoli
- ☐ Pizza & pasta

☐ WORLD HERITAGE SITES
- ☐ Rock Drawings in Valcamonica
- ☐ Church and Dominican Convent of Santa Maria delle Grazie with "The Last Supper" by Leonardo da Vinci
- ☐ Historic Centre of Rome, the Properties of the Holy See in that City Enjoying Extraterritorial Rights and San Paolo Fuori le Mura
- ☐ Historic Centre of Florence

- [ ] Piazza del Duomo, Pisa
- [ ] Venice and its Lagoon
- [ ] Historic Centre of San Gimignano
- [ ] The Sassi and the Park of the Rupestrian Churches of Matera
- [ ] City of Vicenza and the Palladian Villas of the Veneto
- [ ] Crespi d'Adda
- [ ] Ferrara, City of the Renaissance, and its Po Delta
- [ ] Historic Centre of Naples
- [ ] Historic Centre of Siena
- [ ] Castel del Monte
- [ ] Early Christian Monuments of Ravenna
- [ ] Historic Centre of the City of Pienza
- [ ] The *Trulli* of Alberobello
- [ ] 18th-Century Royal Palace at Caserta with the Park, the Aqueduct of Vanvitelli, and the San Leucio Complex
- [ ] Archaeological Area of Agrigento
- [ ] Archaeological Areas of Pompei, Herculaneum and Torre Annunziata
- [ ] Botanical Garden (Orto Botanico), Padua
- [ ] Cathedral, Torre Civica and Piazza Grande, Modena
- [ ] Costiera Amalfitana
- [ ] Portovenere, Cinque Terre, and the Islands (Palmaria, Tino and Tinetto)
- [ ] Residences of the Royal House of Savoy
- [ ] Su Nuraxi di Barumini
- [ ] Villa Romana del Casale
- [ ] Archaeological Area and the Patriarchal Basilica of Aquileia
- [ ] Cilento and Vallo di Diano National Park with the Archeological Sites of Paestum and Velia, and the Certosa di Padula
- [ ] Historic Centre of Urbino
- [ ] Villa Adriana (Tivoli)
- [ ] Assisi, the Basilica of San Francesco and Other Franciscan Sites

- [ ] City of Verona
- [ ] Isole Eolie (Aeolian Islands)
- [ ] Villa d'Este, Tivoli
- [ ] Late Baroque Towns of the Val di Noto (South-Eastern Sicily)
- [ ] *Sacri Monti* of Piedmont and Lombardy
- [ ] Monte San Giorgio
- [ ] Etruscan Necropolises of Cerveteri and Tarquinia
- [ ] Val d'Orcia
- [ ] Syracuse and the Rocky Necropolis of Pantalica
- [ ] Genoa: *Le Strade Nuove* and the system of the *Palazzi dei Rolli*
- [ ] Ancient and Primeval Beech Forests of the Carpathians and Other Regions of Europe
- [ ] Mantua and Sabbioneta
- [ ] Rhaetian Railway in the Albula / Bernina Landscapes
- [ ] The Dolomites
- [ ] Longobards in Italy. Places of the Power (568-774 A.D.)
- [ ] Prehistoric Pile Dwellings around the Alps
- [ ] Medici Villas and Gardens in Tuscany
- [ ] Mount Etna
- [ ] Vineyard Landscape of Piedmont: Langhe-Roero and Monferrato
- [ ] Arab-Norman Palermo and the Cathedral Churches of Cefalú and Monreale
- [ ] Venetian Works of Defence between the 16th and 17th Centuries: *Stato da Terra – Western Stato da Mar*
- [ ] Ivrea, industrial city of the 20th century
- [ ] Le Colline del Prosecco di Conegliano e Valdobbiadene
- [ ] Padua's fourteenth-century fresco cycles
- [ ] The Great Spa Towns of Europe
- [ ] The Porticoes of Bologna

- [ ] **LATVIA**
  - [ ] FUNNY NAMES TO VISIT
    - [ ] Ogre

- ☐ WORLD HERITAGE SITES
  - ☐ Historic Centre of Riga
  - ☐ Struve Geodetic Arc
- ☐ **LIECHTENSTEIN**
- ☐ **LITHUANIA**
  - ☐ Hill of Crosses
  - ☐ WORLD HERITAGE SITES
    - ☐ Vilnius Historic Centre
    - ☐ Curonian Spit
    - ☐ Kernavė Archaeological Site (Cultural Reserve of Kernavė)
    - ☐ Struve Geodetic Arc
- ☐ **LUXEMBOURG**
  - ☐ Explore Casemates du Bock (Luxembourg City) and Chateau de Vianden (Altstadt Vianden)
  - ☐ WORLD HERITAGE SITES
    - ☐ City of Luxembourg: its Old Quarters and Fortifications
- ☐ **MALTA**
  - ☐ The Blue Grotto
  - ☐ WORLD HERITAGE SITES
    - ☐ City of Valletta
    - ☐ Ħal Saflieni Hypogeum
    - ☐ Megalithic Temples of Malta
- ☐ **MOLDOVA**
  - ☐ WORLD HERITAGE SITES
    - ☐ Struve Geodetic Arc
- ☐ **MONACO**
  - ☐ "Pretend to be rich" in Monaco
  - ☐ Gamble at Casino Monte Carlo
  - ☐ EVENTS/FESTIVALS
    - ☐ Attend the Formula Grand Prix
- ☐ **MONTENEGRO**
  - ☐ WORLD HERITAGE SITES
    - ☐ Natural and Culturo-Historical Region of Kotor
    - ☐ Durmitor National Park
    - ☐ Stećci Medieval Tombstone Graveyards

☐ Venetian Works of Defence between the 16th and 17th Centuries: *Stato da Terra –* Western *Stato da Mar*

☐ **NETHERLANDS**

    ☐ Kinderdijk Windmills

    ☐ Smoke weed in Amsterdam | Holland

    ☐ Visit Holland during the spring and see the flowers bloom

    ☐ Keukenhof, Lisse gardens

  ☐ MUSEUMS

    ☐ Explore the Van Gogh Museum | Amsterdam

    ☐ Rijksmuseum | Amsterdam

    ☐ Anne Frank House | Amsterdam

    ☐ Mauritshuis | The Hague

    ☐

  ☐ FOOD DRINKS

    ☐ Eat soused herring in Holland

  ☐ WORLD HERITAGE SITES

    ☐ Schokland and Surroundings

    ☐ Dutch Water Defence Lines

    ☐ Historic Area of Willemstad, Inner City and Harbour, Curaçao

    ☐ Mill Network at Kinderdijk-Elshout

    ☐ Ir.D.F. Woudagemaal (D.F. Wouda Steam Pumping Station)

    ☐ Droogmakerij de Beemster (Beemster Polder)

    ☐ Rietveld Schröderhuis (Rietveld Schröder House)

    ☐ Wadden Sea

    ☐ Seventeenth-Century Canal Ring Area of Amsterdam inside the Singelgracht

    ☐ Van Nellefabriek

    ☐ Colonies of Benevolence

    ☐ Frontiers of the Roman Empire – The Lower German Limes

☐ **NORTH MACEDONIA**

  ☐ WORLD HERITAGE SITES

    ☐ Natural and Cultural Heritage of the Ohrid region

    ☐ Ancient and Primeval Beech Forests of the Carpathians and Other Regions of Europe

☐ **NORWAY**
- ☐ Stand on "Prekestolen" (AKA the Pulpit Rock) or sit on the edge
- ☐ See the "famous" harbour in Bergen
- ☐ Stand on Trolltunga and stand on Kjeragbolten
- ☐ Stay at the Sorrisniva Igloo Hotel | Alta
- ☐ Fish in northern Norway (known for its abundance of fish)
- ☐ Go with Hurtigruten the whole length
- ☐ Explore several of the big fjords of Norway
- ☐ Float down the Geirangerfjord

☐ MUSEUMS
- ☐ Viking Ship Museum | Oslo

☐ EVENTS/FESTIVALS
- ☐ Go to Hammerfest and Svalbard
- ☐ Bicycle race "Trondheim-Oslo" (580km) on a tandem bike
- ☐ Participate in "Toughest"
- ☐ Complete all the "Birkebeiner" races (Cycling, running, skiing)

☐ FOOD/DRINKS
- ☐ Sheep's head (Smalahove)

☐ FUNNY NAMES TO VISIT
- ☐ Hell

☐ WORLD HERITAGE SITES
- ☐ Bryggen
- ☐ Urnes Stave Church
- ☐ Røros Mining Town and the Circumference
- ☐ Rock Art of Alta
- ☐ Vegaøyan – The Vega Archipelago
- ☐ Struve Geodetic Arc
- ☐ West Norwegian Fjords – Geirangerfjord and Nærøyfjord
- ☐ Rjukan-Notodden Industrial Heritage Site

☐ **POLAND**
- ☐ Go through the Crooked Forest
- ☐ Take a carriage ride through Krakow's Old Town
- ☐ Warsaw Uprising Museum | Warsaw
- ☐ Royal Castle Warsaw

- ☐ MUSEUMS
  - ☐ Auschwitz-Birkenau State Museum | Oświęcim
  - ☐ National Museum | Krakow
- ☐ WORLD HERITAGE SITES
  - ☐ Historic Centre of Kraków
  - ☐ Wieliczka and Bochnia Royal Salt Mines
  - ☐ Auschwitz Birkenau : German Nazi Concentration and Extermination Camp (1940-1945)
  - ☐ Białowieża Forest
  - ☐ Historic Centre of Warsaw
  - ☐ Old City of Zamość
  - ☐ Castle of the Teutonic Order in Malbork
  - ☐ Medieval Town of Toruń
  - ☐ Kalwaria Zebrzydowska: the Mannerist Architectural and Park Landscape Complex and Pilgrimage Park
  - ☐ Churches of Peace in Jawor and Świdnica
  - ☐ Wooden Churches of Southern Małopolska
  - ☐ Muskauer Park / Park Mużakowski
  - ☐ Centennial Hall in Wrocław
  - ☐ Ancient and Primeval Beech Forests of the Carpathians and Other Regions of Europe
  - ☐ Wooden *Tserkvas* of the Carpathian Region in Poland and Ukraine
  - ☐ Tarnowskie Góry Lead-Silver-Zinc Mine and its Underground Water Management System
  - ☐ Krzemionki Prehistoric Striped Flint Mining Region
- ☐ **PORTUGAL**
  - ☐ Historic Centre of Porto
  - ☐ Umbrella Street
  - ☐ Bell-Mouth Spillway
  - ☐ Stand on the end of the continent
- ☐ MUSEUMS
  - ☐ Calouste Gulbenkian Museum | Lisbon
- ☐ FOOD/DRINKS
  - ☐ Francesinha
  - ☐ Drink Port in Porto

- ☐ WORLD HERITAGE SITES
    - ☐ Central Zone of the Town of Angra do Heroismo in the Azores
    - ☐ Convent of Christ in Tomar
    - ☐ Monastery of Batalha
    - ☐ Monastery of the Hieronymites and Tower of Belém in Lisbon
    - ☐ Historic Centre of Évora
    - ☐ Monastery of Alcobaça
    - ☐ Cultural Landscape of Sintra
    - ☐ Historic Centre of Oporto, Luiz I Bridge and Monastery of Serra do Pilar
    - ☐ Prehistoric Rock Art Sites in the Côa Valley and Siega Verde
    - ☐ Laurisilva of Madeira
    - ☐ Alto Douro Wine Region
    - ☐ Historic Centre of Guimarães
    - ☐ Landscape of the Pico Island Vineyard Culture
    - ☐ Garrison Border Town of Elvas and its Fortifications
    - ☐ University of Coimbra – Alta and Sofia
    - ☐ Royal Building of *Mafra* – Palace, Basilica, Convent, *Cerco* Garden and Hunting Park (*Tapada*)
    - ☐ Sanctuary of Bom Jesus do Monte in Braga
- ☐ **ROMANIA**
    - ☐ Dracula's Castle | Transylvania
    - ☐ Bigar Cascade Falls
    - ☐ FOOD/DRINKS
        - ☐ Sarmale
    - ☐ WORLD HERITAGE SITES
        - ☐ Danube Delta
        - ☐ Churches of Moldavia
        - ☐ Monastery of Horezu
        - ☐ Villages with Fortified Churches in Transylvania
        - ☐ Dacian Fortresses of the Orastie Mountains
        - ☐ Historic Centre of Sighişoara

- ☐ Wooden Churches of Maramureş
- ☐ Ancient and Primeval Beech Forests of the Carpathians and Other Regions of Europe
- ☐ Roşia Montană Mining Landscape

☐ **RUSSIA**

- ☐ Take the Trans-Siberian Express
- ☐ St. Petersburg

☐ MUSEUMS

- ☐ The State Hermitage Museum | St. Petersburg
- ☐ Russian Museum | St. Petersburg
- ☐ State Tretyakov Gallery | Moscow
- ☐ Multimedia Art Museum | Moscow
- ☐ Pushkin State Museum of Fine Arts | Moscow
- ☐ Kazan Kremlin | Kazan

☐ FOOD/DRINKS

- ☐ Drink vodka

☐ EVENTS/FESTIVALS

- ☐ White Knight Festival in St. Petersburg : Between April 21 – August 21

☐ WORLD HERITAGE SITES

- ☐ Historic Centre of Saint Petersburg and Related Groups of Monuments
- ☐ Kizhi Pogost
- ☐ Kremlin and Red Square, Moscow
- ☐ Cultural and Historic Ensemble of the Solovetsky Islands
- ☐ Historic Monuments of Novgorod and Surroundings
- ☐ White Monuments of Vladimir and Suzdal
- ☐ Architectural Ensemble of the Trinity Sergius Lavra in Sergiev Posad
- ☐ Church of the Ascension, Kolomenskoye
- ☐ Virgin Komi Forests
- ☐ Lake Baikal
- ☐ Volcanoes of Kamchatka
- ☐ Golden Mountains of Altai
- ☐ Western Caucasus
- ☐ Curonian Spit
- ☐ Ensemble of the Ferapontov Monastery

- ☐ Historic and Architectural Complex of the Kazan Kremlin
- ☐ Central Sikhote-Alin
- ☐ Citadel, Ancient City and Fortress Buildings of Derbent
- ☐ Uvs Nuur Basin
- ☐ Ensemble of the Novodevichy Convent
- ☐ Natural System of Wrangel Island Reserve
- ☐ Historical Centre of the City of Yaroslavl
- ☐ Struve Geodetic Arc
- ☐ Putorana Plateau
- ☐ Lena Pillars Nature Park
- ☐ Bolgar Historical and Archaeological Complex
- ☐ Assumption Cathedral and Monastery of the town-island of Sviyazhsk
- ☐ Landscapes of Dauria
- ☐ Churches of the Pskov School of Architecture
- ☐ Petroglyphs of Lake Onega and the White Sea

☐ **SAN MARINO**
- ☐ WORLD HERITAGE SITES
  - ☐ San Marino Historic Centre and Mount Titano

☐ **SERBIA**
- ☐ WORLD HERITAGE SITES
  - ☐ Stari Ras and Sopoćani
  - ☐ Studenica Monastery
  - ☐ Medieval Monuments in Kosovo
  - ☐ Gamzigrad-Romuliana, Palace of Galerius
  - ☐ Stećci Medieval Tombstone Graveyards

☐ **SLOVAKIA**
- ☐ WORLD HERITAGE SITES
  - ☐ Historic Town of Banská Štiavnica and the Technical Monuments in its Vicinity
  - ☐ Levoča, Spišský Hrad and the Associated Cultural Monuments
  - ☐ Vlkolínec
  - ☐ Caves of Aggtelek Karst and Slovak Karst
  - ☐ Bardejov Town Conservation Reserve
  - ☐ Ancient and Primeval Beech Forests of the Carpathians and Other Regions of Europe

- [ ] Wooden Churches of the Slovak part of the Carpathian Mountain Area
- [ ] Frontiers of the Roman Empire – The Danube Limes (Western Segment)

- [ ] **SLOVENIA**
  - [ ] Lake Bled
  - [ ] WORLD HERITAGE SITES
    - [ ] Škocjan Caves
    - [ ] Ancient and Primeval Beech Forests of the Carpathians and Other Regions of Europe
    - [ ] Prehistoric Pile Dwellings around the Alps
    - [ ] Heritage of Mercury. Almadén and Idrija
    - [ ] The works of Jože Plečnik in Ljubljana – Human Centred Urban Design

- [ ] **SPAIN**
  - [ ] Watch the Montjuic Magic Fountain | Barcelona
  - [ ] See the remnants of Gaudi & Sagrada Familia | Barcelona
  - [ ] Rio Tinto River
  - [ ] Girona
  - [ ] See a Flamenco show
  - [ ] Watch a Bull Fight
  - [ ] MUSEUMS
    - [ ] Guggenheim Museum Bilbao | Bilbao
    - [ ] Dalí Theatre and Museum | Figueres
    - [ ] Museu Picasso | Barcelona
    - [ ] Museo Nacional Del Prado | Madrid
    - [ ] Museo Reina Sofía | Madrid
    - [ ] Thyssen-Bornemisza Museum | Madrid
  - [ ] EVENTS/FESTIVALS
    - [ ] Participate in La Tomatina (world's biggest food fight) | Bunol
    - [ ] Run with the bulls in Pamplona
    - [ ] See the human tower competition
    - [ ] Las Fallas | Valencia
    - [ ] San Vino Wine Fight
  - [ ] FOOD/DRINKS
    - [ ] Jamón Ibérico and Paella
  - [ ] WORLD HERITAGE SITES
    - [ ] hambra, Generalife and Albayzín, Granada

- ☐ Burgos Cathedral
- ☐ Historic Centre of Cordoba
- ☐ Monastery and Site of the Escurial, Madrid
- ☐ Works of Antoni Gaudí
- ☐ Cave of Altamira and Paleolithic Cave Art of Northern Spain
- ☐ Monuments of Oviedo and the Kingdom of the Asturias
- ☐ Old Town of Ávila with its Extra-Muros Churches
- ☐ Old Town of Segovia and its Aqueduct
- ☐ Santiago de Compostela (Old Town)
- ☐ Garajonay National Park
- ☐ Historic City of Toledo
- ☐ Mudejar Architecture of Aragon
- ☐ Old Town of Cáceres
- ☐ Cathedral, Alcázar and Archivo de Indias in Seville
- ☐ Old City of Salamanca
- ☐ Poblet Monastery
- ☐ Archaeological Ensemble of Mérida
- ☐ Routes of Santiago de Compostela: *Camino Francés* and Routes of Northern Spain
- ☐ Royal Monastery of Santa María de Guadalupe
- ☐ Doñana National Park
- ☐ Historic Walled Town of Cuenca
- ☐ La Lonja de la Seda de Valencia
- ☐ Las Médulas
- ☐ Palau de la Música Catalana and Hospital de Sant Pau, Barcelona
- ☐ Pyrénées - Mont Perdu
- ☐ San Millán Yuso and Suso Monasteries
- ☐ Prehistoric Rock Art Sites in the Côa Valley and Siega Verde
- ☐ Rock Art of the Mediterranean Basin on the Iberian Peninsula
- ☐ University and Historic Precinct of Alcalá de Henares
- ☐ Ibiza, Biodiversity and Culture
- ☐ San Cristóbal de La Laguna

- [ ] Archaeological Ensemble of Tarraco
- [ ] Archaeological Site of Atapuerca
- [ ] Catalan Romanesque Churches of the Vall de Boí
- [ ] Palmeral of Elche
- [ ] Roman Walls of Lugo
- [ ] Aranjuez Cultural Landscape
- [ ] Renaissance Monumental Ensembles of Úbeda and Baeza
- [ ] Vizcaya Bridge
- [ ] Ancient and Primeval Beech Forests of the Carpathians and Other Regions of Europe
- [ ] Teide National Park
- [ ] Tower of Hercules
- [ ] Cultural Landscape of the Serra de Tramuntana
- [ ] Heritage of Mercury. Almadén and Idrija
- [ ] Antequera Dolmens Site
- [ ] Caliphate City of Medina Azahara
- [ ] Risco Caido and the Sacred Mountains of Gran Canaria Cultural Landscape
- [ ] Paseo del Prado and Buen Retiro, a landscape of Arts and Sciences

- [ ] **SWEDEN**
  - [ ] Gamla Stan
  - [ ] Hike Kungsleden
  - [ ] Hike Sarek National Park
  - [ ] MUSEUMS
    - [ ] The Vasa Museum | Stockholm
  - [ ] EVENTS/FESTIVALS
    - [ ] Attend a midsummer party
  - [ ] HOTELS
    - [ ] Visit the Ice Hotel and watch the Northern Lights
  - [ ] FOOD/DRINKS
    - [ ] Swedish Meatballs
  - [ ] WORLD HERITAGE SITES
    - [ ] Royal Domain of Drottningholm
    - [ ] Birka and Hovgården
    - [ ] Engelsberg Ironworks
    - [ ] Rock Carvings in Tanum
    - [ ] Skogskyrkogården

- ☐ Hanseatic Town of Visby
- ☐ Church Town of Gammelstad, Luleå
- ☐ Laponian Area
- ☐ Naval Port of Karlskrona
- ☐ Agricultural Landscape of Southern Öland
- ☐ High Coast / Kvarken Archipelago
- ☐ Mining Area of the Great Copper Mountain in Falun
- ☐ Grimeton Radio Station, Varberg
- ☐ Struve Geodetic Arc
- ☐ Decorated Farmhouses of Hälsingland

☐ **SWITZERLAND**
- ☐ Ski the Swiss Alps
- ☐ Basel, Luzern and Vienna

☐ HIKES
- ☐ Matterhorn Trail | Matterhorn in Zermatt
- ☐ San Grato Park
- ☐ Grindelwald

☐ HOTEL
- ☐ Outdoor Jacuzzi at Iglu-Dorf Hotel

☐ FOOD/DRINKS
- ☐ fondue
- ☐ Eat in the world's oldest vegetarian restaurant

☐ WORLD HERITAGE SITES
- ☐ Abbey of St Gall
- ☐ Benedictine Convent of St John at Müstair
- ☐ Old City of Berne
- ☐ Three Castles, Defensive Wall and Ramparts of the Market-Town of Bellinzona
- ☐ Swiss Alps Jungfrau-Aletsch
- ☐ Monte San Giorgio
- ☐ Ancient and Primeval Beech Forests of the Carpathians and Other Regions of Europe
- ☐ Lavaux, Vineyard Terraces
- ☐ Rhaetian Railway in the Albula / Bernina Landscapes
- ☐ Swiss Tectonic Arena Sardona
- ☐ La Chaux-de-Fonds / Le Locle, Watchmaking Town Planning
- ☐ Prehistoric Pile Dwellings around the Alps

☐ The Architectural Work of Le Corbusier, an Outstanding Contribution to the Modern Movement

☐ **UKRAINE**

☐ Go through the Tunnel of Love | Klevan

☐ FOOD/DRINKS

☐ Varenyky (Pierogi)

☐ WORLD HERITAGE SITES

☐ Kyiv: Saint-Sophia Cathedral and Related Monastic Buildings, Kyiv-Pechersk Lavra

☐ L'viv – the Ensemble of the Historic Centre

☐ Struve Geodetic Arc

☐ Ancient and Primeval Beech Forests of the Carpathians and Other Regions of Europe

☐ Residence of Bukovinian and Dalmatian Metropolitans

☐ Ancient City of Tauric Chersonese and its Chora

☐ Wooden *Tserkvas* of the Carpathian Region in Poland and Ukraine

☐ **UNITED KINGDOM**

☐ ENGLAND

☐ Walk Across Abbey Road in London | England

☐ Watch the Changing of the Guard at Buckingham Palace, ten bucks more if you can make them smile.

☐ Meet one of the Royals of England

☐ Big Ben

☐ Ely Cathedral

☐ Longleat Maze | Longleat, Warminster, Wiltshire

☐ Platform 9 3/4 at Kings Cross

☐ Glastonbury Abbey

☐ Attend a proper British afternoon tea

☐ Make a phone call from a red telephone booth

☐ Relish cheap seats at Shakespeare's Globe Theatre

☐ Ride the Orient Express (ceased to operate, ride The Venice-Simplon Orient Express instead)
☐ Kew Royal Botanic Gardens
☐ Arundel Castle Gardens
☐ Stourhead Warminster
☐ Hike Hadrian's Wall Path, England
☐ Museums
   ☐ The Beatles Story | Liverpool
   ☐ Pitt Rivers Museum | Oxford
   ☐ The National Gallery | London
   ☐ The British Museum | London
   ☐ Tate Modern | London
   ☐ Somerset House | London
   ☐ The Natural History Museum | London
   ☐ Victoria and Albert Museum | London
   ☐ The Science Museum | London
   ☐ Wellcome Collection | London
   ☐ Portsmouth Historic Dockyard | Portsmouth
☐ FOOD/DRINKS
   ☐ Eat Roast beef and Yorkshire pudding
   ☐ Do The Monopoly Pub Crawl (26 pubs) | London
   ☐ Eat fish & chips
   ☐ Dine at the Rules | London
☐ EVENTS/FESTIVALS
   ☐ Attend Wimbledon | London
   ☐ Attend the Glastonbury Festival | Pilton
   ☐ Black Pool Illuminations Light Festival
   ☐ See a Manchester United game at Old Trafford
☐ GIBRALTAR
☐ SCOTLAND
   ☐ Fingal's Cave on the island of Staffa
   ☐ Play a golf round at St. Andrews
   ☐ Go in search of the Loch Ness monster
   ☐ Hogmanay
   ☐ Wear a kilt in Scotland

63

- ☐ Sleep in a Castle in Scotland
- ☐ Crathes Castle
- ☐ The Garden of Cosmic Speculation
- ☐ HIKES
  - ☐ Cape Wrath Trail, Scotland
  - ☐ Scottish National Park, Scotland
- ☐ MUSEUMS
  - ☐ The National Museum of Scotland | Edinburgh
  - ☐ Scottish National Gallery
- ☐ FOOD/DRINKS
  - ☐ Eat Haggis in Scotland
- ☐ EVENTS/FESTIVALS
  - ☐ Up Helly Aa Fire Festival
  - ☐ Edinburgh Fringe Festival
- ☐ WORLD HERITAGE SITES – Includes, England, Scotland, Northern Ireland and Wales
  - ☐ Castles and Town Walls of King Edward in Gwynedd
  - ☐ Durham Castle and Cathedral
  - ☐ Giant's Causeway and Causeway Coast
  - ☐ Ironbridge Gorge
  - ☐ St Kilda
  - ☐ Stonehenge, Avebury and Associated Sites
  - ☐ Studley Royal Park including the Ruins of Fountains Abbey
  - ☐ Blenheim Palace
  - ☐ City of Bath
  - ☐ Frontiers of the Roman Empire
  - ☐ Palace of Westminster and Westminster Abbey including Saint Margaret's Church
  - ☐ Canterbury Cathedral, St Augustine's Abbey, and St Martin's Church
  - ☐ Henderson Island
  - ☐ Tower of London
  - ☐ Gough and Inaccessible Islands
  - ☐ Old and New Towns of Edinburgh
  - ☐ Maritime Greenwich
  - ☐ Heart of Neolithic Orkney
  - ☐ Blaenavon Industrial Landscape

- ☐ Historic Town of St George and Related Fortifications, Bermuda
- ☐ Derwent Valley Mills
- ☐ Dorset and East Devon Coast
- ☐ New Lanark
- ☐ Saltaire
- ☐ Royal Botanic Gardens, Kew
- ☐ Cornwall and West Devon Mining Landscape
- ☐ Pontcysyllte Aqueduct and Canal
- ☐ The Forth Bridge
- ☐ Gorham's Cave Complex
- ☐ The English Lake District
- ☐ Jodrell Bank Observatory
- ☐ The Great Spa Towns of Europe
- ☐ The Slate Landscape of Northwest Wales

☐ _____

☐ _____

☐ _____

☐ _____

☐ _____

☐ _____

☐ _____

☐ _____

☐ _____

☐ _____

☐ _____

☐ _____

☐ _____

☐ _____

☐ _____

NORTH AMERICA BUCKET LIST

- [ ] **ANGUILLA**
  - [ ] Shal Bay Village
- [ ] **ANTIGUA AND BARBUDA**
  - [ ] WORLD HERITAGE SITES
    - [ ] Antigua Naval Dockyard and Related Archaeological Sites
- [ ] **ARUBA**
- [ ] **BAHAMAS**
  - [ ] Swim with pigs at Big Major Cay in Exuma
  - [ ] Walk on the Pink Sand Beach
  - [ ] Swim and Free dive at Dean's Blue Hole
  - [ ] WORLD'S DANGEROUS WATERSLIDES
    - [ ] Leap of Faith
- [ ] **BARBADOS**
  - [ ] WORLD HERITAGE SITES
    - [ ] Historic Bridgetown and its Garrison
- [ ] **BERMUDA**
- [ ] **BELIZE**
  - [ ] The Great Blue Hole
  - [ ] WORLD HERITAGE SITES
    - [ ] Belize Barrier Reef Reserve System
- [ ] **BRITISH VIRGIN ISLANDS**
- [ ] **CANADA**
  - [ ] Do the Edge Walk at CN Tower
  - [ ] Walk the Capilano Suspension Bridge | Vancouver
  - [ ] Moraine Lake | Alberta
  - [ ] Abraham Lake | Alberta
  - [ ] Bed down in an Igloo | Quebec
  - [ ] Queen Charlotte Islands/Haida Gwaii | British Columbia
  - [ ] Western Brook Pond | Newfoundland
  - [ ] Cavendish Beach, Prince Edward Island
  - [ ] See 125+ Year Old Rhododendron "Tree"

☐ Butchart Gardens, British Columbia
☐ HIKES
    ☐ Long Range traverse, Newfoundland
    ☐ Chilkoot Trail
    ☐ Tonquin Valley, Alberta
    ☐ West Coast Trail
    ☐ West Coast Trail, British Columbia
☐ MUSEUMS
    ☐ Royal Ontario Museum | Toronto
    ☐ National Gallery of Canada | Ottawa
    ☐ Canadian Museum of History | Gatineau
    ☐ Montreal Museum of Fine Arts | Montreal
☐ FOOD/DRINKS
    ☐ Poutine
    ☐ Maple Syrup Pancakes
☐ WORLD HERITAGE SITES
    ☐ L'Anse aux Meadows National Historic Site
    ☐ Nahanni National Park
    ☐ Dinosaur Provincial Park
    ☐ Kluane / Wrangell-St. Elias / Glacier Bay / Tatshenshini-Alsek
    ☐ Head-Smashed-In Buffalo Jump
    ☐ SGang Gwaay
    ☐ Wood Buffalo National Park
    ☐ Canadian Rocky Mountain Parks
    ☐ Historic District of Old Québec
    ☐ Gros Morne National Park
    ☐ Old Town Lunenburg
    ☐ Waterton Glacier International Peace Park
    ☐ Miguasha National Park
    ☐ Rideau Canal
    ☐ Joggins Fossil Cliffs
    ☐ Landscape of Grand Pré
    ☐ Red Bay Basque Whaling Station
    ☐ Mistaken Point
    ☐ Pimachiowin Aki
    ☐ Writing-on-Stone / Áísínai'pi
☐ **CAYMAN ISLANDS**

- ☐ **CARIBBEAN**
    - ☐ FOOD/DRINKS
        - ☐ Tamarind Balls
- ☐ **COSTA RICA**
    - ☐ National Museum of Costa Rica | San Jose
    - ☐ WORLD HERITAGE SITES
        - ☐ Talamanca Range-La Amistad Reserves / La Amistad National Park
        - ☐ Cocos Island National Park
        - ☐ Area de Conservación Guanacaste
        - ☐ Precolumbian Chiefdom Settlements with Stone Spheres of the Diquís
- ☐ **CUBA**
    - ☐ Smoke a Cuban cigar
    - ☐ WORLD HERITAGE SITES
        - ☐ Old Havana and its Fortification System
        - ☐ Trinidad and the Valley de los Ingenios
        - ☐ San Pedro de la Roca Castle, Santiago de Cuba
        - ☐ Desembarco del Granma National Park
        - ☐ Viñales Valley
        - ☐ Archaeological Landscape of the First Coffee Plantations in the South-East of Cuba
        - ☐ Alejandro de Humboldt National Park
        - ☐ Urban Historic Centre of Cienfuegos
        - ☐ Historic Centre of Camagüey
- ☐ **CURACAO**
- ☐ **DOMINICA**
    - ☐ WORLD HERITAGE SITES
        - ☐ Morne Trois Pitons National Park
- ☐ **DOMINICAN REPUBLIC**
    - ☐ WORLD HERITAGE SITES
        - ☐ Colonial City of Santo Domingo
- ☐ **EL SALVADOR**
    - ☐ WORLD HERITAGE SITES
        - ☐ Joya de Cerén Archaeological Site
- ☐ **FALKLAND ISLANDS**
- ☐ **GREENLAND**
    - ☐ HIKES
        - ☐ Polar Route
        - ☐ Arctic Circle Trail

68

- ☐ **GRENADA**
- ☐ **GUADELOUPE**
- ☐ **GUAM**
- ☐ **GUATEMALA**
    - ☐ Hike the Active Pacaya Volcano
    - ☐ WORLD HERITAGE SITES
        - ☐ Antigua Guatemala
        - ☐ Tikal National Park
        - ☐ Archaeological Park and Ruins of Quirigua
- ☐ **HAITI**
    - ☐ WORLD HERITAGE SITES
        - ☐ National History Park – Citadel, Sans Souci, Ramiers
- ☐ **HONDURAS**
    - ☐ WORLD HERITAGE SITES
        - ☐ Maya Site of Copan
        - ☐ Río Plátano Biosphere Reserve
- ☐ **JAMAICA**
    - ☐ Bob Marley Museum | Kingston
    - ☐ FOOD/DRINKS
        - ☐ Ugli Fruit
    - ☐ WORLD HERITAGE SITES
        - ☐ Blue and John Crow Mountains
- ☐ **MARTINIQUE**
- ☐ **MEXICO**
    - ☐ Aztec Ruins
    - ☐ Mayan Ruins | Chichen Itza
    - ☐ Paricuting Volcano
    - ☐ Visit the Naica Mines
    - ☐ Visit Mexico and see the Teotihuacan, among others
    - ☐ Swim in a Cenote
    - ☐ Swim with Whale Sharks
    - ☐ Spring Break in Cabo San Lucas, Cancun or Puerto Vallarta
    - ☐ Tulum
    - ☐ Ixtapa and Zihuatanejo
    - ☐ Grutas Tolantongo
    - ☐ Hierve el Aqua
    - ☐ Suytun Cenote

69

- ☐ Cenote Tak Bi Ha
- ☐ Tamasopo
- ☐ Play Balandra in La Paz
☐ GARDENS
- ☐ Edward James Surrealist Garden "Las Pozas"
☐ MUSEUMS
- ☐ Snorkel the Underwater Museum
- ☐ Cancún Underwater Museum | Cancún
- ☐ The National Museum of Anthropology | Mexico City
- ☐ Museo Soumaya | Mexico City
- ☐ The Frida Kahlo Museum | Mexico City
☐ EVENTS AND FESTIVALS
- ☐ Día de Los Muertos (Day of the Dead) | Mexico City, November 1-2
☐ FOOD/DRINKS
- ☐ Dragon fruit
- ☐ Mole sauce
☐ WORLD HERITAGE SITES
- ☐ Historic Centre of Mexico City and Xochimilco
- ☐ Historic Centre of Oaxaca and Archaeological Site of Monte Albán
- ☐ Historic Centre of Puebla
- ☐ Pre-Hispanic City and National Park of Palenque
- ☐ Pre-Hispanic City of Teotihuacan
- ☐ Sian Ka'an
- ☐ Historic Town of Guanajuato and Adjacent Mines
- ☐ Pre-Hispanic City of Chichen-Itza
- ☐ Historic Centre of Morelia
- ☐ El Tajin, Pre-Hispanic City
- ☐ Historic Centre of Zacatecas
- ☐ Rock Paintings of the Sierra de San Francisco
- ☐ Whale Sanctuary of El Vizcaino
- ☐ Earliest 16th-Century Monasteries on the Slopes of Popocatepetl
- ☐ Historic Monuments Zone of Querétaro
- ☐ Pre-Hispanic Town of Uxmal
- ☐ Hospicio Cabañas, Guadalajara
- ☐ Archaeological Zone of Paquimé, Casas Grandes

- ☐ Historic Monuments Zone of Tlacotalpan
- ☐ Archaeological Monuments Zone of Xochicalco
- ☐ Historic Fortified Town of Campeche
- ☐ Ancient Maya City and Protected Tropical Forests of Calakmul, Campeche
- ☐ Franciscan Missions in the Sierra Gorda of Querétaro
- ☐ Luis Barragán House and Studio
- ☐ Islands and Protected Areas of the Gulf of California
- ☐ Agave Landscape and Ancient Industrial Facilities of Tequila
- ☐ Central University City Campus of the *Universidad Nacional Autónoma de México* (UNAM)
- ☐ Monarch Butterfly Biosphere Reserve
- ☐ Protective town of San Miguel and the Sanctuary of Jesús Nazareno de Atotonilco
- ☐ Camino Real de Tierra Adentro
- ☐ Prehistoric Caves of Yagul and Mitla in the Central Valley of Oaxaca
- ☐ El Pinacate and Gran Desierto de Altar Biosphere Reserve
- ☐ Aqueduct of Padre Tembleque Hydraulic System
- ☐ Archipiélago de Revillagigedo
- ☐ Tehuacán-Cuicatlán Valley: originary habitat of Mesoamerica

☐ **MONTSERRAT**

☐ **NICARAGUA**

- ☐ Board Down a Volcano | Nicaragua
- ☐ WORLD HERITAGE SITES
  - ☐ Ruins of León Viejo
  - ☐ León Cathedral

☐ **PANAMA**

- ☐ Biomuseo | Panama City
- ☐ WORLD HERITAGE SITES
  - ☐ Fortifications on the Caribbean Side of Panama: Portobelo-San Lorenzo
  - ☐ Darien National Park

- ☐ Talamanca Range-La Amistad Reserves / La Amistad National Park
- ☐ Archaeological Site of Panamá Viejo and Historic District of Panamá
- ☐ Coiba National Park and its Special Zone of Marine Protection
- ☐ **PUERTO RICO**
- ☐ **SAINT KITTS AND NEVIS**
  - ☐ WORLD HERITAGE SITES
    - ☐ Brimstone Hill Fortress National Park
- ☐ **SAINT LUCIA**
  - ☐ WORLD HERITAGE SITES
    - ☐ Pitons Management Area
- ☐ **SAINT PIERRE & MIQUELON**
- ☐ **SAINT VINCENT AND THE GRENADINES**
- ☐ **SINT MAARTEN**
- ☐ **TRINIDAD AND TOBAGO**
- ☐ **TURKS AND CAICOS**
- ☐ **UNITED STATES**
  - ☐ Drive Route 66
  - ☐ Go to all the US National Parks
    - ☐ Acadia
    - ☐ American Samoa
    - ☐ Arches
    - ☐ Badlands
    - ☐ Big Bend
    - ☐ Biscayne
    - ☐ Black Canyon of the Gunnison
    - ☐ Bryce Canyon
    - ☐ Canyonlands
    - ☐ Capitol Reef
    - ☐ Carlsbad Caverns
    - ☐ Channel Islands
    - ☐ Congaree
    - ☐ Crater Lake
    - ☐ Cuyahoga Valley
    - ☐ Death Valley
    - ☐ Denali
    - ☐ Dry Tortugas
    - ☐ Everglades

- ☐ Gates of the Arctic
- ☐ Gateway Arch
- ☐ Glacier Bay
- ☐ Glacier
- ☐ Grand Canyon
- ☐ Grand Teton
- ☐ Great Basin
- ☐ Great Sand Dunes
- ☐ Great Smoky Mountains
- ☐ Guadalupe Mountains
- ☐ Haleakala
- ☐ Hawai'i Volcanoes
- ☐ Hot Springs
- ☐ Indiana Dunes
- ☐ Isle Royale
- ☐ Joshua Tree
- ☐ Katmai
- ☐ Kenai Fjords
- ☐ Kings Canyon
- ☐ Kobuk Valley
- ☐ Lake Clark
- ☐ Lassen Volcanic
- ☐ Mammoth Cave
- ☐ Mesa Verde
- ☐ Mount Rainier
- ☐ New River Gorge
- ☐ North Cascades
- ☐ Olympic
- ☐ Petrified Forest
- ☐ Pinnacles
- ☐ Redwood
- ☐ Rocky Mountain
- ☐ Saguaro
- ☐ Sequoia
- ☐ Shenandoah
- ☐ Theodore Roosevelt
- ☐ Virgin Islands
- ☐ Voyageurs
- ☐ White Sands
- ☐ Wind Cave

- [ ] Wrangell – St. Elias
- [ ] Yellowstone
- [ ] Yosemite
- [ ] Zion
- [ ] Lay on the Four Corners (4 States at Once)
- [ ] Go on a road trip through the United States
- [ ] Watch an NBA game
- [ ] Watch an NHL Game
- [ ] Stanley Cup
- [ ] World Series Baseball
- [ ] Super Bowl
- [ ] Visit All 50 States
- [ ] Visit my State Capitol
- [ ] Eat a huge (4LB) hamburger
- [ ] Hike the Appalachian Trail

- [ ] ALABAMA
- [ ] ALASKA
  - [ ] Trek the Mendenhall Glacier Caves
  - [ ] See the Northern Lights
  - [ ] Dogsledding
- [ ] ARIZONA
  - [ ] See the Grand Canyon by plane/helicopter
  - [ ] Grand Canyon Rim-to-Rim Hike
  - [ ] See "The Wave" | Utah/Arizona, US
  - [ ] Hike into Antelope Canyon
  - [ ] Paria Canyon-Vermilion Cliffs
  - [ ] Desert Botanical Garden
- [ ] ARKANSAS
  - [ ] Visit Anthony Chapel in Garvan Woodland Gardens
- [ ] CALIFORNIA
  - [ ] Go to the Santa Monica Pier and ride the Ferris Wheel | Los Angeles
  - [ ] Stand under the Hollywood sign | Los Angeles
  - [ ] Visit the Hollywood Walk of Fame | Los Angeles

74

- ☐ Go to Madame Tussaud's Wax Museum
- ☐ The Getty Center | Los Angeles
- ☐ Tour Beverly Hills and shop Rodeo Drive
- ☐ Warner Brothers Studio Tour
- ☐ Stay at the Beverly Hills Hotel
- ☐ Party at the Playboy Mansion
- ☐ Hug a redwood tree (Sequoioideae) | Redwood Nt. Park
- ☐ The President, Third-Largest Giant Sequoia
- ☐ See the Golden Gate Bridge | San Francisco
- ☐ See the Beach Art by Andres Amador
- ☐ Fisherman's Wharf | San Francisco
- ☐ Visit Alcatraz | San Francisco
- ☐ Alcatraz Island Museum | San Francisco
- ☐ de Young Museum | San Francisco
- ☐ Drive/go down Lombard Street | San Francisco
- ☐ Ride a cable car in San Francisco
- ☐ Walk Across the Golden Gate Bridge
- ☐ Do the Half-Dome Ascent in Yosemite
- ☐ Drive the Pacific Coast Highway
- ☐ Rappel into Moaning Caverns
- ☐ Walk on a Glass Beach
- ☐ Wine Taste in the Napa Valley
- ☐ Hike Yosemite Grand Traverse, California
- ☐ USS Midway Museum | San Diego
- ☐ FUNNY NAMES TO VISIT
  - ☐ Yolo County
- ☐ RESTAURANTS/BARS
  - ☐ French Laundry
- ☐ COLORADO
  - ☐ Go Sandboarding at Great Sand Dunes National Park
  - ☐ See the Ice Castles at Silverthorne
  - ☐ Ski Aspen
  - ☐ Take the Viaferada (Iron Route)
  - ☐ Hike The Narrows, Colorado

75

☐ FUNNY NAMES TO VISIT
    ☐ No Name
☐ DELAWARE
☐ FLORIDA
    ☐ Explore the Everglades
    ☐ Have Fun at Walt Disney World
    ☐ Take a Selfie at the Southernmost Point in the Continental US
    ☐ Kennedy Space Center Visitor Complex | Titusville
    ☐ The Salvador Dali Museum | St. Petersburg
  ☐ EVENTS/FESTIVALS
    ☐ Art Basal | Miami
☐ GEORGIA
☐ HAWAII
    ☐ Attend a luau
    ☐ Wear a fresh lei
    ☐ Climb the Haiku Stairs of Oahu
    ☐ Learn the Hula
    ☐ Drive the Road to Hana
    ☐ Walk on Waianapanapa Black Sand Beach
    ☐ Volcanoes
    ☐ Turtle Bay
    ☐ Rainbow Eucalyptus, Kauai
    ☐ Hike Kalalau Trail, Hawaii
    ☐ Hike Muliwai Trail, Hawaii
  ☐ FOOD/DRINKS
    ☐ Eat Ahi Poke
    ☐ Eat Poi
    ☐ Eat at a shrimp truck
☐ IDAHO
    ☐ White water rafting in Middle Fork Salmon River
☐ ILLINOIS
    ☐ Catch a Baseball Game at Wrigley Field
    ☐ The Art Institute of Chicago

☐ The Field Museum of Natural History | Chicago

☐ INDIANA
☐ IOWA
    ☐ FOOD/DRINKS
        ☐ Eat Food-on-a-Stick at the State Fair
☐ KANSAS
    ☐ WORLD'S DANGEROUS WATERSLIDES
        ☐ Verrückt
☐ KENTUCKY
    ☐ Wear a Fancy Hat at the Kentucky Derby
    ☐ FOOD/DRINKS
        ☐ Eat KFC
☐ LOUISIANA
    ☐ Listen to Jazz in the French Quarter
    ☐ The National WWII Museum | New Orleans
    ☐ EVENTS/FESTIVALS
        ☐ Throw Beads at Mardi Gras in New Orleans
☐ MAINE
    ☐ FOOD/DRINKS
        ☐ Eat Maine Lobster
        ☐ Eat Lobster Rolls from a seaside shack
☐ MARYLAND
☐ MASSACHUSETTS
    ☐ Spend the Night in Martha's Vineyard
    ☐ Experience the Fall Foliage
    ☐ Go to Walden Pond and read Thoreau while drifting in a canoe
    ☐ MUSEUMS
        ☐ Museum of Fine Arts | Boston
        ☐ The Museum of Bad Art Somerville | Massachusetts
☐ MICHIGAN
    ☐ Frederik Meijer Gardens & Sculpture Park
    ☐ MUSEUMS

☐ The Henry Ford Museum | Dearborn
☐ MINNESOTA
☐ MISSISSIPPI
☐ MISSOURI
 ☐ Explore the Ozark Caverns
 ☐ MUSEUMS
  ☐ Nelson-Atkins Museum of Art | Kansas City
☐ MONTANA
 ☐ HIKES
  ☐ Hike Through Glacier National Park
☐ NEBRASKA
☐ NEVADA
 ☐ See a show in Las Vegas
 ☐ Gamble and win in Las Vegas
 ☐ Walk the Las Vegas Strip
 ☐ See a Cirque du Soleil show
 ☐ Go to a hotel pool party
 ☐ HIKES
  ☐ Hike Sierra High Route, Nevada
 ☐ RESTAURANTS/BARS
  ☐ Dine at Dick's Last Resort
 ☐ EVENTS/FESTIVALS
  ☐ Burning Man
☐ NEW HAMPSHIRE
☐ NEW JERSEY
☐ NEW MEXICO
 ☐ Explore the Carlsbad Caverns
 ☐ EVENTS/FESTIVALS
  ☐ Albuquerque International Balloon Fiesta
☐ NEW YORK
 ☐ Hail Ride a Yellow Cab
 ☐ Bronx Zoo
 ☐ Have "Breakfast at Tiffany's"
 ☐ Metropolitan Museum of Art and the Museum of Modern Art
 ☐ Be on top of the Empire State Building
 ☐ Ice skate at the Rockefeller Center during Christmas time

- ☐ See a Broadway Musical
- ☐ Climb the stairs to the top of the Statue of Liberty
- ☐ Be a spectator at Carnegie Hall
- ☐ Play at Coney Island
- ☐ Walk Through Grand Central Station
- ☐ Stand in Times Square
- ☐ See Niagara Falls
- ☐ Spend summer in the Hamptons
- ☐ GARDENS
  - ☐ Brooklyn Botanic Gardens
- ☐ MUSEUMS
  - ☐ National 9/11 Memorial & Museum
  - ☐ Intrepid Sea, Air & Space Museum
  - ☐ The Metropolitan Museum of Art
  - ☐ The Museum of Modern Art
  - ☐ Solomon R. Guggenheim Museum
- ☐ FUNNY NAMES TO VISIT
  - ☐ Bitch Mountain
- ☐ FOOD/DRINKS
  - ☐ Eat Buffalo Wings in Buffalo
  - ☐ Eat Red Velvet Cake in Waldorf-Astoria Hotel
- ☐ EVENTS/FESTIVALS
  - ☐ Macy's Thanksgiving Day Parade
  - ☐ Westminster Dog Show
  - ☐ Celebrate New Year's in Times Square
  - ☐ Village Halloween Parade
  - ☐ Coney Island polar bear plunge | Jan. 1
  - ☐ Participate in the Coney Island hot dog eating contest
- ☐ NORTH CAROLINA
  - ☐ Tour the Biltmore Estates
- ☐ NORTH DAKOTA
- ☐ OHIO
- ☐ OKLAHOMA
- ☐ OREGON
  - ☐ Get Lost in Powell's Books
  - ☐ See Multnomah Falls

- ☐ Beautiful Japanese Maple in Portland
- ☐ Antarctic Beech Draped in Hanging Moss
- ☐ Maple Tree Tunnel

☐ PENNSYLVANIA
- ☐ Go to a Mud Sale in Lancaster County
- ☐ MUSEUMS
  - ☐ Philadelphia Museum of Art | Philadelphia
  - ☐ Mütter Museum | Philadelphia
- ☐ FOOD/DRINKS
  - ☐ Eat a Philly Cheese Steak in Philadelphia

☐ RHODE ISLAND
☐ SOUTH CAROLINA
- ☐ Angel Oak in John's Island
- ☐ Avenue of Oaks at Dixie Plantation

☐ SOUTH DAKOTA
- ☐ See Mount Rushmore
- ☐ Explore Badlands National Park

☐ TENNESSEE
- ☐ Party at Honky Tonk
- ☐ See the Grand Ole Opry in Nashville
- ☐ Stay in Summer City when it is summer

☐ TEXAS
- ☐ Visit the Alamo

- ☐ MUSEUMS
  - ☐ Kimbell Art Museum | Fort Worth
- ☐ EVENTS/FESTIVALS
  - ☐ Sandfest

☐ UTAH
- ☐ Explore Bryce Canyon
- ☐ Visit Zion National Park
- ☐ EVENTS/FESTIVALS
  - ☐ Electric Run
  - ☐ Sundance Film Festival

☐ VERMONT

- [ ] VIRGINIA
- [ ] WASHINGTON
    - [ ] Catch a Fish at Pike Place Market
    - [ ] Leave a Contribution on Seattle's Gum Wall
    - [ ] Visit Skagit Valley Tulip Fields
- [ ] WASHINGTON DC
    - [ ] Tour the White House
    - [ ] See the Thomas Jefferson Memorial
    - [ ] MUSEUMS
        - [ ] Smithsonian National Air and Space Museum
        - [ ] Smithsonian American Art Museum
        - [ ] The National Gallery of Art
        - [ ] International Spy Museum
    - [ ] EVENTS FESTIVALS
        - [ ] National Cherry Blossom Festival
- [ ] WEST VIRGINIA
- [ ] WISCONSIN
    - [ ] The Milwaukee Art Museum
- [ ] WYOMING
    - [ ] Attend the Biggest Outdoor Rodeo
    - [ ] Go to Grand Prismatic Spring
    - [ ] Devil's Tour
    - [ ] Go camping
- [ ] WORLD HERITAGE SITES
    - [ ] Mesa Verde National Park
    - [ ] Yellowstone National Park
    - [ ] Everglades National Park
    - [ ] Grand Canyon National Park
    - [ ] Independence Hall
    - [ ] Kluane / Wrangell-St. Elias / Glacier Bay / Tatshenshini-Alsek
    - [ ] Redwood National and State Parks
    - [ ] Mammoth Cave National Park
    - [ ] Olympic National Park
    - [ ] Cahokia Mounds State Historic Site
    - [ ] Great Smoky Mountains National Park
    - [ ] La Fortaleza and San Juan National Historic Site in Puerto Rico

- ☐ Statue of Liberty
- ☐ Yosemite National Park
- ☐ Chaco Culture
- ☐ Hawaii Volcanoes National Park
- ☐ Monticello and the University of Virginia in Charlottesville
- ☐ Taos Pueblo
- ☐ Carlsbad Caverns National Park
- ☐ Papahānaumokuākea
- ☐ Monumental Earthworks of Poverty Point
- ☐ San Antonio Missions
- ☐ The 20th-Century Architecture of Frank Lloyd Wright

☐ **U.S. VIRGIN ISLANDS**

- ☐ _____
- ☐ _____
- ☐ _____
- ☐ _____
- ☐ _____
- ☐ _____
- ☐ _____

OCEANIA BUCKET LIST

☐ **AUSTRALIA**
    ☐ Dive or snorkel in Great Barrier Reef
    ☐ Climb the Sydney Harbour Bridge
    ☐ Visit Bondi Beach | Sydney
    ☐ See an Opera at the Sydney Opera House
    ☐ Melbourne
    ☐ Visit the outback
    ☐ See the Red Crab Migration in Christmas Island
    ☐ Stay on the Christmas Islands when it is Christmas
    ☐ Sail the Whitsundays
    ☐ See the Tessellated Pavement | Tasmania
    ☐ Royal Botanic Garden

☐ HIKES
    ☐ Overland Track, Australia
    ☐ Bay of Fires, Australia
    ☐ Bibbulmun Track, Australia
    ☐ Great Ocean Walk, Victoria, Australia

☐ MUSEUMS
    ☐ Queensland Art Gallery | South Brisbane
    ☐ Gallery of Modern Art | Bisbane
    ☐ The Australian Centre for the Moving Image | Melbourne
    ☐ National Gallery of Victoria | Melbourne

☐ FOOD/DRINKS
    ☐ Vegemite
    ☐ Kangaroo

☐ WORLD HERITAGE SITES
    ☐ Great Barrier Reef
    ☐ Kakadu National Park
    ☐ Willandra Lakes Region
    ☐ Lord Howe Island Group
    ☐ Tasmanian Wilderness

- ☐ Gondwana Rainforests of Australia
- ☐ Uluru-Kata Tjuta National Park
- ☐ Wet Tropics of Queensland
- ☐ Shark Bay, Western Australia
- ☐ K'gari (Fraser Island)
- ☐ Australian Fossil Mammal Sites (Riversleigh / Naracoorte)
- ☐ Heard and McDonald Islands
- ☐ Macquarie Island
- ☐ Greater Blue Mountains Area
- ☐ Purnululu National Park
- ☐ Royal Exhibition Building and Carlton Gardens
- ☐ Sydney Opera House
- ☐ Australian Convict Sites
- ☐ Ningaloo Coast
- ☐ Budj Bim Cultural Landscape

☐ **FIJI**
- ☐ Mamnuca Islands
- ☐ The Yasawa Islands
    - ☐ WORLD HERITAGE SITES
        - ☐ Levuka Historical Port Town

☐ **KIRIBATI**
- ☐ WORLD HERITAGE SITES
    - ☐ Phoenix Islands Protected Area

☐ **MARSHALL ISLANDS**
- ☐ WORLD HERITAGE SITES
    - ☐ Bikini Atoll Nuclear Test Site

☐ **MELANESIA**

☐ **MICRONESIA**
- ☐ WORLD HERITAGE SITES
    - ☐ Nan Madol: Ceremonial Centre of Eastern Micronesia

☐ **NAURU**

☐ **NEW ZEALAND**
- ☐ See Kiwis (the bird not the fruit...)
- ☐ Visit Hobbiton
- ☐ See Rotorua & the Champagne Pool
- ☐ Explore the Waitomo Glowworm Cave
- ☐ Go Black Water Rafting
- ☐ Kayak Milford Sound

- ☐ Kaaikoura dolphin swim experience
- ☐ See Wind-Swept Trees
- ☐ Spend a night in a haunted location (Waitomo Caves Hotel)
- ☐ HIKES
  - ☐ Queen Charlotte Track
  - ☐ Tongariro Alpine Crossings
  - ☐ Overland Track
  - ☐ Routeburn Track
  - ☐ The Franz Josef Glacier
- ☐ WORLD HERITAGE SITES
  - ☐ Te Wahipounamu – South West New Zealand
  - ☐ Tongariro National Park
  - ☐ New Zealand Sub-Antarctic Islands

☐ **PALAU**
- ☐ Swim in Jellyfish Lake
- ☐ Get a natural and bath in Palau's Milky Way
- ☐ WORLD HERITAGE SITES
  - ☐ Rock Islands Southern Lagoon

☐ **PAPUA NEW GUINEA**
- ☐ WORLD HERITAGE SITES
  - ☐ Kuk Early Agricultural Site

☐ **POLYNESIA**

☐ **SAMOA**
- ☐ To Sua Ocean Trench in the Lotofoga village

☐ **SOLOMON ISLANDS**
- ☐ WORLD HERITAGE SITES
  - ☐ East Rennell
  - ☐ AlSuriname
  - ☐ Central Suriname Nature Reserve
  - ☐ Historic Inner City of Paramaribo

☐ **TONGA**

☐ **TUVALU**

☐ **VANUATU**
- ☐ WORLD HERITAGE SITES
  - ☐ Chief Roi Mata's Domain

☐ _____

☐ _____

BUCKET LIST

- ☐ _____
- ☐ _____
- ☐ _____
- ☐ _____
- ☐ _____
- ☐ _____
- ☐ _____
- ☐ _____
- ☐ _____
- ☐ _____
- ☐ _____
- ☐ _____
- ☐ _____
- ☐ _____
- ☐ _____
- ☐ _____
- ☐ _____
- ☐ _____
- ☐ _____
- ☐ _____
- ☐ _____
- ☐ _____
- ☐ _____
- ☐ _____
- ☐ _____
- ☐ _____

SOUTH AMERICA BUCKET LIST

☐ **ARGENTINA**
  ☐ See the Patagonian grasslands | Argentina/Chile
  ☐ Do the Argentine Tango
  ☐ Hike Fitz Roy Trek, Argentina
  ☐ Museo De Arte Latinoamericano De Buenos Aires | Buenos Aires
  ☐ WORLD HERITAGE SITES
    ☐ Los Glaciares National Park
    ☐ Jesuit Missions of the Guaranis: San Ignacio Mini, Santa Ana, Nuestra Señora de Loreto and Santa Maria Mayor (Argentina), Ruins of Sao Miguel das Missoes (Brazil)
    ☐ Iguazu National Park
    ☐ Cueva de las Manos, Río Pinturas
    ☐ Península Valdés
    ☐ Ischigualasto / Talampaya Natural Parks
    ☐ Jesuit Block and Estancias of Córdoba
    ☐ Quebrada de Humahuaca
    ☐ Qhapaq Ñan, Andean Road System
    ☐ The Architectural Work of Le Corbusier, an Outstanding Contribution to the Modern Movement
    ☐ Los Alerces National Park
☐ **BOLIVIA**
  ☐ Walk on the Salar de Uyuni Salt Flat
  ☐ Hike Cordillera Apolobamba, Bolivia
  ☐ FUNNY NAMES TO VISIT
    ☐ Lake Titicaca
  ☐ WORLD HERITAGE SITES
    ☐ City of Potosí
    ☐ Jesuit Missions of the Chiquitos
    ☐ Historic City of Sucre
    ☐ Fuerte de Samaipata
    ☐ Noel Kempff Mercado National Park

- ☐ Tiwanaku: Spiritual and Political Centre of the Tiwanaku Culture
- ☐ Qhapaq Ñan, Andean Road System

☐ **BRAZIL**

- ☐ Harbour of Rio de Janeiro
- ☐ See the Iguazu Falls
- ☐ Christ the Redeemer
- ☐ Visit the Amazon
- ☐ Swim with Pink Dolphins | Amazon
- ☐ Hang gliding preferably in Rio
- ☐ Stand on the Equator line
- ☐ Flamboyant Tree, Brazil
- ☐ Instituto Ricardo Brennand | Recife
- ☐ Instituto Inhotim | Brumadinho
- ☐ Centro Cultural Banco Do Brasil | Rio De Janeiro
- ☐ Pinacoteca Do Estado De São Paulo | São Paulo
- ☐ Museu Do Futebol | São Paulo

☐ WORLD'S DANGEROUS WATERSLIDES
- ☐ Insano

☐ EVENTS/FESTIVALS
- ☐ Participate in the Carnival in Rio de Janeiro

☐ FOOD/DRINKS
- ☐ Jabuticaba
- ☐ Feijoada

☐ WORLD HERITAGE SITES
- ☐ Historic Town of Ouro Preto
- ☐ Historic Centre of the Town of Olinda
- ☐ Jesuit Missions of the Guaranis: San Ignacio Mini, Santa Ana, Nuestra Señora de Loreto and Santa Maria Mayor (Argentina), Ruins of Sao Miguel das Missoes (Brazil)
- ☐ Historic Centre of Salvador de Bahia
- ☐ Sanctuary of Bom Jesus do Congonhas
- ☐ Iguaçu National Park
- ☐ Brasilia
- ☐ Serra da Capivara National Park
- ☐ Historic Centre of São Luís
- ☐ Atlantic Forest South-East Reserves
- ☐ Discovery Coast Atlantic Forest Reserves

- ☐ Historic Centre of the Town of Diamantina
- ☐ Central Amazon Conservation Complex
- ☐ Pantanal Conservation Area
- ☐ Brazilian Atlantic Islands: Fernando de Noronha and Atol das Rocas Reserves
- ☐ Cerrado Protected Areas: Chapada dos Veadeiros and Emas National Parks
- ☐ Historic Centre of the Town of Goiás
- ☐ São Francisco Square in the Town of São Cristóvão
- ☐ Rio de Janeiro: Carioca Landscapes between the Mountain and the Sea
- ☐ Pampulha Modern Ensemble
- ☐ Valongo Wharf Archaeological Site
- ☐ Paraty and Ilha Grande – Culture and Biodiversity
- ☐ Sítio Roberto Burle Marx

☐ CHILE

- ☐ Stay on the Easter Islands when it is Easter
- ☐ Trek the Torres del Paine (Cordillera Paine)
- ☐ Swim in the world's largest pool
- ☐ Hike Torres del Paine Circuit, Chile

☐ WORLD HERITAGE SITES

- ☐ Rapa Nui National Park
- ☐ Churches of Chiloé
- ☐ Historic Quarter of the Seaport City of Valparaíso
- ☐ Humberstone and Santa Laura Saltpeter Works
- ☐ Sewell Mining Town
- ☐ Qhapaq Ñan, Andean Road System
- ☐ Settlement and Artificial Mummification of the Chinchorro Culture in the Arica and Parinacota Region

☐ COLOMBIA

- ☐ Hike La Ciudad | Perdida
- ☐ Gold Museum | Bogotá

☐ WORLD HERITAGE SITES

- ☐ Port, Fortresses and Group of Monuments, Cartagena
- ☐ Los Katíos National Park

- ☐ Historic Centre of Santa Cruz de Mompox
- ☐ National Archeological Park of Tierradentro
- ☐ San Agustín Archaeological Park
- ☐ Malpelo Fauna and Flora Sanctuary
- ☐ Coffee Cultural Landscape of Colombia
- ☐ Qhapaq Ñan, Andean Road System
- ☐ Chiribiquete National Park – "The Maloca of the Jaguar"

☐ **ECUADOR**
- ☐ Explore the Galapagos Islands
- ☐ Swing at the "End of the World"
- ☐ See the Blue-Footed Booby bird mating dance.
  - ☐ WORLD HERITAGE SITES
    - ☐ City of Quito
    - ☐ Galápagos Islands
    - ☐ Sangay National Park
    - ☐ Historic Centre of Santa Ana de los Ríos de Cuenca
    - ☐ Qhapaq Ñan, Andean Road System

☐ **FRENCH GUIANA**

☐ **GUYANA**
- ☐ Marvel at Kaieteur Falls

☐ **PARAGUAY**
- ☐ Museo Del Barro | Asuncion
  - ☐ WORLD HERITAGE SITES
    - ☐ Jesuit Missions of La Santísima Trinidad de Paraná and Jesús de Tavarangue

☐ **PERU**
- ☐ See the Inca Ruins
- ☐ City of Cuzco
- ☐ Hike Inca Trail, Machu Picchu
- ☐ Hike Santa Cruz Trek, Peru
  - ☐ WORLD HERITAGE SITES
    - ☐ Historic Sanctuary of Machu Picchu
    - ☐ Chavin (Archaeological Site)
    - ☐ Huascarán National Park
    - ☐ Chan Chan Archaeological Zone
    - ☐ Manú National Park
    - ☐ Historic Centre of Lima

- ☐ Río Abiseo National Park
- ☐ Lines and Geoglyphs of Nasca and Palpa
- ☐ Historical Centre of the City of Arequipa
- ☐ Sacred City of Caral-Supe
- ☐ Qhapaq Ñan, Andean Road System
- ☐ Chankillo Archaeoastronomical Complex

☐ **SURINAME**

☐ **URUGUAY**

    ☐ WORLD HERITAGE SITES

- ☐ Historic Quarter of the City of Colonia del Sacramento
- ☐ Fray Bentos Industrial Landscape
- ☐ The work of engineer Eladio Dieste: Church of Atlántida

☐ **VENEZUELA**

    ☐ WORLD HERITAGE SITES

- ☐ Coro and its Port
- ☐ Canaima National Park
- ☐ Ciudad Universitaria de Caracas

☐ _____

☐ _____

☐ _____

☐ _____

☐ _____

☐ _____

☐ _____

☐ _____

☐ _____

☐ _____

☐ _____

☐ _____

☐ _____

EVENTS BUCKET LIST

- ☐ Throw out the first pitch at a Major League Baseball game
- ☐ Attend a unique Small-Town Festival
- ☐ Attend a Professional Golf Tournament
- ☐ Go to a World Series Game
- ☐ Go to a rugby match
- ☐ Go on a big match in an extremely "random/weird" sport
- ☐ Attend the World Cup
- ☐ Attend the Summer Olympics
- ☐ Attend the Winter Olympics
- ☐ Champions League final (soccer)
- ☐ Attend a TED Talk
- ☐ Attend a masquerade
- ☐ Attend a boxing match
- ☐ Attend a film premiere
- ☐ Attend a gay pride event
- ☐ Get VIP passes to a show
- ☐ Go to a Comicon
- ☐ Attend an Adult Entertainment Expo
- ☐ Attend a big fashion show
- ☐ Attend the Super Bowl
- ☐ Watch your favorite sports team on their home turf
- ☐ Attend an Improv Show
- ☐ Attend the US Open
- ☐ Catch a ball in the stands of an MLB Game
- ☐ See your favorite band live
- ☐ Go to Nascar
- ☐ Go to an IndyCar race
- ☐ Attend a Jazz Festival
- ☐ Attend a Music Festival
- ☐ Black Tie Gala
- ☐ Gallery opening
- ☐ Native American Pow Wow
- ☐ Poetry Reading
- ☐ White Party
- ☐ WWE Match

- ☐ MMA Fight
- ☐ Dance at a Rave
- ☐ Go to a Blues bar
- ☐ Go to a book signing
- ☐ Go to a Miniature Museum
- ☐ Roller Derby
- ☐ Dinner Theatre
- ☐ Renaissance Festival
- ☐ Tattoo Festival
- ☐ Party in a private booth at a nightclub
- ☐ Wimbledon
- ☐ Opera
- ☐ See a rodeo show
- ☐ Go to a 3D/Trick-eye Museum
- ☐ Ride on a parade float
- ☐ Attend a foam party
- ☐ Go to a toga party

☐ _____

☐ _____

☐ _____

☐ _____

☐ _____

☐ _____

☐ _____

☐ _____

☐ _____

☐ _____

☐ _____

☐ _____

FESTIVALS BUCKET LIST

January

- ☐ Thaipusam Festival – Malaysia
- ☐ Timkat Festival – Ethiopia
- ☐ Hogmanay Festival – Scotland
- ☐ Kumbh Mela Festival – India

February

- ☐ Venice Carnival – Venice
- ☐ Sky Lantern Festival – China
- ☐ Rio de Janeiro Carnival – Brazil
- ☐ Tapati Rapa Nui – Chile
- ☐ Taj Mahotsav – India
- ☐ Jaislmer Desert Festival – India
- ☐ Bergen International Literary Festival – Norway
- ☐ Envision – Costa Rica
- ☐ Quebec Winter Carnival – Canada
- ☐ Sauti za Busara – Zanzibar
- ☐ Charleston Wine and Food – USA
- ☐ Adelaide Fringe – Australia
- ☐ Saidaiji Eyo Hadaka Matsuri – Japan
- ☐ Taiwan Latern Festival – Taiwan
- ☐ Lemon Festival – France

March

- ☐ Holi Festival – India
- ☐ St. Patrick's Day Festival – Ireland
- ☐ Mardi Gras – New Orleans, USA
- ☐ Las Fallas Festival – Valencia, Spain
- ☐ SXSW – USA
- ☐ Narvik Winter Festival – Norway
- ☐ Food and Fun Fest – Iceland
- ☐ Cape Town Jazz Fest – South Africa

- ☐ Mendoza Grape Harvest Festival – Argentina
- ☐ Spring Equinox Festival – Chichen Itza, Mexico
- ☐ Starkbierzeit Festival – Germany
- ☐ Kakku Pagoda Festival – Shan State, Myanmar

April

- ☐ The Penis Festival – Japan
- ☐ Songkran Water Festival – Thailand
- ☐ Kings Day – Netherlands
- ☐ Coachella – California, USA
- ☐ New Orleans Jazz Festival – New Orleans, Louisiana

May

- ☐ Cannes Film Festival – France
- ☐ Pahiyas Festival – Philippines
- ☐ Cooper's Hill Cheese Rolling Festival – England
- ☐ Cheung Chau Bun Festival – Hong Kong
- ☐ Vivid Sydney - Australia

June

- ☐ Isle of Wight Festival – England
- ☐ Karneval de Kulturen – Germany
- ☐ Rock in Rio – Parque Olimpico, Cidade do Rock, Brazil
- ☐ Glastonbury Festival – Glastonbury, England
- ☐ Summerfest – Wisconsin, USA

July

- ☐ EXIT Festival – Novi Sad, Serbia
- ☐ Montreux Jazz Festival – Montreux, Switzerland
- ☐ White Nights – St. Petersburg, Russia
- ☐ Dawson City Music Festival – Dawson City, Canada
- ☐ Down the Rabbit Hole – Ewijk, Netherlands

August

- ☐ Reggae Sumfest – Montego Bay, Jamaica
- ☐ Ghosts Festival – China
- ☐ La Tomatina – Bunol, Spain
- ☐ Burning Man – Nevada, USA
- ☐ Notting Hill Carnival – Notting Hill, England
- ☐ Victorious Festival – Portsmouth, UK
- ☐ Fuji Rock Festival – Yuzawa-cho, Niigata Pref, Japan

September

- ☐ La Merce – Barcelona, Spain
- ☐ Lake of Stars – Malawi
- ☐ The Venice Film Festival – Venice, Italy
- ☐ Mid-Autumn Festival – China
- ☐ Regatta Storica – Venice, Italy
- ☐ Hermanus Whale Festival – Hermanus, South Africa
- ☐ Mid-Autumn Festival in France – Montpellier, France
- ☐ ViniMilo – Sicily, Italy
- ☐ Fiesta Rey en Jaume – Majorca, Spain
- ☐ Mooncake Festival – China

October

- ☐ Oktoberfest – Germany
- ☐ Festival of the Lights – India
- ☐ Dusshera – India
- ☐ Hachiman Matsuri – Japan
- ☐ Concurs de Castells – Spain
- ☐ The Albuquerque International Balloon Fiesta – New Mexico, USA
- ☐ Rubber Duck Race – Germany
- ☐ Cirio de Nazare – Brazil
- ☐ New York City's Village Halloween Parade – USA
- ☐ MassKara Festival – Philippines
- ☐ Paris Nuit Blanche – France
- ☐ Naga Fireball Festival – Thailand
- ☐ Barcolana Regatta – Italy

☐ Inle Lake Pagoda Festival – Myanmar
☐ Feria del Mole – Mexico

November

☐ Day of the Dead – Mexico
☐ Iceland Airwaves – Iceland
☐ Lewes Bonfire – England
☐ BaconFest in Pennsylvania – USA
☐ Chang Mai Lantern Festival – Thailand
☐ Monkey Buffet Festival – Thailand
☐ Blackpool Christmas Lights – England
☐ VooDoo Fest – New Orleans, USA
☐ Niagara Falls Festival of Lights – Canada
☐ New York's Macy's Thanksgiving Day Parade – USA
☐ Strawberry Fields – Australia
☐ Kite Festival – Santiago Sacatepéquez, Guatemala
☐ Pushkar Camel Fair – Rajasthan, India
☐ Kendal Mountain Festival – England
☐ Dia de Todos los Santos – Spain

December

☐ Snowglobe – Lake Tahoe, California
☐ Fete des Lumieres – Lyon, France
☐ Burning the Clocks – Brighton
☐ Hogmanay – Scotland
☐ Krampusnacht Festival – Vienna
☐ Chichibu Yomatsuri – Japan
☐ Junkanoo Parade – Bahamas
☐ Al Dhafra Festival – Abu Dhabi
☐ St. Kitts Nevis Carnival
☐ Rakastella – Miami, Florida
☐ Art Basel – Miami, Florida
☐ Rise Festival – Les Deux Alpes, France
☐ Night of the Radishes – Mexico
☐ Cosmic Convergence Festival – Guatemala

RESTAURANTS

- [ ] St. John – London
- [ ] elBulli – Girona, Spain
- [ ] Sin Huat Eating House – Singapore
- [ ] Le Bernardin – New York
- [ ] Salumi – Seattle
- [ ] Russ & Daughters – New York
- [ ] Mamoun's – New York
- [ ] Etxebarri – Axpe, Spain
- [ ] Sukiyabashi Jiro – Tokyo
- [ ] Hot Doug's – Chicago, Illinois
- [ ] Oklahoma Joe's Barbecue – Kansas City
- [ ] Ristorante Grotta Palazzese – Puglia, Italy
- [ ] Northern Lights Bar in Ion Hotel – Iceland
- [ ] Aiguille Du Midi Restaurant – Chamonix, France
- [ ] Giraffe Manor – Langata, Kenya
- [ ] Ithaa Undersea Restaurant – Alif Dhaal Atoll, Maldives
- [ ] Remvi Restaurant – Santorini, Greece
- [ ] White Rabbit – Moscow, Russia
- [ ] Le Panoramic – Border of France and Switzerland
- [ ] Truth Coffee – Cape Town, South Africa
- [ ] The Snowcastle of Kemi – Kemi, Finland
- [ ] The Rock – Michamvi Pingue, Zanzibar
- [ ] Labassin Waterfall Restaurant, Villa Escudero Resort – Philippines
- [ ] El Diablo – Lanzarote, Spain
- [ ] The Green Dragon Pub – New Zealand
- [ ] Wildman Wilderness Lodge - Australia
- [ ] Ali Barbour's Cave Restaurant – Kenya
- [ ] Hr Giger Museum Bar – Gruyeres, Switzerland
- [ ] Sci-Fi Dine-in Theater Restaurant, Disney's Hollywood Studios – Florida, USA
- [ ] Espresso Patronum – Toronto, Canada
- [ ] Alice in a Labyrinth – Tokyo, Japan
- [ ] Redwoods Treehouse – Warkworth, New Zealand

- [ ] Stratosfare – New Zealand
- [ ] Dog Café – Los Angeles, California
- [ ] World's Only Hot Air Balloon Restaurant – Culiair, Netherlands
- [ ] Bistrot Chez Remy, Disneyland – Paris, France
- [ ] Walter's Lab, Walter's coffee Roastery – Istanbul, Turkey
- [ ] Tsavo Lion Restaurant – Bali
- [ ] 6.8 Palopo – Guatemala
- [ ] Bateaux Dubai - Dubai
- [ ] Dinner in the Sky – All Around the World
- [ ] Game of Thrones Feast – London, UK
- [ ] Bicycle Bar – Bucharest, Romania
- [ ] Street Dinner – Ferrara, Italy
- [ ] Dans Le Noir – Around the World
- [ ] Phu Nhuan's Café Babo – Saigon Vietnam
- [ ] Soneva Kiri - Thailand
- [ ] Hajime Robot Restaurant – Bangkok, Thailand
- [ ] The Grotto – Thailand
- [ ] Vertigo 61 – Bangkok, Thailand
- [ ] Prison of Fire – Tianjin, China
- [ ] Barbie Café – Taipei, Taiwan
- [ ] Modern Toilet – Tapei, Taiwan
- [ ] The Clinic Bar – Singapore
- [ ] La Refuge Des Fondus – Paris, France
- [ ] 58 Tour Eiffel – Paris, France
- [ ] Fa Hua Dumplings – Shanghai, China
- [ ] Banh Cuon Thien Huong – Ho Chi Minh City, Vietnam
- [ ] Kappacasein – London, UK
- [ ] Abu Hassan – Tel Aviv, Israel
- [ ] The Bright Star – Bessemer, Alabama
- [ ] Big Bob Gibson Bar-B-Que – Decatur, Alabama
- [ ] The Saltry – Cove, Alaska
- [ ] Sugar Bowl – Scottsdale, Arizona
- [ ] Spago – Beverly Hills, California
- [ ] Swan Oyster Depot – San Francisco, California
- [ ] Buckhorn Exchange – Denver, Colorado
- [ ] Louis' Lunch – New Haven, Connecticut
- [ ] Jessop's Tavern – New Castle, Delaware
- [ ] Joe's Stone Crab – Miami Beach, Florida
- [ ] The Colonnade – Atlanta, Georgia

- [ ] Beverly's – Coeur d'Alene, Idaho
- [ ] Lou Malnati's – Chicago, Illinois
- [ ] Portillo's – Chicago, Illinois
- [ ] St. Elmo Steak House – Indianapolis, Indiana
- [ ] Canteen Lunch in the Alley – Ottumwa, Iowa
- [ ] The Cozy Inn – Salina, Kansas
- [ ] The Brown Hotel – Louisville, Kentucky
- [ ] Café du Monde – New Orleans, Louisiana
- [ ] Commander's Palace – New Orleans, Louisiana
- [ ] Five Islands Lobster Co. – Georgetown, Maine
- [ ] Faidley Seafood – Baltimore, Maryland
- [ ] Union Oyster House – Boston, Massachusetts
- [ ] Matt's Bar and Grill – Minneapolis, Minnesota
- [ ] Ajax Diner – Oxford, Mississippi
- [ ] Arthur Bryant's – Kansas City, Missouri
- [ ] Polebridge Mercantile – Polebridge, Montana
- [ ] The Drover – Omaha, Nebraska
- [ ] The Golden Steer – Las Vegas, Nevada
- [ ] Pickity Place – Mason, New Hampshire
- [ ] Tops Diner – East Newark, New Jersey
- [ ] El Pinto – Albuquerque, New Mexico
- [ ] Keens Steakhouse - New York City, New York
- [ ] Trinity Place – New York City, New York
- [ ] The Angus Barn – Raleigh, North Carolina
- [ ] Wurst Bier Hall – Fargo, North Dakota
- [ ] Camp Washington Chili – Cincinnati, Ohio
- [ ] Schmidt's Sausage House – Columbus, Ohio
- [ ] Cattlemen's Steakhouse – Oklahoma City, Oklahoma
- [ ] Jake's Famous Crawfish – Portland, Oregon
- [ ] Voodoo Doughnut – Portland, Oregon
- [ ] Pat's King of Steaks – Philadelphia, Pennsylvania
- [ ] Ralph's Italian Restaurant – Philadelphia, Pennsylvania
- [ ] Primanti Bros. – Pittsburgh, Pennsylvania
- [ ] Matunuck Oyster Bar – South Kingston, Rhode Island
- [ ] Alpine Inn – Hill City, South Dakota
- [ ] Gus's World Famous Fried Chicken – Memphis, Tennessee
- [ ] Salt Lick BBQ – Driftwood, Texas
- [ ] Red Iquana – Salt Lake City, Utah
- [ ] Henof the Wood – Waterbury, Vermont
- [ ] The Inn at Little Washington – Washington, Virginia

- ☐ Maneki – Seattle, Washington
- ☐ Old Ebbitt Grill – Washington, D.C.
- ☐ Ben's Chili Bowl – Washington, D.C.
- ☐ Hillbilly Hot Dogs – Lesage, West Virginia
- ☐ Frank's Diner – Kenosha, Wisconsin
- ☐ The Safe House - Milwaukee
- ☐ The Irma – Cody, Wyoming
- ☐ El Tovar Lodge – Grand Canyon National Park

Famous by Movies and TV shows

- ☐ Monk's Café (Seinfeld) – Tom's Restaurant, Manhattan's Morningside Heights
- ☐ Katz's Delicatessen (When Harry Met Sally) – New York
- ☐ Le Polidor (Midnight in Paris)
- ☐ Double R Diner (Twin Peaks) – Twede's Café, North Bend, WA
- ☐ L Street Tavern (Good Will Hunting)
- ☐ Mystic Pizza (Mystic Pizza) – Mystic, CT
- ☐ Café Lalo (You've Got Mail)
- ☐ Cheers (Cheers) – Boston's Beacon Hill
- ☐ New York Bar (Lost in Translation) – Tokyo, Japan
- ☐ Holsten's (The Sopranos) – Bloomfield, NJ
- ☐ The Bluebird Café (Nashville)
- ☐ 21 Club (Wall Street)
- ☐ The Voltaire (Pretty Woman) – Cicada, Los Angeles, California
- ☐ Randy's Donuts (Many movies) – Inglewood, California
- ☐ Coyote Ugly (Coyote Ugly) – East Village
- ☐ Top Notch Hamburgers (Dazed and Confused) – Austin, Texas
- ☐ Kansas City Barbeque (Top Gun) – San Diego, California
- ☐ Johnie's Coffee Shop (Many movies) – Los Angeles, California
- ☐ Smith & Wollensky (American Psycho) – New York City
- ☐ 101 Coffee Shop (Swingers)
- ☐ 7B Horseshoe Bar (The Godfather Part II) – New York City
- ☐ Bridges Restaurant and Bar (Mrs. Doubtfire) – Danville, California
- ☐ The Brazilian Steakhouse (Bridesmaids) – Van Nuys, California

☐ MacLaren's Bar (How I Met Your Mother) – McGee's Pub, New York

All Michelin-Starred Restaurants
☐ Washington - The Inn at Little Washington
☐ New York
    ☐ Eleven Madison Park
    ☐ Chef's Table at Brooklyn Fare
    ☐ Le Bernardin
    ☐ Per Se
    ☐ Masa
☐ Chicago – Alinea
☐ San Diego – Addison
☐ Los Gatos – Manresa
☐ San Francisco
    ☐ Benu
    ☐ Quince
    ☐ Atelier Crenn
☐ Napa Valley – The French Laundry
☐ Healdsburg – SingleThread
☐ United Kingdom
    ☐ L'Enclume – Cartmel
    ☐ Fat Duck – Bray
    ☐ Waterside Inn – Bray
    ☐ CORE by Clare Smyth – London
    ☐ Restaurant Gordon Ramsay – London
    ☐ Alain Ducasse at The Chorchester – London
    ☐ Helene Darroze at The Connaught – London
    ☐ Sketh (The Lecture Room & Library) – London
☐ Spain
    ☐ Atrio – Caceres
    ☐ Aponiente – El Puerto de Santa Maria
    ☐ Cenador de Amos – Villaverde de Pontones
    ☐ Azurmendi – Larrabetzu
    ☐ DiverXO – Madrid
    ☐ Akelare – Donostia/San Sebastian
    ☐ Martin Berasategui – Lasarte
    ☐ Arzak - Donostia/San Sebastian
    ☐ Quique Dacosta - Denia

- ☐ ABaC – Barcelona
- ☐ Cocina Hermanos Torres – Barcelona
- ☐ Lasarte – Barcelona
- ☐ El Celler de Can Roca = Girona
- ☐ France
  - ☐ Christopher Coutanceau – La Rochelle
  - ☐ Les Pres d'Eugenie – Michel Guerard – Eugenie-les-Bains
  - ☐ Le Pre Catelan – Paris
  - ☐ Pierre Gagnaire – Paris
  - ☐ Le Cinq – Paris
  - ☐ Epicure – Paris
  - ☐ Alleno Paris au Pavillon Ledoyen – Paris
  - ☐ Arpege – Paris
  - ☐ Guy Savoy – Paris
  - ☐ Kei – Paris
  - ☐ Plenitude – Cheval Blanc Paris
  - ☐ L'Ambroisie – Paris
  - ☐ Assiette Champenoise – Reims
  - ☐ Troisgros – Le Bois sans Feuilles – Ouches
  - ☐ Auberge du Vieux Puits – Fontjoncourse
  - ☐ Maison Lameloise – Chagny
  - ☐ Regis et Jacques Marcon – Saint-Bonnet-le-Froid
  - ☐ Georges Blanc – Vonnas
  - ☐ Pic – Valence
  - ☐ L'Oustau de Baumaniere – Les Baux-de-Provence
  - ☐ Le Clos des Sens – Annecy
  - ☐ Le Petit Nice – Marseille
  - ☐ AM par Alexandre Mazzia – Marseille
  - ☐ Flocons de Sel
  - ☐ Megeve
  - ☐ Rene et Maxime Meilleur – Saint-Martin-de-Belleville
  - ☐ Le Villa Madie – Cassis
  - ☐ Le 1947 a Cheval Blanc – Courchevel
  - ☐ Christophe Bacquie – Le Castellet
  - ☐ La Vague d'Or – Cheval Blanc – St. Tropez
  - ☐ Le Louis XV – Alain Ducasse a l'Hotel de Paris – Monaco
  - ☐ Mirazur - Menton

- ☐ Belgium
  - ☐ Boury
  - ☐ Hof van Cleve
  - ☐ Zilte - Antwerpen
- ☐ Netherlands
  - ☐ Inter Scaldes – Kruiningen
  - ☐ De Librije - Zwolle
- ☐ Norway – Maaemo
- ☐ Germany
  - ☐ Victor's Fine Dining by Christian bau
  - ☐ Waldhotel Sonnora – Dreis
  - ☐ Schanz. Restaurant . – Piesport
  - ☐ The Table Kevin Fehling – Hamburg
  - ☐ Restaurant Bareiss – Baiersbronn
  - ☐ Schwarzwaldstube – Baiersbronn
  - ☐ Aqua – Wolfsburg
  - ☐ Rutz – Berlin
  - ☐ Restaurant Uberfahrt Christian Jurgens – Rottach-Egern
- ☐ Switherzerland
  - ☐ Restaurant de 'lHotel de Ville – Crissier
  - ☐ Cheval Blanc by Peter Knogl – Basel
  - ☐ Memories – Bad Ragaz
  - ☐ Schloss Schauenstein - Furstenau
- ☐ Denmark
  - ☐ Geranium – Copenhagen
  - ☐ Noma – Copenhagen
- ☐ Italy
  - ☐ Villa Crespi – Orta San Giulio
  - ☐ Piazza Duomo – Alba
  - ☐ Enrico Bartolini al Mudec – Milan
  - ☐ Da Vittorio – Brsaporto
  - ☐ Dal Pescatore – Runate
  - ☐ St. Hubertus – San Cassiano
  - ☐ Osteria Francescana – Modena
  - ☐ Le Calandre – Rubano
  - ☐ Enoteca Pinchiorri – Florence
  - ☐ Uliassi – Senigallia
  - ☐ La Pergola – Rome
  - ☐ Reale – Castel di Sangro

- ☐ Sweden – Frantzen – Stockholm
- ☐ Austria – Amador – Vienna
- ☐ Japan
    - ☐ Kohaku – Tokyo
    - ☐ Kagurazaka Ishikawa – Tokyo
    - ☐ RyuGin – Tokyo
    - ☐ L'OSIER – Tokyo
    - ☐ Sushi Yoshitake – Tokyo
    - ☐ Kanda – Tokyo
    - ☐ Azuabu Kadowaki – Tokyo
    - ☐ L'Effervescence – Tokyo
    - ☐ Sazenka – Tokyo
    - ☐ Joel Robuchon – Tokyo
    - ☐ Quintessence – Tokyo
    - ☐ Makimura – Tokyo
    - ☐ Hyotei – Kyoto
    - ☐ Mizai – Kyoto
    - ☐ Kikunoi Honten – Kyoto
    - ☐ Isshisoden Nakamura – Kyoto
    - ☐ Maeda – Kyoto
    - ☐ Gion Sasaki – Kyoto
    - ☐ Kashiwaya Osaka Senriyama – Osaka
    - ☐ Hajime – Osaka
    - ☐ Taian – Osaka
- ☐ South Korea
    - ☐ Gaon – Seoul
    - ☐ Mosu – Seoul
- ☐ China
    - ☐ Xin rong Ji – Beijing
    - ☐ King's Joy – Beijing
    - ☐ Ultraviolet by Paul Pairet – Shanghai
    - ☐ Tain Table – Shanghai
- ☐ Taipei – Le Palais
- ☐ Hong Kong
    - ☐ T'ang Court
    - ☐ Forum
    - ☐ Caprice
    - ☐ Lung King Heen
    - ☐ 8 ½ Otto e Mezzo – Bombana
    - ☐ L'Atelier de Joel Robuchon

☐ Sushi Shikon
☐ Macau
    ☐ The Eight
    ☐ Robuchon au Dome
    ☐ Jade Dragon
☐ Singapore
    ☐ Les Amis
    ☐ Odette
    ☐ Zen

☐ _____
☐ _____
☐ _____
☐ _____
☐ _____
☐ _____
☐ _____
☐ _____
☐ _____
☐ _____
☐ _____
☐ _____
☐ _____
☐ _____
☐ _____

BARS

- ☐ The Rooftop (Cabo San Lucas)
- ☐ The Aviary (Chicago)
- ☐ Untitled Supper Club (Chicago)
- ☐ Bordel (Chicago)
- ☐ El Floridita (Havana)
- ☐ Sloppy Joe's Bar (Havana)
- ☐ The Chandelier Lounge (Las Vegas)
- ☐ Gallery Bar (Los Angeles)
- ☐ Gianni Bar (Los Angeles)
- ☐ The Spare Room (Los Angeles)
- ☐ Black Rum Bar (Negril)
- ☐ Beach Bum Berry's Latitude 29 (New Orleans)
- ☐ Carousel Bar (New Orleans)
- ☐ Blacktail Bar (NYC)
- ☐ The Bar Room (NYC)
- ☐ The Blond (NYC)
- ☐ Campell Bar (NYC)
- ☐ Dante (NYC)
- ☐ The Dead Rabbit (NYC)
- ☐ Employees Only (NYC)
- ☐ Nomad Bar (NYC)
- ☐ Attaboy (NYC)
- ☐ Mace (NYC)
- ☐ Monarch Rooftop (NYC)
- ☐ Mr. Purple (NYC)
- ☐ Trick Dog (San Francisco)
- ☐ RED2ONE (Santiago)
- ☐ Canon Bar (Seattle)
- ☐ Rumba (Seattle)
- ☐ Bar Raval (Toronto)
- ☐ Flying Dutchmen Cocktails (Amsterdam)
- ☐ Tales & Spirits (Amsterdam)
- ☐ Belroy's Bijou (Antwerp)
- ☐ Dogma (Antwerp)
- ☐ Alexander's Bar (Athens)
- ☐ The Clumsies (Athens)
- ☐ Apotheke (Barcelona)

- [ ] El Nacional (Barcelona)
- [ ] Dry Martini Bar (Barcelona)
- [ ] Edgbaston Bar (Birmingham)
- [ ] Humus x Hortense (Brussels)
- [ ] Seiberts Bar (Cologne)
- [ ] Prince of Wales Bar (Cong)
- [ ] Buza Bar (Dubrovnik)
- [ ] The Cobbler (Ghent)
- [ ] Jiggers (Ghent)
- [ ] HR Giger Bar (Gruyères)
- [ ] Boilerman Bar (Hamburg)
- [ ] Le Lion Bar De Paris (Hamburg)
- [ ] The Allis (Istanbul)
- [ ] Kilimanjaro (Istanbul)
- [ ] Gra Z Vognem (Kiev)
- [ ] Stollen 1930 (Kufstein)
- [ ] Red Frog Bar (Lisbon)
- [ ] 81LTD (Liverpool)
- [ ] The Alchemist (London)
- [ ] Aqua Shard (London)
- [ ] Beaufort Bar (London)
- [ ] The American Bar (London)
- [ ] Connaught Bar (London)
- [ ] Bloomsbury Club Bar (London)
- [ ] Christopher's Martini Bar (London)
- [ ] German Gymnasium (London)
- [ ] Dandelyan (London)
- [ ] The Gibson (London)
- [ ] Sexy Fish (London)
- [ ] Hyde Bar (London)
- [ ] K Bar (London)
- [ ] Jailhouse Bar (London)
- [ ] Milk & Honey (London)
- [ ] Mr. Frog's Taven (London)
- [ ] Nightjar (London)
- [ ] Oriole (London)
- [ ] Scarfes Bar (London)
- [ ] Shanghai Bar (London)
- [ ] Colebrook Row (London)
- [ ] Sky Pod Bar (London)

- ☐ Wave Bar (London)
- ☐ Zth Cocktail Lounge (London)
- ☐ Le Parfum (London)
- ☐ City Space Bar (Moscow)
- ☐ Schumann's (Munich)
- ☐ Die Goldene Bar (Munich)
- ☐ Candelaria (Paris)
- ☐ Castor Club (Paris)
- ☐ Le Bar Botaniste (Paris)
- ☐ Dirty Dick (Paris)
- ☐ Le Bar Georges V (Paris)
- ☐ Little Red Door (Paris)
- ☐ Le Bar Du Plaza Athene (Paris)
- ☐ Sherry Butt (Paris)
- ☐ Hemingway Bar (Prague)
- ☐ The Jerry Thomas Project (Rome)
- ☐ Linje Tio (Stockholm)
- ☐ Mr. Simon (Udine)
- ☐ Harry's Bar (Venice)
- ☐ Baiser Bar (Xanthi)
- ☐ Widder Bar (Zurich)
- ☐ Sky Bar (Bangkok)
- ☐ Bamboo Bar (Bangkok)
- ☐ Red Sky (Bangkok)
- ☐ Zoom Sky Bar (Bangkok)
- ☐ Gold on 27 (Dubai)
- ☐ Vault (Dubai)
- ☐ The Chinnery (Hong Kong)
- ☐ Castello 4 (Hong Kong)
- ☐ Club Qing (Hong Kong)
- ☐ Djapa Bar (Hong Kong)
- ☐ Dr. Fern's Gin Parlour (Hong Kong)
- ☐ J Boroski (Hong Kong)
- ☐ Lobster Bar And Grill (Hong Kong)
- ☐ Mo Bar (Hong Kong)
- ☐ Ophelia (Hong Kong)
- ☐ Otto E Mezzo Bombana (Hong Kong)
- ☐ Please Don't Tell (Hong Kong)
- ☐ Quinary (Hong Kong)
- ☐ Stockton (Hong Kong)

- ☐ Bar Palladio (Jaipur)
- ☐ Rock Bar (Jimbaran)
- ☐ Aer Lounge (Mumbai)
- ☐ Charles H. Bar (Seoul)
- ☐ Speak Low (Shanghai)
- ☐ 28 Hongkong Street (Singapore)
- ☐ Atlas Bar (Singapore)
- ☐ Employees Only (Singapore)
- ☐ Tippling Club (Singapore)
- ☐ Gibson Bar (Singapore)
- ☐ Jigger and Pony (Singapore)
- ☐ Long Bar (Singapore)
- ☐ Manhattan (Singapore)
- ☐ Operation Dagger (Singapore)
- ☐ Smoke & Mirrors (Singapore)
- ☐ Imperial Craft (Tel Aviv)
- ☐ Whiskey Bar & Museum (Tel Aviv)
- ☐ Bar Benfeddich (Tokyo)
- ☐ Bar High Five (Tokyo)
- ☐ Bar/S (Tokyo)
- ☐ Bar Tram (Tokyo)
- ☐ Bar Trench (Tokyo)
- ☐ Cobbler Bar (Brisbane)
- ☐ Seymour's Cocktails & Oysters (Brisbane)
- ☐ Atrium Bar on 35 (Melbourne)
- ☐ The Everleigh (Melbourne)
- ☐ Black Pearl (Melbourne)
- ☐ 1806 (Melbourne)
- ☐ Abode Bistro & Bar (Sydney)
- ☐ Baxter Inn (Sydney)
- ☐ Beta Bar (Sydney)
- ☐ 360 Bar and Dining (Sydney)
- ☐ PS40 (Sydney)

FOOD AND DRINK BUCKET LIST

DISHES

- Pizza
- Doner Kebab
- Hamburger
- Falafel
- Gyro
- Hummus
- Cavier
- Peking Duck
- Dim Sum
- Spaghetti
- Lasagna
- Bolognese Sauce
- Baba Ganoush
- Mutabbal
- Biryani Rice
- Thali
- Chicken Tandoori
- Paella
- Escargots de Bourgogne
- French Onion Soup
- Mexican Mole
- Burrito
- Tacos
- Sushi
- Sashimi
- Poke
- Ceviche
- Ramen Soup
- Pho

- Spring Rolls
- Pad Thai
- Shakshuka
- Kosheri
- Couscous
- Tagine
- Injera
- Asados
- Goulash
- Moussaka
- Wiener Schnitzel
- Bratwurst
- Moules Frites
- Yorkshire Pudding
- Stilton Cheese
- Fondue
- Poutine
- Cevapcici
- Ajvar
- Gravce Tavce
- Bacalahu
- Balcao Al Pil Pil
- Feijoada
- Kimchi (makes your breathe smell terrible)
- Chicken Adobo
- Knedliky
- Pierogi
- Gnocci
- Chicken Satay
- Borscht

- ☐ Khachapuri
- ☐ Air-Cured Ham
- ☐ Lobster Roll
- ☐ Boudin
- ☐ Bagel with Lox
- ☐ Avocado Toast
- ☐ French Toast
- ☐ Waffles
- ☐ Eggs Benedict
- ☐ Key Lime Pie
- ☐ Traditional Texas BBQ
- ☐ Philly Cheesesteak
- ☐ Cochinita Pibil
- ☐ Chile en Nogada
- ☐ Fry Jacks
- ☐ Nutella
- ☐ Cuy (Guinea Pig)
- ☐ Chocolate Chip Cookie
- ☐ Ice Cream
- ☐ Sorbet
- ☐ Greek Yogurt
- ☐ Frozen Yogurt
- ☐ Custard
- ☐ Jerk Chicken
- ☐ Ropa Vieja
- ☐ Carbonara
- ☐ Kaiserschmarrn
- ☐ Bled Crème Cake
- ☐ Better than Sex Cake
- ☐ Pineapple Cake
- ☐ Tiramisu
- ☐ Eclaires
- ☐ Macarons
- ☐ Ratatouille
- ☐ Tartare
- ☐ Crepes
- ☐ Fish and Chips

- ☐ Surf and Turf
- ☐ Herring and Onions
- ☐ Souvlaki
- ☐ Mousaka
- ☐ Colzido das Furnas
- ☐ Khachapuri
- ☐ Churchkhela
- ☐ Tarator Soup
- ☐ Lobster Bisque
- ☐ Chicken and Dumplings
- ☐ Chili
- ☐ Mac and Cheese
- ☐ Grilled Cheese with Tomato Soup
- ☐ Risotto
- ☐ Pasus Tolma and Mashosh
- ☐ Cepelinai
- ☐ Borscht
- ☐ Fesendjoon
- ☐ Mango Sticky Rice
- ☐ Shish Barak
- ☐ Bobotie
- ☐ Bunny Chow
- ☐ Harira
- ☐ Koshari
- ☐ Bubar Ayam
- ☐ Xiao Long Bao
- ☐ Milmyeon
- ☐ Matcha
- ☐ Pineapple Buns
- ☐ Lamingtons
- ☐ Chiko Roll
- ☐ Vegemite
- ☐ Dal
- ☐ Bisque
- ☐ Kare

- ☐ Flan
- ☐ Panna cotta
- ☐ Kushiyaki
- ☐ Tortas
- ☐ Chow Mein
- ☐ Coleslaw
- ☐ Yakisoba
- ☐ Nigiri
- ☐ Sarma
- ☐ Pilaf
- ☐ Pavlova
- ☐ S'more
- ☐ BLT
- ☐ Apple Pie
- ☐ Nougat
- ☐ Fudge
- ☐ Jeon
- ☐ Quiche
- ☐ Chorizo
- ☐ Dondurma
- ☐ Barbacoa
- ☐ Bruschetta
- ☐ Kimbap
- ☐ Borek
- ☐ Banchan
- ☐ Pulled Pork
- ☐ Ribs
- ☐ Churros
- ☐ Miso
- ☐ Milkshake

- ☐ Churrasco
- ☐ Mooncake
- ☐ Doughnut
- ☐ Bibimbap
- ☐ Bulgogi
- ☐ Naan
- ☐ Chutney
- ☐ Quesadilla
- ☐ Fajitas
- ☐ Guacamole
- ☐ Queso
- ☐ Tonkatsu
- ☐ Dashi
- ☐ Ravioli
- ☐ Tamal
- ☐ Shabu-shabu
- ☐ Wagashi
- ☐ Fried Chicken
- ☐ Nachos
- ☐ Brownies
- ☐ Wonton
- ☐ Gyoza
- ☐ Cupcake
- ☐ Mochi
- ☐ Onigiri
- ☐ Roti
- ☐ Yakitori
- ☐ Jiaozi
- ☐ Yakiniku
- ☐ Croissant

FRUITS

- ☐ Cupuaçu (Amazon Basin)
- ☐ Cherimoya (Andes)

- ☐ Monstera Deliciosa
- ☐ Sweetsop
- ☐ Jackfruit

113

☐ Araza
☐ Spanish Lime
☐ African Horned Cucumber
☐ Durian
☐ Ciruela
☐ Mangosteen
☐ Ackee
☐ Feijoa
☐ Snake Fruit
☐ Jabuticaba
☐ Naseberry
☐ Guava
☐ Pomelo
☐ Passionfruit
☐ Mamey Sapote
☐ Langsat
☐ Miracle fruit
☐ Lulo
☐ Dragon Fruit
☐ Kiwano
☐ Korean Melon
☐ Loquat
☐ Longan
☐ Physalia
☐ Mulberry
☐ Jujube
☐ Chom Chom
☐ Star Fruit
☐ Persimmon
☐ Sapodilla

VEGETABLES

☐ Black Radish
☐ Okinawan Purple Sweet Potato
☐ Chinese Artichokes
☐ Fiddleheads
☐ Ramps

☐ Dulse
☐ Jicama
☐ Kohlrabi
☐ Romanesco Broccoli
☐ Salsify
☐ Samphire
☐ Sunchoke
☐ Tomatillo
☐ White Asparagus
☐ Oca
☐ Tiger Nut
☐ Celeriac
☐ Kai Lan
☐ Nopal
☐ Manioc
☐ Apollo Broccoli AKA Broccolini
☐ Dragon Carrot
☐ Red Perilla (Shiso)
☐ Chinese Flowering Leek
☐ Winter Squash
☐ Winter Melon
☐ Wax Gourd
☐ Chinese Water Spinach
☐ Lotus Root
☐ Bitter Melon
☐ Silk Squash
☐ Bamboo Shoot
☐ Saltwort
☐ Daikon Radish
☐ Calabash AKA Bottle Gourd
☐ Yardlong Beans
☐ Karela
☐ Garlic Scapes
☐ Wan Shen
☐ Cassava
☐ Malabar Spinach
☐ Peter Pepper
☐ Hen of the Woods

☐ Watercress
☐ Daikon

☐ Escarole

COCKTAILS

☐ Adios Mother F*cker
☐ Alabama Slammer
☐ Amaretto Sour
☐ Americano
☐ Aperol Spritz
☐ Apple Jacks
☐ Bahama Mama
☐ Bay Breeze
☐ Bellini
☐ Black'n'Tan
☐ Bloody Mary
☐ Blow Job
☐ Buttery Nipple
☐ Captain and Coke
☐ Cement Mixer
☐ Champagne
☐ Cosmopolitan
☐ Creamsicle
☐ Daiquiri
☐ Dirty Martini
☐ Eggnog
☐ Fuzzy Navel
☐ Gimlet
☐ Gin and Tonic
☐ Grasshopper
☐ Harvey Wallbanger
☐ Horny Bull
☐ Hot Toddy
☐ Hurricane

☐ Irish Car Bomb
☐ Irish Coffee
☐ Jell-O Shot
☐ Lemon Drop
☐ Mai Tai
☐ Manhattan
☐ Margarita
☐ Martini
☐ Miami Vice
☐ Midori Sour
☐ Mimosa
☐ Mojito
☐ Moscow Mule
☐ Mudslide
☐ Old Fashioned
☐ Pina Colada
☐ Red-Headed Slut
☐ Screwdriver
☐ Sea Breeze
☐ Seven and Seven
☐ Sex on the Beach
☐ Tequila Rose and Mountain Dew
☐ Tequila Sunrise
☐ Tom Collins
☐ Washington Apple
☐ Whiskey Straight
☐ White Russian

WINE

☐ Albariño
☐ Aligoté

☐ Amarone
☐ Arneis

- ☐ Asti Spumante
- ☐ Auslese
- ☐ Banylus
- ☐ Bardolino
- ☐ Barolo
- ☐ Beaujolais
- ☐ Blanc de Blancs
- ☐ Blanc de Noirs
- ☐ Boal or Bual
- ☐ Brunello
- ☐ Cabernet Franc
- ☐ Cabernet Sauvignon
- ☐ Carignan
- ☐ Cava
- ☐ Charbono
- ☐ Champagne
- ☐ Chardonnay
- ☐ Châteauneuf-du-Pape
- ☐ Chianti
- ☐ Chianti Classico
- ☐ Claret
- ☐ Colombard
- ☐ Constantia
- ☐ Cortese
- ☐ Dolcetto
- ☐ Eiswein
- ☐ Frascati
- ☐ Gamay
- ☐ Gamay Beaujolais
- ☐ Gattinara
- ☐ Gewürztraminer
- ☐ Grappa
- ☐ Grenache
- ☐ Kir
- ☐ Lambrusco
- ☐ Liebfraumich
- ☐ Madeira
- ☐ Malbec
- ☐ Marc
- ☐ Marsala
- ☐ Marsanne
- ☐ Mead
- ☐ Meritage
- ☐ Merlot
- ☐ Montepulciano
- ☐ Mourvedre
- ☐ Müller-Thurgau
- ☐ Muscat
- ☐ Nebbiolo
- ☐ Petit Verdot
- ☐ Petit Sirah
- ☐ Pinot Blanc
- ☐ Pinot Grigio/Pino Gris
- ☐ Pino Meunier
- ☐ Pinot Noir
- ☐ Pinotage
- ☐ Port
- ☐ Resina
- ☐ Riesling
- ☐ Rose
- ☐ Roussane
- ☐ Sangiovese
- ☐ Sauterns
- ☐ Sauvignon Blanc
- ☐ Sémillon
- ☐ Sherry
- ☐ Soave
- ☐ Trebbiano
- ☐ Valpolicella
- ☐ Verdicchio
- ☐ Viognier
- ☐ Zinfandel

BEER

- ☐ Amber
- ☐ American Lager
- ☐ American Pale Ale
- ☐ Bock
- ☐ Blonde Ale
- ☐ Dunkel
- ☐ English Pale Ale
- ☐ German Helles
- ☐ Hefeweizen

- ☐ Indian Pale Ale
- ☐ Kolsch
- ☐ Pilsner
- ☐ Porter
- ☐ Sour
- ☐ Stout
- ☐ Tripel
- ☐ Wheat

- ☐ Belgian-Style Flanders Oud Bruin or Oud Red Ales
- ☐ Belgian-Style Dubbel
- ☐ Belgian-Style Tripel
- ☐ Belgian-Style Quadrupel
- ☐ Belgian-Style Blonde Ale
- ☐ Belgian-Style Pale Ale
- ☐ Belgian-Style Pale Strong Ale
- ☐ Belgian-Style Dark Strong Ale
- ☐ Belgian-Style White (or Wit) / Belgian-Style Wheat
- ☐ Belgian-Style Lambic
- ☐ Belgian-Style Gueuze Lambic
- ☐ Belgian-Style Fruit Lambic
- ☐ Belgian-Style Table Beer
- ☐ Other Belgian-Style Ales
- ☐ French-Style Bière de Garde
- ☐ French & Belgian-Style Saison
- ☐ Classic English-Style Pale Ale
- ☐ English-Style India Pale Ale
- ☐ Ordinary Bitter
- ☐ Special Bitter or Best Bitter
- ☐ Extra Special Bitter
- ☐ English-Style Summer Ale
- ☐ Scottish-Style Light Ale
- ☐ Scottish-Style Heavy Ale
- ☐ Scottish-Style Export Ale
- ☐ English-Style Pale Mild Ale

117

- ☐ English-Style Dark Mild Ale
- ☐ English-Style Brown Ale
- ☐ Old Ale
- ☐ Strong Ale
- ☐ Scotch Ale
- ☐ British-Style Imperial Stout
- ☐ British-Style Barley Wine Ale
- ☐ Brown Porter
- ☐ Robust Porter
- ☐ Sweet or Cream Stout
- ☐ Oatmeal Stout
- ☐ Double Red Ale
- ☐ Contemporary Gose
- ☐ German-Style Kölsch / Köln-Style Kölsch
- ☐ Berliner-Style Weisse (Wheat)
- ☐ Leipzig-Style Gose
- ☐ South German-Style Hefeweizen / Hefeweissbier
- ☐ South German-Style Kristall Weizen / Kristall Weissbier
- ☐ German-Style Leichtes Weizen / Weissbier
- ☐ South German-Style Bernsteinfarbenes Weizen / Weissbier
- ☐ South German-Style Dunkel Weizen / Dunkel Weissbier
- ☐ South German-Style Weizenbock / Weissbock
- ☐ Bamberg-Style Weiss (Smoke) Rauchbier (Dunkel or Helles)
- ☐ German-Style Altbier
- ☐ Kellerbier (Cellar beer) or Zwickelbier - Ale
- ☐ Adambier
- ☐ International-Style Pale Ale
- ☐ Australian-Style Pale Ale
- ☐ Irish-Style Red Ale
- ☐ Classic Irish-Style Dry Stout
- ☐ Foreign (Export)-Style Stout
- ☐ American-Style Pale Ale
- ☐ Fresh "Wet" Hop Ale
- ☐ Pale American-Belgo-Style Ale
- ☐ Dark American-Belgo-Style Ale
- ☐ American-Style Strong Pale Ale
- ☐ American-Style India Pale Ale
- ☐ Imperial or Double India Pale Ale
- ☐ American-Style Amber/Red Ale
- ☐ Imperial Red Ale

118

- ☐ American-Style Barley Wine Ale
- ☐ American-Style Wheat Wine Ale
- ☐ Golden or Blonde Ale
- ☐ American-Style Brown Ale
- ☐ Smoke Porter
- ☐ American-Style Sour Ale
- ☐ American-Style Black Ale
- ☐ American-Style Stout
- ☐ American-Style Imperial Stout
- ☐ Specialty Stouts
- ☐ American-Style Imperial Porter
- ☐ Session India Pale Ale
- ☐ German-Style Pilsener
- ☐ Bohemian-Style Pilsener
- ☐ German-Style Leichtbier
- ☐ Münchner (Munich)-Style Helles
- ☐ Dortmunder / European-Style Export
- ☐ Vienna-Style Lager
- ☐ German-Style Märzen
- ☐ German-Style Oktoberfest / Wiesen (Meadow)
- ☐ European-Style Dark / Münchner Dunkel
- ☐ German-Style Schwarzbier
- ☐ Bamberg-Style Märzen Rauchbier
- ☐ Bamberg-Style Helles Rauchbier
- ☐ Bamberg-Style Bock Rauchbier
- ☐ Traditional German-Style Bock
- ☐ German-Style Heller Bock/Maibock
- ☐ German-Style Eisbock
- ☐ Kellerbier (Cellar beer) or Zwickelbier - Lager
- ☐ Brett Beer
- ☐ Session Beer
- ☐ American-Style Cream Ale or Lager
- ☐ California Common Beer
- ☐ Ginjo Beer or Sake-Yeast Beer
- ☐ Light American Wheat Ale or Lager with Yeast
- ☐ Light American Wheat Ale or Lager without Yeast
- ☐ Fruit Wheat Ale or Lager with or without Yeast
- ☐ Dark American Wheat Ale or Lager with Yeast
- ☐ Dark American Wheat Ale or Lager without Yeast
- ☐ Rye Ale or Lager with or without Yeast

- [ ] German-Style Rye Ale (Roggenbier) with or without Yeast
- [ ] Fruit Beer
- [ ] Field Beer
- [ ] Pumpkin Beer
- [ ] Chocolate / Cocoa-Flavored Beer
- [ ] Coffee-Flavored Beer
- [ ] Herb and Spice Beer
- [ ] Specialty Beer
- [ ] Specialty Honey Lager or Ale
- [ ] Gluten-Free Beer
- [ ] Indigenous Beer (Lager or Ale)
- [ ] Smoke Beer (Lager or Ale)
- [ ] Experimental Beer (Lager or Ale)
- [ ] Historical Beer
- [ ] Wood- and Barrel-Aged Beer
- [ ] Wood- and Barrel-Aged Pale to Amber Beer
- [ ] Wood- and Barrel-Aged Dark Beer
- [ ] Wood- and Barrel-Aged Strong Beer
- [ ] Wood- and Barrel-Aged Sour Beer
- [ ] Aged Beer (Ale or Lager)
- [ ] Other Strong Ale or Lager
- [ ] Non-Alcoholic (Beer) Malt Beverages
- [ ] Belgian-style Fruit Beer
- [ ] Chili Pepper Beer
- [ ] Mixed Culture Brett Beer
- [ ] Wild Beer
- [ ] International-Style Pilsener
- [ ] Dry Lager
- [ ] American-Style Lager
- [ ] American-Style Light (Low Calorie) Lager
- [ ] American-Style Low-Carbohydrate Light Lager
- [ ] American-Style Amber (Low Calorie) Lager
- [ ] American-Style Premium Lager
- [ ] American-Style Pilsener
- [ ] American-Style Ice Lager
- [ ] American-Style Malt Liquor
- [ ] American-Style Amber Lager
- [ ] American-Style Märzen / Oktoberfest
- [ ] American-Style Dark Lager

OTHER FOOD THINGS TO DO AND TRY

- ☐ Attend a Beer Festival
- ☐ Attend a Low Country Boil
- ☐ Attend a Pig Roast
- ☐ Attend a Winemakers Dinner
- ☐ Bake a Cake for Someone Special
- ☐ Bake a Loaf of Bread
- ☐ Boil a Lobster
- ☐ Bottle a Recipe & Sell it
- ☐ Catch, Cook & Eat a Fish
- ☐ Cook a Traditional Dish from a Different Culture
- ☐ Cook Christmas Dinner
- ☐ Cook Every Dish in One Cookbook
- ☐ Cook with a Celebrity Chef
- ☐ Cook with a Partner
- ☐ Create a New Ice Cream Flavor
- ☐ Create Food Art
- ☐ Create Latte Art
- ☐ Create your Own Cocktail
- ☐ Create your Own Recipe
- ☐ Create you Signature Dish
- ☐ Dismember a Chicken
- ☐ Drink a Bottle of Expensive Champagne
- ☐ Drink Absinthe
- ☐ Drink at a Distillery
- ☐ Drink at a Dive Bar
- ☐ Drink at an Ice Bar
- ☐ Drink Juice from a Fresh Coconut
- ☐ Drink Fresh Milk from the Cow
- ☐ Drink Moonshine
- ☐ Drink Sake
- ☐ Drink Tea at a Tea House
- ☐ Eat Breakfast in Bed
- ☐ Eat a Meal Cooked by a Celebrity Chef
- ☐ Eat a Molecular Gastronomy Dinner
- ☐ Eat a Raw Diet for a Day
- ☐ Eat Alone at a Restaurant
- ☐ Eat an Insect
- ☐ Eat at a Food Truck

- ☐ Eat Caviar
- ☐ Eat in a Pitch-Black Restaurant
- ☐ Eat Fondue
- ☐ Eat Southern BBQ in the South
- ☐ Enter Something in a Food Competition
- ☐ Extract Honey from a Bee Hive
- ☐ Fillet a Fish
- ☐ Go Oyster Hunting
- ☐ Go to a Vodka Lounge
- ☐ Go Wine Tasting
- ☐ Have a Dinner Party
- ☐ Have a Progressive Dining Experience
- ☐ Have a Wine and Whiskey Collection
- ☐ Host a Cookie Exchange
- ☐ Hunt for Wild Mushrooms
- ☐ Learn a Flair Bartending Trick
- ☐ Learn to Use Chopsticks
- ☐ Make a Gingerbread House
- ☐ Make Cheese
- ☐ Make Fresh Pasta
- ☐ Make Ice Cream
- ☐ Make Jam
- ☐ Make Sushi
- ☐ Make Wine
- ☐ Order from the Secret Menu at In-n-Out
- ☐ Order One of Everything on a Menu
- ☐ Own a Food Cart
- ☐ Own an Award-Winning Restaurant
- ☐ Partake in a Food Fight
- ☐ Partake in Afternoon Tea
- ☐ Participate in a Private Wine Tasting
- ☐ Pick Fruit from the Tree & Make a Pie
- ☐ Recreate a Childhood Recipe
- ☐ Recreate a Classic Dish
- ☐ Shuck Oysters
- ☐ Start an Herb Garden
- ☐ Toss Pizza Dough in the Air
- ☐ Try Deep-Fried Twinkies
- ☐ Wade in a Cranberry Bog
- ☐ Alligator

- ☐ Alpaca
- ☐ Ants
- ☐ Balut (Fertilized Egg)
- ☐ Bird Nest Soup
- ☐ Bone Marrow
- ☐ Cactus
- ☐ Casu Marzu
- ☐ Cheeks
- ☐ Conch
- ☐ Elk
- ☐ Escargot
- ☐ Flowers
- ☐ Frickles
- ☐ Frog Legs
- ☐ Guinea Pig
- ☐ Head Cheese
- ☐ Heart
- ☐ Lamb Tongue
- ☐ Lambs Brain
- ☐ Lambs Rump
- ☐ Liver
- ☐ Mushy Peas
- ☐ Octopus
- ☐ Pigs Ear
- ☐ Pigs Feet
- ☐ Pigs Head
- ☐ Pigs Tail
- ☐ Pig Brain
- ☐ Sea Horse
- ☐ Rabbit
- ☐ Reindeer (smoked)
- ☐ Rocky Mountain Oysters
- ☐ Scrapple
- ☐ Sea Slug
- ☐ Wild Boar
- ☐ Worm Cakes
- ☐ Yak
- ☐ Eat raw oyster
- ☐ Eat at a Michelin restaurant
- ☐ Dine in the Sky

- ☐ Participate in an eating competition
- ☐ Eat in an underwater restaurant
- ☐ Try every kind of fruit in the world
- ☐ Order a 3+ course dinner in a nice restaurant in the opposite order
- ☐ Eat black and white truffle
- ☐ Try deep fried Mars and Snickers
- ☐ Try national dishes in every country you visit
- ☐ Decide for one cookbook then cook ALL the dishes in it
- ☐ Eat in a five-star restaurant/hotel
- ☐ Eat a McDonald's burger that looks like the picture (good luck...)
- ☐ Eat patbingsu (shaved ice)
- ☐ Eat in a floating restaurant
- ☐ Cronut
- ☐ Invent your own meal/dish
- ☐ Build a giant gingerbread house
- ☐ Leave a 100% tip to a server
- ☐ Eat in various themed restaurants:
  - ☐ Fish your own Fish restaurant
  - ☐ Robot Restaurant
  - ☐ Maid Café
  - ☐ Prison Restaurant
  - ☐ Zombie Restaurant
- ☐ Go to a cat café
- ☐ Have a complete picnic in the park
- ☐ Eat "a sausage in a sausage"
- ☐ Eat beef tongue
- ☐ Try one of the world's hottest chillies
- ☐ Attend a tea tasting
- ☐ Create your own signature smoothie
- ☐ Eat Foie Gras
- ☐ Eat dim sum
- ☐ Eat boar
- ☐ Prepare a whole dinner for your family
- ☐ Cut off sugar for a month
- ☐ Hunt for truffles
- ☐ Eat at the top five restaurants in your home town
- ☐ Be vegetarian for a month
- ☐ Have a chocolate fountain

- ☐ Bake a cake from scratch
- ☐ Order food in a foreign language
- ☐ Eat at one of chef Gordon Ramsay's restaurants
- ☐ Go on a dinner cruise
- ☐ Not waste a single grocery item for at least 3 months
- ☐ Order whatever your finger lands on the menu, eyes closed
- ☐ Try a dish you can't pronounce
- ☐ Try bubble tea
- ☐ Try hot white chocolate
- ☐ Try Borscht
- ☐ Visit a chocolate factory
- ☐ Try all the dishes in your favorite restaurant
- ☐ Make a rainbow cake
- ☐ Make vodka gummy bears
- ☐ Make a "drunken watermelon"
- ☐ Do a cafe latte art workshop
- ☐ Do a coffee barista course
- ☐ Akutaq
- ☐ Balut
- ☐ Bird nest soup
- ☐ Blood sausage
- ☐ Bone marrow
- ☐ Cactus
- ☐ Casu marzu
- ☐ Century egg
- ☐ Chicken feet
- ☐ Crickets
- ☐ Crocodile
- ☐ Durian (both raw and deep-fried)
- ☐ Escamoles
- ☐ Eel
- ☐ Fugu blowfish
- ☐ Gizzard
- ☐ Grasshoppers
- ☐ Green tuna fruit
- ☐ Intestines
- ☐ Jellyfish
- ☐ Mealworms
- ☐ Ostrich
- ☐ Pidgeon

- ☐ "Prairie Oysters"
- ☐ Scorpion
- ☐ Sea cucumber
- ☐ Shark
- ☐ Snails
- ☐ Snake
- ☐ Spider
- ☐ Spoon worms (Echiura)
- ☐ Squid ink
- ☐ Starfish
- ☐ Tequila worm
- ☐ Tripe
- ☐ Whale meat
- ☐ Eat in a "Toilet Resaurant"
- ☐ Brew Beer
- ☐ Visit a Barbie Café
- ☐ Fake a birthday in a restaurant to get a free dessert
- ☐ Go barhopping dressed as nuns
- ☐ Smash a pie in someone's face
- ☐ Drink from an ice luge
- ☐ Eat in a lion restaurant
- ☐ Dance on a bar
- ☐ Do a body shot
- ☐ Saber a Champagne bottle
- ☐ Have a drink at an Ice bar
- ☐ Go to an oxygen bar

THE MOVIE BUCKET LIST

This Bucket List is compiled of the Academy Award Winners (Best Picture, Best Original and Adapted Screenplays, Best Actor/Supporting Actor, Best Actress/Supporting Actress, IMDB Top 250 List, American Film Institute 100 Years…100 Movies and numerous other lists to make this complete. This list is complete with all genres like Action/Adventure, Animation, Biographical/Historical, Comedy, Crime/Mystery/Thriller/Suspense, Cult Classics, Disney Films, Drama, Family, Foreign Language, Holiday, Horror, Musical, Romance, Science Fiction/Fantasy, Sports, Teen Angst and War/Westerns to make this list over 1,300 must-see movies before you die.

#

- ☐ 3 Idiots
- ☐ 3.10 to Uma
- ☐ 7th Heaven
- ☐ 8 ½
- ☐ 9 to 5
- ☐ 9 ½ Weeks
- ☐ 10
- ☐ 10 Things I Hate About You
- ☐ 12 Angry Men
- ☐ 12 Years a Slave
- ☐ 28 Days Later…
- ☐ The 40-Year-Old Virgin
- ☐ 42nd Street
- ☐ 127 Hours
- ☐ 200 Cigarettes
- ☐ The 400 Blows
- ☐ 500 Days of Summer
- ☐ 1917
- ☐ 2001: A Space Odyssey

A

- ☐ About a Boy
- ☐ About Time
- ☐ The Accidental Tourist
- ☐ The Accused
- ☐ Adam's Rib
- ☐ The Addams Family
- ☐ Adventures in Babysitting (1987)
- ☐ The Adventures of Robin Hood
- ☐ An Affair to Remember
- ☐ Affliction
- ☐ The African Queen
- ☐ Age of Innocence
- ☐ Aguirre, The Wrath of God
- ☐ A.I. Artificial Intelligence
- ☐ Airplane!
- ☐ Airport
- ☐ Akeelah and the Bee
- ☐ Aladdin
- ☐ Ali
- ☐ Alice Doesn't Live Here Anymore
- ☐ Alice in Wonderland
- ☐ Alien
- ☐ Aliens
- ☐ All About Eve

- ☐ All About My Mother
- ☐ All Dogs Go to Heaven
- ☐ All of Me
- ☐ All Quiet on the Western Front
- ☐ All That Jazz
- ☐ All the King's Men
- ☐ All the President's Men
- ☐ All the Right Moves
- ☐ Almost Famous
- ☐ Amadeus
- ☐ Amelie
- ☐ American Beauty
- ☐ American Graffiti
- ☐ American History X
- ☐ An American in Paris
- ☐ American Pie
- ☐ American Psycho
- ☐ American Sniper
- ☐ An American Tail
- ☐ An American Werewolf in London
- ☐ Amistad
- ☐ Amores Perros
- ☐ Amour
- ☐ Anastasia (1956)
- ☐ Anastasia (1997)
- ☐ Anatomy of a Murder
- ☐ Anchorman
- ☐ Andhadhun
- ☐ Andrei Rublev
- ☐ Angel at My Table
- ☐ Angel Heart
- ☐ Angels in the Outfield
- ☐ Animal House
- ☐ Annie (1982)
- ☐ Annie Hall
- ☐ Anthony Adverse
- ☐ Any Given Sunday
- ☐ The Apartment

- ☐ The Apple Dumpling Gang
- ☐ Apocalypse Now
- ☐ Apollo 13
- ☐ Argo
- ☐ Arise My Love
- ☐ Army of Darkness
- ☐ Around the World in 80 Days
- ☐ Arsenic and Old Lace
- ☐ The Artist
- ☐ Arthur
- ☐ As Good as It Gets
- ☐ Ashes and Diamonds
- ☐ The Asphalt Jungle
- ☐ Attack of the Killer Tomatoes!
- ☐ Au Hasard Balthazar
- ☐ Audition
- ☐ Austin Powers
- ☐ Autumn Sonata
- ☐ Avatar
- ☐ The Aviator
- ☐ Avengers: End Game
- ☐ Avengers: Infinite War
- ☐ The Awful Truth

B

- ☐ Babe
- ☐ Babes in Toyland
- ☐ The Bachelor and the Bobby-Soxer
- ☐ Back to the Future
- ☐ The Bad and the Beautiful
- ☐ Bad Girl
- ☐ The Bad News Bears (1976)
- ☐ Bad Santa
- ☐ Balto

- ☐ Bambi
- ☐ The Band Wagon
- ☐ The Bandit
- ☐ The Barefoot Contessa
- ☐ Barefoot in the Park
- ☐ Barry Lyndon
- ☐ Basic Instinct
- ☐ The Basketball Diaries
- ☐ Batman Begins
- ☐ The Battle of Algiers
- ☐ A Beautiful Mind
- ☐ Beauty and the Beast
- ☐ Becket
- ☐ Bedknobs and Broomsticks
- ☐ Beethoven
- ☐ Beetlejuice
- ☐ Before I Go to Sleep
- ☐ Before Sunrise
- ☐ Before Sunset
- ☐ Being John Malkovich
- ☐ Being There
- ☐ Bella de Jour
- ☐ Ben-Hur
- ☐ Bend it Like Beckham
- ☐ The Best Man (1999)
- ☐ The Best Years of Our Lives
- ☐ Bicycle Thieves
- ☐ Big
- ☐ The Big Country
- ☐ Big Daddy
- ☐ Big Fish
- ☐ The Big Green
- ☐ The Big Heat
- ☐ Big Hero 6
- ☐ The Big House
- ☐ The Big Lebowski
- ☐ The Big Short
- ☐ The Big Sick

- ☐ The Big Sleep
- ☐ Big Trouble in Little China
- ☐ Bill and Ted's Excellent Adventure
- ☐ The Bird Cage
- ☐ Birdman
- ☐ Birdman of Alcatraz
- ☐ The Birds
- ☐ The Bishop's Wife
- ☐ The Bitter Tears of Petra Van Kant
- ☐ Black Hawk Down
- ☐ Black Panther
- ☐ Black Stallion
- ☐ Black Swan
- ☐ Blackbeard's Ghost
- ☐ BlacKkKlansman
- ☐ Blade Runner
- ☐ The Blair Witch Project
- ☐ Blazing Saddles
- ☐ The Blind Side
- ☐ Blue Chips
- ☐ Blue Crush
- ☐ Blue Jasmine
- ☐ Blue Sky
- ☐ Bluebeard's Eighth Wife
- ☐ The Blues Brothers
- ☐ The Boat
- ☐ Bohemian Rhapsody
- ☐ Bonnie and Clyde
- ☐ Born Yesterday
- ☐ The Boy Who Harnessed the Wind
- ☐ Boyhood
- ☐ Boys Don't Cry
- ☐ Boys Town
- ☐ Brave
- ☐ The Brave Little Toaster

129

- ☐ Braveheart
- ☐ Brazil (1985)
- ☐ Breaking Away
- ☐ Breakfast at Tiffany's
- ☐ The Breakfast Club
- ☐ Breathless
- ☐ Bride of Frankenstein
- ☐ Bridge of Spies
- ☐ The Bridge on the River Kwai
- ☐ Bridge to Terabithia
- ☐ Bridget Jones' Diary
- ☐ Brief Encounter
- ☐ A Brighter Summer Day
- ☐ Bring It On
- ☐ Bringing Up Baby
- ☐ Broadcast News
- ☐ The Broadway Melody
- ☐ Brokeback Mountain
- ☐ Bull Durham
- ☐ Bullitt
- ☐ Bullets Over Broadway
- ☐ Butch Cassidy and the Sundance Kid
- ☐ Butterfield 8
- ☐ Butterflies are Free
- ☐ The Butterfly Effect

C

- ☐ Cabaret
- ☐ Cactus Flower
- ☐ Caddyshack
- ☐ California Suite
- ☐ Call Me by Your Name
- ☐ Camille
- ☐ Camp Nowhere
- ☐ The Candidate
- ☐ Can't Buy Me Love
- ☐ Can't Hardly Wait
- ☐ Capernaum

- ☐ Capote
- ☐ Captain Courageous
- ☐ Carrie
- ☐ Casablanca
- ☐ Casino
- ☐ Casper
- ☐ Cast Away
- ☐ Cat Ballou
- ☐ Catch Me If You Can
- ☐ Catch-22
- ☐ Cavalcade
- ☐ The Champ
- ☐ Charade
- ☐ Chariots of Fire
- ☐ Charlotte's Web
- ☐ Charly
- ☐ Cheaper By the Dozen
- ☐ Chicago
- ☐ Child's Play
- ☐ Children of a Lesser God
- ☐ Children of Heaven
- ☐ Chinatown
- ☐ Chitty Chitty Bang Bang
- ☐ A Christmas Story
- ☐ Chronicles of Narnia
- ☐ The Cider House Rules
- ☐ Cimarron
- ☐ Cinderella
- ☐ Cinderella Man
- ☐ Cinema Paradiso
- ☐ City Lights
- ☐ City of God
- ☐ City Slickers
- ☐ Citizen Kane
- ☐ Clerks
- ☐ A Clockwork Orange
- ☐ Close Encounters of the Third Kind

- ☐ Close-Up
- ☐ Cloudy with a Chance of Meatballs
- ☐ Clueless
- ☐ Coach Carter
- ☐ Coal Miner's Daughter
- ☐ Coco
- ☐ Cocoon
- ☐ Coda
- ☐ Cold Mountain
- ☐ The Color of Money
- ☐ The Color Purple
- ☐ Come and Get it
- ☐ Come and See
- ☐ Come Back, Little Sheba
- ☐ Coming Home
- ☐ Coming to America
- ☐ The Conformist
- ☐ The Constant Gardner
- ☐ The Conversation
- ☐ Cool Hand Luke
- ☐ Cool Runnings
- ☐ Coquette
- ☐ The Country Girl
- ☐ Crash
- ☐ Crazy Heart
- ☐ Crazy Rich Asians
- ☐ Crazy, Stupid, Love
- ☐ Crouching Tiger, Hidden Dragon
- ☐ Cruel Intentions
- ☐ The Crying Game
- ☐ Cyrano de Bergerac

D

- ☐ Dallas Buyer's Club
- ☐ Dances with Wolves
- ☐ Dangerous Liaisons
- ☐ The Danish Girl

- ☐ Darkest Hour
- ☐ The Dark Knight
- ☐ The Dark Knight Rises
- ☐ Darling
- ☐ Dangal
- ☐ Dangerous
- ☐ Darby O'Gill and the Little People
- ☐ Das Boot
- ☐ The Dawn Patrol
- ☐ Day of Wrath
- ☐ The Day the Earth Stood Still (1951)
- ☐ Days of Thunder
- ☐ Dazed and Confused
- ☐ Dead Man Walking
- ☐ Dead of Night
- ☐ Dead Poets Society
- ☐ Deadpool
- ☐ Death Becomes Her
- ☐ The Death of Mr. Lazarescu
- ☐ Decalogue
- ☐ The Deer Hunter
- ☐ The Defiant Ones
- ☐ Definitely, Maybe
- ☐ Deliverance
- ☐ Demon Slayer, Mugen Train
- ☐ Dennis the Menace (1993)
- ☐ The Departed
- ☐ Dersu Uzala
- ☐ The Descendants
- ☐ Designing Woman
- ☐ Despicable Me
- ☐ The Devil Wears Prada
- ☐ Diabolique
- ☐ Dial M for Murder
- ☐ Diary of a Wimpy Kid

- ☐ The Diary of Anne Frank
- ☐ Die Hard
- ☐ Dirty Dancing
- ☐ The Dirty Dozen
- ☐ Dirty Harry
- ☐ Dirty Rotten Scoundrels
- ☐ The Siscreet Charm of Bourgeoisie
- ☐ Disraeli
- ☐ The Divine Bell and for the Butterfly
- ☐ The Divorcee
- ☐ Divorce, Italian Style
- ☐ Django Unchained
- ☐ Do the Right Thing
- ☐ Doctor Dolittle (1998)
- ☐ Doctor Jekyll and Mr. Hyde
- ☐ Doctor Strangelove or: How I Learned to Stop Worrying and Love the Bomb
- ☐ Doctor Zhivago
- ☐ Dog Day Afternoon
- ☐ Dogtown and Z-Boys
- ☐ La Dolce Vita
- ☐ Donnie Brasco
- ☐ Don't Look Now
- ☐ Don't Tell Mom the Babysitter's Dead
- ☐ A Double Life
- ☐ Double Indemnity
- ☐ Downfall
- ☐ Dracula (1992)
- ☐ Dreamgirls
- ☐ Driving Miss Daisy
- ☐ Duck Soup
- ☐ Dumb and Dumber
- ☐ Dumbo

- ☐ Dunkirk

E

- ☐ The Earrings of Madam De…
- ☐ Easter Parade
- ☐ Easy A
- ☐ Eraserhead
- ☐ Earth Girls are Easy
- ☐ East of Eden
- ☐ Easy Rider
- ☐ Ed Wood
- ☐ The Edge of Seventeen
- ☐ Edward Scissorhands
- ☐ Election
- ☐ The Elephant Man
- ☐ Elf
- ☐ Elmer Gantry
- ☐ Empire Records
- ☐ Enchanted
- ☐ The English Patient
- ☐ Enter the Dragon
- ☐ Erin Brockovich
- ☐ Escape from New York
- ☐ Escape to Witch Mountain
- ☐ E.T: The Extra-Terrestrial
- ☐ Eternal Sunshine of the Spotless Mind
- ☐ Event Horizon
- ☐ Ever After
- ☐ Everything Everywhere All at Once
- ☐ The Evil Dead
- ☐ The Exorcist
- ☐ The Eyes of Tammy Faye

F

- [ ] The Fabulous Baker Boys
- [ ] Fahrenheit 451
- [ ] Fame
- [ ] The Family Stone
- [ ] Fanny and Alexander
- [ ] Fantasia
- [ ] Fantastic Four
- [ ] A Fantastic Woman
- [ ] Fargo
- [ ] The Farmer's Daughter
- [ ] Farewell My Concubine
- [ ] The Fast and the Furious
- [ ] Fast Times at Richmond High
- [ ] The Father (2020)
- [ ] Father Goose
- [ ] Fatal Attraction
- [ ] The Fault in Our Stars
- [ ] The Favourite
- [ ] Fear and Loathing in Las Vegas
- [ ] Fences
- [ ] FernGully: The Last Rainforest
- [ ] Ferris Bueller's Day Off
- [ ] Field of Dreams
- [ ] Fight Club
- [ ] The Fighter
- [ ] Finding Nemo
- [ ] Fire Walk with Me
- [ ] A Fish Called Wanda
- [ ] The Fishing King
- [ ] Flowers of Shanghai
- [ ] The Fly
- [ ] The Fog
- [ ] Footloose
- [ ] For a Few Dollars More

- [ ] For Whom the Bell Tolls
- [ ] Forbidden Planet
- [ ] Ford v Ferrari
- [ ] Forrest Gump
- [ ] The Fortune Cookie
- [ ] The Founder
- [ ] Four Weddings and a Funeral
- [ ] Frankenstein (1931)
- [ ] Freaks (1932)
- [ ] Freaky Friday (1976)
- [ ] A Free Soul
- [ ] Free Willy
- [ ] The French Connection
- [ ] The French Lieutenant's Woman
- [ ] Frida
- [ ] Friday
- [ ] Friday the 13th (1980)
- [ ] Fried Green Tomatoes
- [ ] From Here to Eternity
- [ ] Frost/Nixon
- [ ] Frozen
- [ ] The Fugitive
- [ ] Full Metal Jacket
- [ ] Funny Face
- [ ] Funny Girl

G

- [ ] Gandhi
- [ ] The Gang's All Here
- [ ] Gangs of Wasseypur
- [ ] Garden State
- [ ] Gaslight (1944)
- [ ] The General
- [ ] Gentleman Prefer Blondes
- [ ] Gentleman's Agreement
- [ ] Get Out

☐ Ghost
☐ The Ghost and Mrs. Muir
☐ Ghost World
☐ Ghostbusters (1984)
☐ Giant (1956)
☐ Gigi
☐ Girl, Interrupted
☐ The Girl on the Train
☐ The Girl with the Dragon Tattoo
☐ Gladiator
☐ Glengarry, Glen Ross
☐ Glory
☐ The Godfather
☐ The Godfather Part II
☐ Gods and Monsters
☐ Going My Way
☐ Gold Diggers of 1933
☐ The Gold Rush
☐ Goldfinger
☐ Gone Girl
☐ Gone with the Wind
☐ The Good Earth
☐ The Good, The Bad and The Ugly
☐ Good Morning, Vietnam
☐ Good Will Hunting
☐ The Goodbye Girl
☐ Goodbye Mr. Chips
☐ Goodfellas
☐ The Goonies
☐ Gosford Park
☐ The Graduate
☐ Gran Torino
☐ The Grand Budapest Hotel
☐ Grand Hotel
☐ Grand Illusion
☐ The Grapes of Wrath

☐ Grave of the Fireflies
☐ Grease
☐ The Great Debaters
☐ The Great Dictator
☐ The Great Escape
☐ The Great Lie
☐ The Great Ziegfeld
☐ Greater
☐ The Greatest Show on Earth
☐ The Greatest Showman
☐ Green Book
☐ Green Card
☐ The Green Mile
☐ Gremlins
☐ Grosse Pointe Blank
☐ Groundhog Day
☐ Guess Who's Coming to Dinner
☐ Guys and Dolls

H

☐ Hachi: A Dog's Tale
☐ Hacksaw Ridge
☐ La Haine
☐ Hairspray (1988)
☐ Halloween (1978)
☐ Hamilton
☐ Hamlet
☐ The Handmaiden
☐ The Hangover
☐ Hannah and Her Sisters
☐ Happy Feet
☐ Happy Gilmore
☐ Hara-Kiri
☐ A Hard Day's Night
☐ Harold and Maude
☐ Harry and Tonto
☐ Harry Potter and the Deathly Hallows: Part 2

- [ ] Harvey
- [ ] The Haunting (1963)
- [ ] Heartbreaker (2010)
- [ ] Heat
- [ ] Heathers
- [ ] Hedwig and the Angry Inch
- [ ] The Heiress
- [ ] Hello, Dolly!
- [ ] The Help
- [ ] Her
- [ ] Hercules (1997)
- [ ] Here Comes Mr. Jordan
- [ ] Hidden Figures
- [ ] High and Low
- [ ] High Fidelity
- [ ] High Noon
- [ ] High Society
- [ ] Hiroshima Mon Amour
- [ ] His Girl Friday
- [ ] Hitch
- [ ] Hocus Pocus
- [ ] Holes
- [ ] The Holiday
- [ ] Home Alone
- [ ] Homeward Bound
- [ ] Honey, I Shrunk the Kids
- [ ] Hook
- [ ] Hoop Dreams
- [ ] Hoosiers
- [ ] Hope Floats
- [ ] Horse Feathers
- [ ] The Hospital
- [ ] Hotel Rwanda
- [ ] The Hours
- [ ] How Green was My Valley
- [ ] How Stella Got Her Groove Back
- [ ] How the Grinch Stole Christmas (1966)
- [ ] How the West was Won
- [ ] How to Lose a Guy in 10 Days
- [ ] How to Marry a Millionaire
- [ ] How to Train Your Dragon
- [ ] Howards End
- [ ] Howl's Moving Castle
- [ ] Hud
- [ ] Hugo (2001)
- [ ] The Hunchback of Notre Dame (1996)
- [ ] Hunger Games
- [ ] The Hunt
- [ ] The Hurt Locker
- [ ] The Hustler

I

- [ ] I Heart Huckabees
- [ ] I, Tonya
- [ ] I Want to Live!
- [ ] I'll Be Home for Christmas
- [ ] Ice Age
- [ ] Idiocracy
- [ ] If Beale Street Could Talk
- [ ] Ikiru
- [ ] The Imitation Game
- [ ] In Cold Blood
- [ ] In Old Arizona
- [ ] In Old Chicago
- [ ] In the Heat of the Night
- [ ] In the Loop
- [ ] In the Mood for Love
- [ ] In the Name of the Father

- [ ] Incendies
- [ ] Inception
- [ ] The Incredible
  Shrinking Man (1957)
- [ ] The Incredibles
- [ ] Independence Day
- [ ] Indiana Jones and the
  Raiders of the Lost Ark
- [ ] Indiana Jones and the
  Last Crusade
- [ ] The Informer
- [ ] Inglorious Bastards
- [ ] Inherit the Wind
- [ ] Inside Man
- [ ] Inside Out
- [ ] Interstellar
- [ ] Into the Wild
- [ ] Invasion of the Body
  Snatchers (1956)
- [ ] The Intouchables
- [ ] Invictus
- [ ] The Irishman
- [ ] The Iron Giant
- [ ] The Iron Lady
- [ ] It (2017)
- [ ] It Happened One Night
- [ ] It's a Wonderful Life
- [ ] It's Complicated
- [ ] Italian Job

J

- [ ] Jack Frost (1998)
- [ ] Jawbreaker
- [ ] Jaws
- [ ] The Jazz Singer
- [ ] Jeanne Dielman, 23
  Commerce Quay, 1080
  Brussels
- [ ] Jeff, Who Lives at
  Home

- [ ] Jerry Maguire
- [ ] Jezebel
- [ ] JFK
- [ ] Jingle All the Way
- [ ] Jodhaa Akbar
- [ ] Johnny Belinda
- [ ] Johnny Eager
- [ ] Jojo Rabbit
- [ ] Joker
- [ ] Judas and the Black
  Messiah
- [ ] Judgement at
  Nuremberg
- [ ] Judy
- [ ] Julia
- [ ] Jumanji
- [ ] The Jungle Book
- [ ] Juno
- [ ] Jurassic Park

K

- [ ] The Karate Kid (1984)
- [ ] Kentucky
- [ ] Key Largo
- [ ] The Kid
- [ ] Kids
- [ ] Kill Bill Vol. 1
- [ ] The Killing
- [ ] The Killing Fields
- [ ] Kind Hearts and
  Coronets
- [ ] The King and I
- [ ] King Kong
- [ ] King Richard
- [ ] Kingpin
- [ ] The King's Speech
- [ ] The Kissing Booth
- [ ] Kiss of the Spider
  Woman
- [ ] Kitty Foyle

- ☐ Klaus
- ☐ Klute
- ☐ Knives Out
- ☐ Knocked Up
- ☐ Kramer vs. Kramer
- ☐ Kung Fu Panda

L

- ☐ L'Avventura
- ☐ LA Confidential
- ☐ La La Land
- ☐ Labyrinth
- ☐ Lady and the Tramp
- ☐ The Lady Eve
- ☐ The Lady Vanishes
- ☐ The Land Before Time
- ☐ Last Christmas
- ☐ The Last Command
- ☐ The Last Emperor
- ☐ Last Holiday
- ☐ The Last King of Scotland
- ☐ The Last of the Mohicans
- ☐ The Last Picture Show
- ☐ The Last Waltz
- ☐ Lawrence of Arabia
- ☐ A League of their Own
- ☐ Leaving Las Vegas
- ☐ Legally Blonde
- ☐ Lemony Snicket's Series of Unfortunate Events
- ☐ Leon: The Professional
- ☐ The Leopard
- ☐ Les Misérables
- ☐ Letter from an Unknown Woman
- ☐ Letters from Iwo Jima
- ☐ A Letter to Three Wives

- ☐ Liar Liar
- ☐ Life as a House
- ☐ Life is Beautiful
- ☐ Life of Brian
- ☐ The Life of Emile Zola
- ☐ Life of Pi
- ☐ Like Stars on Earth
- ☐ Lilies of the Field
- ☐ Lilo and Stitch
- ☐ Lincoln
- ☐ The Lion in Winter
- ☐ The Lion King
- ☐ The Little Mermaid
- ☐ Little Miss Sunshine
- ☐ A Little Princess
- ☐ Little Rascals
- ☐ Little Shop of Horrors (1986)
- ☐ Little Women (1933)
- ☐ The Lives of Others
- ☐ Lock, Stock and Two Smoking Barrels
- ☐ Logan
- ☐ The Longest Yard
- ☐ The Lord of the Rings: Fellowship of the Ring
- ☐ The Lord of the Rings: The Return of the King
- ☐ The Lord of the Rings: The Two Towers
- ☐ The Lost Boys
- ☐ Lost in America
- ☐ Lost in Translation
- ☐ The Lost Weekend
- ☐ Love Actually
- ☐ Love and Baskeball
- ☐ Love and Mercy
- ☐ The Love Bug
- ☐ Love Me if You Dare
- ☐ Love, Simon

☐ Love Story (1970)
☐ Lust for Life

M

☐ M
☐ Mad Max
☐ Mad Max: Fury Road
☐ The Magnificent Seven
☐ Major League
☐ Malcom X
☐ Maleficent
☐ The Maltese Falcon
☐ A Man and a Woman
☐ A Man for All Seasons
☐ The Man in the White Suit
☐ The Man Who Fell to Earth
☐ Manchester by the Sea
☐ The Manchurian Candidate (1962)
☐ Manhattan Melodrama
☐ Manhunter
☐ Marie-Louise
☐ Marriage Story
☐ Marty
☐ Mary and Max
☐ Mary Poppins
☐ M*A*S*H
☐ Master and Commander
☐ Matilda
☐ The Matrix
☐ Me Before You
☐ Mean Girls
☐ Mean Streets
☐ Meet Me in St. Louis
☐ Meet the Parents
☐ Melvin and Howard
☐ Memento
☐ Memories of Murder

☐ Men in Black
☐ Metropolis
☐ Michael Clayton
☐ Midnight Cowboy
☐ Midnight in Paris
☐ Mighty Aphrodite
☐ The Mighty Ducks
☐ Mighty Joe Young
☐ Mildred Pierce
☐ Milk
☐ Million Dollar Baby
☐ Miller's Crossing
☐ Milo and Otis
☐ Min and Bill
☐ Minari
☐ Minority Report
☐ Miracle
☐ Miracle on 34th Street (1947)
☐ The Miracle Worker
☐ Misery
☐ Mishima
☐ Miss Congeniality
☐ Missing
☐ Mister Roberts
☐ Moana
☐ Modern Times
☐ Moneyball
☐ Monster
☐ Monster's Ball
☐ Monty Python and the Holy Grail
☐ Mommie Dearest
☐ Moonlight
☐ Moonrise Kingdom
☐ Moonstruck
☐ Monsters Inc.
☐ The More the Merrier
☐ Morning Glory
☐ Move Over, Darling

- ☐ Moulin Rouge!
- ☐ Mr. Smith Goes to Washington
- ☐ Mrs. Doubtfire
- ☐ Mrs. Miniver
- ☐ Much Ado About Nothing
- ☐ Mulan
- ☐ Mulholland Drive
- ☐ The Mummy
- ☐ Murder in Cell No. 7
- ☐ Murder on the Orient Express
- ☐ Muriel's Wedding
- ☐ Mutiny on the Bounty
- ☐ My Best Friend's Wedding
- ☐ My Cousin Vinny
- ☐ My Darling Clementine
- ☐ My Fair Lady
- ☐ My Father My Son
- ☐ My Girl
- ☐ My Left Foot
- ☐ My Neighbor Totoro
- ☐ My Night at Maud's
- ☐ Mystic Pizza
- ☐ Mystic River

N

- ☐ The Naked Gun
- ☐ Napoleon Dynamite
- ☐ Nashville
- ☐ National Lampoon's Christmas Vacation
- ☐ National Lampoon's Vacation
- ☐ National Lampoon's Van Wilder
- ☐ National Velvet
- ☐ The Natural

- ☐ Nausicaa of the Valley of the Wind
- ☐ Network
- ☐ New Year's Eve
- ☐ New York New York
- ☐ A Night at the Opera (1935)
- ☐ The Night of the Hunter
- ☐ Night of the Living Dead (1968)
- ☐ Nightcrawler
- ☐ The Nightmare Before Christmas
- ☐ A Nightmare on Elm Street (1984)
- ☐ Ninotchka
- ☐ No Country for Old Men
- ☐ Nocturnal Animals
- ☐ Nomadland
- ☐ None But the Lonely Heart
- ☐ Norma Rae
- ☐ North by Northwest
- ☐ Nosferatu, A Symphony of Terror
- ☐ The Notebook
- ☐ Nothing Sacred
- ☐ Notting Hill
- ☐ Now and Then
- ☐ Now, Voyager

O

- ☐ The Odd Couple
- ☐ Office Space
- ☐ An Officer and a Gentleman
- ☐ Oklahoma! (1955)
- ☐ Old School
- ☐ Old Yeller

- [ ] Oldboy
- [ ] Oliver!
- [ ] The Omen (1976)
- [ ] On the Town
- [ ] Once Upon a Time in America
- [ ] Once Upon a Time in Hollywood
- [ ] Once Upon a Time in the West
- [ ] One Flew Over the Cuckoo's Nest
- [ ] One Hundred and One Dalmatians
- [ ] One Way Passage
- [ ] On Golden Pond
- [ ] On the Waterfront
- [ ] Operation Dumbo Drop
- [ ] Ordinary People
- [ ] The Others (2001)
- [ ] Out of Africa
- [ ] The Outsiders
- [ ] Overboard (1987)

P

- [ ] The Page Master
- [ ] Pal Joey
- [ ] Palm Springs
- [ ] Pan's Labyrinth
- [ ] The Paper Chase
- [ ] Paper Moon
- [ ] Paranormal Activity
- [ ] Parasite
- [ ] The Parent Trap (1961)
- [ ] A Passage to India
- [ ] The Passion of Joan of Arc
- [ ] A Patch of Blue
- [ ] Pather Panchali
- [ ] Paths of Glory
- [ ] The Patriot
- [ ] Patton
- [ ] Peeping Tom
- [ ] The Perks of Being a Wallflower
- [ ] Persona
- [ ] Peter Pan
- [ ] The Phantom of the Opera (1925)
- [ ] Philadelphia
- [ ] The Philadelphia Story
- [ ] Pi
- [ ] The Pianist
- [ ] The Piano
- [ ] Pillow Talk
- [ ] The Pink Panther
- [ ] Pippy Longstocking
- [ ] Pirates of the Caribbean: The Curse of the Black Pearl
- [ ] Pitch Perfect
- [ ] A Place in the Sun
- [ ] Places in the Heart
- [ ] Planes, Trains and Automobiles
- [ ] Planet of the Apes
- [ ] Platoon
- [ ] The Player
- [ ] Playtime
- [ ] Point Break
- [ ] The Polar Express
- [ ] Pollock
- [ ] Poltergeist
- [ ] The Post
- [ ] Precious
- [ ] The Prestige
- [ ] Pretty in Pink
- [ ] Pretty Woman
- [ ] Pride
- [ ] Pride and Prejudice

☐ Pride of the Yankees
☐ The Prime of Miss Jean Brodie
☐ The Prince of Egypt
☐ The Princess Bride
☐ The Princess Diaries
☐ Princess Mononoke
☐ Princess O'Rourke
☐ Prisoners
☐ The Private Life of Henry VIII
☐ Prizzi's Honor
☐ The Producers
☐ Promising Young Woman
☐ Pulp Fiction
☐ Pump Up the Volume
☐ Punch-Drunk Love
☐ The Pursuit of Happyness
☐ Pygmalion (1938)
☐ Psycho

Q

☐ The Queen
☐ The Quiet Man
☐ A Quiet Place
☐ Quiz Show

R

☐ Raatchasen
☐ Radio
☐ Raging Bull
☐ The Raid
☐ Rain Man
☐ Raise the Red Lantern
☐ Raising Arizona
☐ Ran
☐ Random Harvest
☐ Rashomon

☐ Ratatouille
☐ Ray
☐ The Razor's Edge
☐ Th Reader
☐ Real Genius
☐ Rear Window
☐ Rebecca
☐ Rebel Without a Cause
☐ The Red Badge of Courage
☐ The Red Balloon
☐ The Red Shoes
☐ Reds
☐ Reefer Madness (2005)
☐ Remember the Titans
☐ Repo Man
☐ Repo! The Genetic Opera
☐ Requiem for a Dream
☐ Reservoir Dogs
☐ Resident Evil
☐ The Revenant
☐ Revenge of the Nerds
☐ Reversal of Fortune
☐ Richie Rich
☐ Rififi
☐ Ringu
☐ Rio
☐ RoboCop
☐ Rocketman
☐ Rocky
☐ The Rocky Horror Picture Show
☐ Roman Holiday
☐ Road to Morocco
☐ Rookie of the Year
☐ Room
☐ The Room
☐ Room at the Top
☐ A Room with a View

- ☐ Romancing the Stone
- ☐ Romeo and Juliet (1996)
- ☐ Romy and Michele's High School Reunion
- ☐ Rosemary's Baby
- ☐ The Rose Tattoo
- ☐ The Royal Tenenbaums
- ☐ The Rules of the Game
- ☐ Run Lola Run
- ☐ Rush
- ☐ Rushmore
- ☐ Rudy
- ☐ Ryan's Daughter

S

- ☐ Sabrina (1954)
- ☐ Safety Last!
- ☐ Salt
- ☐ The Sandlot
- ☐ Sansho the Bailiff
- ☐ The Santa Clause
- ☐ Saturday Night Fever
- ☐ Save the Tiger
- ☐ Saving Private Ryan
- ☐ Saw
- ☐ Say Anything
- ☐ Sayonara
- ☐ Scarface
- ☐ Scent of a Woman
- ☐ Schindler's List
- ☐ School of Rock
- ☐ Scott Pilgrim vs. the World
- ☐ The Scoundrel
- ☐ Scream
- ☐ Scrooged
- ☐ The Sea Inside
- ☐ Seabiscuit
- ☐ Searching for Bobby Fischer

- ☐ The Searchers
- ☐ The Secret Garden
- ☐ The Secret in Their Eyes
- ☐ The Secret Life of Bees
- ☐ Secret Life of Pets
- ☐ The Secret of NIMH
- ☐ Secondhand Lions
- ☐ Selma
- ☐ Sense and Sensibility
- ☐ Separate Tables
- ☐ A Separation
- ☐ Seraphine
- ☐ Serendipity
- ☐ Sergeant York
- ☐ Serpico
- ☐ Se7en
- ☐ Seven Samurai
- ☐ The Seven-Year Itch
- ☐ The Seventh Seal
- ☐ The Seventh Veil
- ☐ Shadow of a Doubt
- ☐ Shaft
- ☐ The Shaggy Dog
- ☐ Shakespeare in Love
- ☐ Shampoo
- ☐ Shane (1953)
- ☐ The Shape of Water
- ☐ Shark Tale
- ☐ The Shawshank Redemption
- ☐ Shaun of the Dead
- ☐ She Wore a Yellow Ribbon
- ☐ She's All That
- ☐ Sherlock Jr.
- ☐ Shine
- ☐ The Shining
- ☐ Shoah

- ☐ The Shop Around the Corner
- ☐ Show Girls
- ☐ Show People
- ☐ Shrek
- ☐ Shutter Island
- ☐ Sideways
- ☐ The Silence of the Lambs
- ☐ A Silent Voice
- ☐ Silver Linings Playbook
- ☐ The Sin of Madelon Claudet
- ☐ Singin' in the Rain
- ☐ Singles
- ☐ The Sisterhood of the Traveling Pants
- ☐ Sixteen Candles
- ☐ The Sixth Sense
- ☐ Slapshot
- ☐ Sleepless in Seattle
- ☐ Sliding Doors
- ☐ Sling Blade
- ☐ Slueth
- ☐ Slumdog Millionaire
- ☐ Snatch
- ☐ Snow White and the Seven Dwarfs
- ☐ The Social Network
- ☐ Solaris (1972)
- ☐ Some Kind of Wonderful
- ☐ Some Like It Hot
- ☐ The Song of Bernadette
- ☐ Song of the Sea
- ☐ Sophie's Choice
- ☐ Soul
- ☐ The Sound of Music
- ☐ South Pacific
- ☐ Space Jam (1996)
- ☐ Spaceballs
- ☐ Spartacus
- ☐ Speed
- ☐ The Spirit of the Beehive
- ☐ Spirited Away
- ☐ Spider-Man
- ☐ Spider-Man: Into the Spider-Verse
- ☐ Spider-Man: No Way Home
- ☐ Splash
- ☐ Splendor in the Grass
- ☐ Split
- ☐ Spotlight
- ☐ Stagecoach
- ☐ Stalag 17
- ☐ Stalker (1979)
- ☐ Stand By Me
- ☐ A Star is Born (1937)
- ☐ A Star is Born (1954)
- ☐ Star Trek (1979)
- ☐ Star Wars (1977)
- ☐ Star Wars: Episode V
- ☐ Star Wars: Episode VI
- ☐ Steel Magnolias
- ☐ Step Brothers
- ☐ Still Alice
- ☐ The Sting
- ☐ The Story of Louis Pasteur
- ☐ Straight Outta Compton
- ☐ Stranger than Paradise
- ☐ Strangers on a Train
- ☐ Street Angel
- ☐ A Streetcar Named Desire
- ☐ Strike Up the Band
- ☐ The Subject was Roses
- ☐ Suffragette

☐ Sullivan's Travels
☐ Sunset Blvd.
☐ The Sunshine Boys
☐ Super Troopers
☐ Superbad
☐ Superman (1978)
☐ Suspicion
☐ Sweet Bird of Youth
☐ Sweet November
☐ Sweet Smell of Success
☐ Swiss Family Robinson (1960)
☐ Syriana

T

☐ Talk to Her
☐ Tall Tale
☐ Taxi Driver
☐ Teen Wolf (1985)
☐ Tender Mercies
☐ The Terminator
☐ Terminator 2
☐ Terms of Endearment
☐ The Texas Chainsaw Massacre (1974)
☐ Thelma and Louise
☐ The Theory of Everything
☐ There Will Be Blood
☐ There's Something About Mary
☐ They Shoot Horses, Don't They?
☐ They Were Expendable
☐ The Thing
☐ The Third Man
☐ This is Spinal Tap
☐ This is the End
☐ The Thomas Crown Affair

☐ A Thousand Clowns
☐ Three Billboards Outside Ebbing, Missouri
☐ Three Colors, Red
☐ The Three Faces of Eve
☐ Thumbelina
☐ Time Bandits
☐ The Time Traveler's Wife
☐ Tin Cup
☐ Titanic
☐ To All the Boys I've Loved Before
☐ To Be or Not to Be
☐ To Catch a Thief
☐ To Each His Own
☐ To Kill a Mockingbird
☐ To Wong Foo thanks for Everything, Julie Newmar
☐ Tokyo Story
☐ Tom Jones
☐ Tomb Raider
☐ Tombstone
☐ Tommy Boy
☐ Tootsie
☐ Top Gun
☐ Top Gun: Maverick
☐ Top Hat
☐ Topkapi
☐ Tora! Tora! Tora!
☐ Total Recall
☐ A Touch of Class
☐ Touch of Evil
☐ The Towering Inferno
☐ Toy Story
☐ Toy Story 3
☐ Trading Places
☐ Traffic

- ☐ Trainspotting
- ☐ The Treasure of the Sierra Madre
- ☐ A Tree Grows in Brooklyn
- ☐ Tremors
- ☐ The Trip to Bountiful
- ☐ Tron (1982)
- ☐ Troy
- ☐ True Grit
- ☐ True Lies
- ☐ The Truman Show
- ☐ Twelve Monkeys
- ☐ Twelve O'Clock High
- ☐ Two Women

U

- ☐ The Umbrellas of Cherbourg
- ☐ Uncle Buck
- ☐ Underworld
- ☐ Unforgiven
- ☐ The Untouchables
- ☐ Up
- ☐ Up in Smoke
- ☐ The Usual Suspects

V

- ☐ V for Vendetta
- ☐ Valley Girl (1983)
- ☐ Valley of the Dolls
- ☐ Varsity Blues
- ☐ Vertigo
- ☐ Vicky Cristina Barcelona
- ☐ La Vie en Rose
- ☐ Village of the Damned
- ☐ The VIPs
- ☐ Viridiana
- ☐ Vision Quest

- ☐ Viva Las Vegas
- ☐ Viva Zapata

W

- ☐ The Wages of Fear
- ☐ Waiting…
- ☐ Waiting for Guffman
- ☐ Waking Ned Devine
- ☐ Walk the Line
- ☐ Wall Street
- ☐ Wall-E
- ☐ War and Peace
- ☐ War of the Worlds (1953)
- ☐ Warrior
- ☐ The Warriors
- ☐ Watch on the Rhine
- ☐ Waterloo Bridge
- ☐ The Way Back
- ☐ The Way of All Flesh
- ☐ Way Out West
- ☐ The Way We Were
- ☐ We Are Marshall
- ☐ Wedding Crashers
- ☐ The Wedding Singer
- ☐ Welcome to the Dollhouse
- ☐ The Westerner
- ☐ West Side Story
- ☐ West Side Story (2022)
- ☐ Westworld (1973)
- ☐ Wet Hot American Summer
- ☐ What About Bob?
- ☐ What's Up Doc?
- ☐ Whatever Happened to Baby Jane?
- ☐ When a Man Loves a Woman
- ☐ When Harry Met Sally

- [ ] Where a Woman Ascends the Stairs
- [ ] While You Were Sleeping
- [ ] Whiplash
- [ ] White Men Can't Jump
- [ ] White Oleander
- [ ] Who Framed Roger Rabbit
- [ ] Who's Afraid of Virginia Woolf?
- [ ] The Wicker Man (1973)
- [ ] The Wild Bunch (1969)
- [ ] Wild Hearts Can't Be Broken
- [ ] Wild Strawberries
- [ ] Wild Tales
- [ ] Willow
- [ ] Willy Wonka and the Chocolate Factory
- [ ] Wilson
- [ ] Wings
- [ ] Wings of Desire
- [ ] Winter's Bone
- [ ] The Witches
- [ ] The Witches of Eastwick
- [ ] Withnail & I
- [ ] Witness
- [ ] Witness for the Prosecution
- [ ] The Wiz
- [ ] The Wizard of Oz
- [ ] The Wolf of Wall Street

- [ ] Woman of the Year
- [ ] Women in Love
- [ ] Women on the Verge of a Breakdown
- [ ] Woodstock
- [ ] Working Girl
- [ ] The Wrestler
- [ ] Written on the Wind
- [ ] Wuthering Heights

X

- [ ] X-Men

Y

- [ ] Yankee Doodle Dandy
- [ ] The Year of Living Dangerously
- [ ] Yi Yi (One and a Two)
- [ ] Yojimbo
- [ ] You Can't Take It with You
- [ ] You Were Never Lovelier
- [ ] You've Got Mail
- [ ] Young Frankenstein
- [ ] Young Guns
- [ ] Youngblood
- [ ] Your Name

Z

- [ ] Zero Dark Thirty
- [ ] Zodiac
- [ ] Zoolander
- [ ] Zorba the Greek

THE TELEVISION SHOW
BUCKET LIST

I would count this as long as you watched at least one or two episodes.

- ☐ The Ed Sullivan Show
- ☐ The Lone Ranger
- ☐ The Jack Benny Program
- ☐ What's My Line
- ☐ Dragnet
- ☐ I Love Lucy
- ☐ American Bandstand
- ☐ Superman
- ☐ Father Knows Best
- ☐ The Tonight Show Starring Johnny Carson
- ☐ Alfred Hitchcock Presents
- ☐ Gunsmoke
- ☐ The Benny Hill Show
- ☐ The Honeymooners
- ☐ The Price is Right
- ☐ Leave it to Beaver
- ☐ Maverick
- ☐ Perry Mason
- ☐ Bonanza
- ☐ Twilight Zone
- ☐ Rawhide
- ☐ The Andy Griffith Show
- ☐ The Flintstones
- ☐ Car 54, Where are You?
- ☐ Mr. Ed
- ☐ The Dick Van Dyke Show
- ☐ The Beverly Hillbillies
- ☐ Doctor Who
- ☐ Let's Make a Deal
- ☐ The Outer Limits
- ☐ Bewitched

- ☐ Gilligan's Island
- ☐ Peyton Place
- ☐ The Addams Family
- ☐ Jeopardy
- ☐ The Munsters
- ☐ I Dream of Jeannie
- ☐ Green Acres
- ☐ Hogan's Heroes
- ☐ Lost in Space
- ☐ I Spy
- ☐ Days of Our Lives
- ☐ The Dating Game
- ☐ Batman
- ☐ Star Trek
- ☐ The Phil Donahue Show
- ☐ The Carol Burnette Show
- ☐ The Forsyte Saga
- ☐ Hawaii Five-O
- ☐ The Brady Bunch
- ☐ All My Children
- ☐ The Odd Couple
- ☐ The Partridge Family
- ☐ The Mary Tyler Moore Show
- ☐ All in the Family
- ☐ Soul Train
- ☐ Columbo
- ☐ The Waltons
- ☐ M*A*S*H
- ☐ Maude
- ☐ Barnaby Jones
- ☐ Happy Days

- [ ] Good Times
- [ ] The Six Million Dollar Man
- [ ] Little House on the Prairie
- [ ] The Rockford Files
- [ ] Starsky & Hutch
- [ ] Barney Miller
- [ ] Wonder Woman
- [ ] Saturday Night Live
- [ ] Wheel of Fortune
- [ ] The Jeffersons
- [ ] Laverne & Shirley
- [ ] Charlie's Angels
- [ ] The Bionic Woman
- [ ] The Muppet Show
- [ ] The Gong Show
- [ ] The Sullivans
- [ ] Roots
- [ ] Three's Company
- [ ] Chips
- [ ] The Love Boat
- [ ] Fantasy Island
- [ ] Different Strokes
- [ ] Dallas
- [ ] Mork & Mindy
- [ ] Taxi
- [ ] WKRP in Cincinnati
- [ ] The Dukes of Hazzard
- [ ] The Facts of Life
- [ ] Magnum P.I.
- [ ] Dynasty
- [ ] The Borgias
- [ ] Cagney and Lacey
- [ ] Remington Steele
- [ ] Knight Rider
- [ ] Cheers
- [ ] The A-Team
- [ ] Murder, She Wrote
- [ ] Night Court
- [ ] The Cosby Show
- [ ] Miami Vice
- [ ] Moonlighting
- [ ] The Golden Girls
- [ ] Larry King Live
- [ ] Alf
- [ ] The Oprah Winfrey Show
- [ ] The Garry Shandling's Show
- [ ] L.A. Law
- [ ] Matlock
- [ ] Married with Children
- [ ] Tutti Frutti
- [ ] Thirtysomething
- [ ] Full House
- [ ] Roseanne
- [ ] Murphy Brown
- [ ] The Wonder Years
- [ ] The Kids in the Hall
- [ ] The Simpsons
- [ ] The Arsenio Hall Show
- [ ] Baywatch
- [ ] Quantum Leap
- [ ] Seinfeld
- [ ] Beverly Hills, 90210
- [ ] The Fresh Prince of Bel-Air
- [ ] Twin Peaks
- [ ] Northern Exposure
- [ ] Mr. Bean
- [ ] Law & Order
- [ ] House of Cards
- [ ] The Jerry Springer Show
- [ ] Prime Suspect
- [ ] Melrose Place
- [ ] The Real World
- [ ] Absolutely Fabulous
- [ ] The Larry Sanders Show
- [ ] Boy Meets World
- [ ] The X-Files
- [ ] Walker Texas Ranger
- [ ] Late Show with David Letterman

☐ NYPD Blue
☐ Beavis and Butt-Head
☐ Frasier
☐ Lois & Clark
☐ Babylon 5
☐ All-American Girl
☐ ER
☐ My So-Called Life
☐ Friends
☐ Ellen
☐ Xena: Warrior Princess
☐ 3rd Rock from the Sun
☐ The Daily Show
☐ Pop-Up Video
☐ The Newsroom
☐ La Femme Nikita
☐ Ally McBeal
☐ Stargate SG-1
☐ Buffy the Vampire Slayer
☐ King of the Hill
☐ South Park
☐ Dawson's Creek
☐ That '70s Show
☐ Charmed
☐ Sex and the City
☐ Who Wants to Be a
   Millionaire
☐ Will & Grace
☐ Strangers with Candy
☐ Family Guy
☐ Angel
☐ Queer as Folk
☐ The West Wing
☐ The Sopranos
☐ Roswell
☐ Big Brother
☐ Futurama
☐ Freaks and Geeks
☐ Survivor
☐ CSI: Miami

☐ Deal or No Deal
☐ Jackass
☐ Malcolm in the Middle
☐ Gilmore Girls
☐ Curb Your Enthusiasm
☐ Alias
☐ 24
☐ Smallville
☐ Scrubs
☐ Six Feet Under
☐ The Office (UK)
☐ The Shield
☐ Monk
☐ The Wire
☐ Without a Trace
☐ The Bachelor
☐ The Osbournes
☐ Angels in America
☐ America's Next Top Model
☐ One Tree Hill
☐ Arrested Development
☐ Reno 911!
☐ Two and a half Men
☐ NCIS
☐ Nip/Tuck
☐ The OC
☐ Dog: The Bounty Hunter
☐ Battlestar Galactica
☐ Entourage
☐ Veronica Mars
☐ Desperate Housewives
☐ The 4400
☐ Boston Legal
☐ Project Runway
☐ House
☐ Lost
☐ Deadwood
☐ Shameless
☐ The L Word
☐ The X-Factor

- ☐ American Idol
- ☐ Supernatural
- ☐ Robot Chicken
- ☐ It's Always Sunny in Philadelphia
- ☐ Criminal Minds
- ☐ The Colbert Report
- ☐ Bones
- ☐ Prison Break
- ☐ Dancing with the Stars
- ☐ Medium
- ☐ The Office (US)
- ☐ Numbers
- ☐ Extras
- ☐ Grey's Anatomy
- ☐ How I Met Your Mother
- ☐ Weeds
- ☐ Ugly Betty
- ☐ 30Rock
- ☐ America's Got Talent
- ☐ Big Love
- ☐ Jericho
- ☐ Eureka
- ☐ The Unit
- ☐ Friday Night Lights
- ☐ The Real Housewives of Orange County
- ☐ Brothers and Sisters
- ☐ Dexter
- ☐ Heroes
- ☐ Wilfred
- ☐ Burn Notice
- ☐ Damages
- ☐ Chuck
- ☐ Reaper
- ☐ Gossip Girl
- ☐ Secret Diary of a Call Girl
- ☐ Californication
- ☐ Flight of the Conchords
- ☐ Keeping up with the Kardashians
- ☐ The Big Bang Theory
- ☐ Pushing Daisies
- ☐ The Tudors
- ☐ Mad Men
- ☐ The Mentalist
- ☐ True Blood
- ☐ Breaking Bad
- ☐ Merlin
- ☐ Man vs. Food
- ☐ Children's Hospital
- ☐ Fringe
- ☐ Sons of Anarchy
- ☐ Archer
- ☐ United States of Tara
- ☐ Castle
- ☐ Modern Family
- ☐ The League
- ☐ Nurse Jackie
- ☐ RuPaul's Drag Race
- ☐ Community
- ☐ The Good Wife
- ☐ Parks and Recreation
- ☐ Southland
- ☐ Vampire Diaries
- ☐ Glee
- ☐ The Voice
- ☐ Boardwalk Empire
- ☐ Raising Hope
- ☐ Downton Abbey
- ☐ The Great British Bake Off
- ☐ The Big C
- ☐ Parenthood
- ☐ Pretty Little Liars
- ☐ Sherlock
- ☐ The Walking Dead
- ☐ Mrs. Brown's Boys
- ☐ Bob's Burgers
- ☐ New Girl

- ☐ Portlandia
- ☐ Episodes
- ☐ Game of Thrones
- ☐ Grimm
- ☐ Revenge
- ☐ Homeland
- ☐ American Horror Story
- ☐ Scandal
- ☐ Nashville
- ☐ Arrow
- ☐ Veep
- ☐ Hatfields & McCoys
- ☐ The Newsroom
- ☐ Duck Dynasty
- ☐ Brooklyn Nine-Nine
- ☐ Orange is the New Black
- ☐ The Blacklist
- ☐ Agents of S.H.I.E.L.D
- ☐ Peaky Blinders
- ☐ Ray Donovan
- ☐ The Flash
- ☐ Gotham
- ☐ Penny Dreadful
- ☐ Jane the Virgin
- ☐ How to Get Away with Murder
- ☐ Empire
- ☐ Unbreakable Kimmy Schmidt
- ☐ Better Call Saul
- ☐ The Squid Game
- ☐ Hart of Dixie
- ☐ Yellowstone
- ☐ Emily in Paris
- ☐ The Good Doctor

THE BOOK BUCKET LIST

- ☐ Read a Banned Book
- ☐ Read a Classic Novel
- ☐ Read a Story to a Child
- ☐ Read a Trilogy

#

- ☐ The 13 Clocks – James Thurber
- ☐ The 120 Days of Sodom – Marquis de Sade
- ☐ 2001: A Space Odyssey – Arthur C. Clarke
- ☐ 2666 – Roberto Bolano

A

- ☐ Aaron's Rod – D.H. Lawrence
- ☐ The Abbot C – Georges Bataille
- ☐ Absalom, Absalom! – William Faulkner
- ☐ The Absentee – Maria Edgeworth
- ☐ Absolute Beginners – Colin MacInnes
- ☐ The Accidental – Ali Smith
- ☐ Ada – Vladimir Nabokov
- ☐ Adam Bede – George Eliot
- ☐ Adjunct: An Undigest – Peter Manson
- ☐ The Adventures and Misadventures of Magroll – Alvaro Mutis
- ☐ The Adventures of Augie March – Saul Bellow
- ☐ The Adventures of Caleb Williams – William Godwin
- ☐ The Adventures of Huckleberry Finn – Mark Twain
- ☐ The Adventures of Sherlock Holmes – Sir Arthur Conan Doyle
- ☐ The Adventures of Tom Sawyer – Mark Twain
- ☐ The Adventurous Simplicissimus – Hans von Girmmelshausen
- ☐ Aesop's Fables – Aesopus
- ☐ After the Death of Don Juan – Sylvie Townsend Warner
- ☐ After the Quake – Haruki Murakami
- ☐ The Afternoon of a Writer – Peter Handke
- ☐ Against the Day – Thomas Pynchon
- ☐ Against the Grain – Joris-Karl Huysmans

- ☐ The Age of Innocence – Edith Wharton
- ☐ Aithiopika – Heliodorus
- ☐ Alamut – Vladimir Bartol
- ☐ Albert Angelo – B.S. Johnson
- ☐ Alberta and Jacob – Cora Sandel
- ☐ The Albigenses – Charles Robert Maturin
- ☐ Alias Grace – Margaret Atwood
- ☐ Alice's Adventures in Wonderland – Lewis Carroll
- ☐ All About H. Hatterr – G.V. Desani
- ☐ All Quiet on the Western Front – Erich Maria Remarque
- ☐ All Souls – Javier Marias
- ☐ All Souls Day – Cees Nooteboom
- ☐ All the Pretty Horses – Cormac McCarthy
- ☐ Almost Transparent Blue – Ryu Murakami
- ☐ Amadis of Gaul – Garci Rodriguez de Montalvo
- ☐ Amateurs – Donald Barthelm
- ☐ The Amazing Adventures of Kavalier & Clay – Michael Chabon
- ☐ The Ambassadors – Henry James
- ☐ Amelia – Henry Fielding
- ☐ American Pastoral – Philip Roth
- ☐ American Psycho – Bret Easton Ellis
- ☐ American Rust – Philipp Meyer
- ☐ Amerika – Franz Kafka
- ☐ Amok – Stefan Zweig
- ☐ Amongst Women – John McGahern
- ☐ Amsterdam – Ian McEwan
- ☐ Anagrams – Lorrie Moore
- ☐ Ancestral Voices – Etienne van Heerden
- ☐ Andrea – Carmen Laforet
- ☐ Agnes Grey – Anne Brontë
- ☐ Animal Farm – George Orwell
- ☐ Animal's People – Indra Sinha
- ☐ Anna Karenina – Leo Tolstoy
- ☐ Annie John – Jamaica Kincaid
- ☐ Another World – Pat Barker
- ☐ Antic Hay – Aldous Huxley
- ☐ Anton Reiser – Karl Phillip Moritz
- ☐ The Apes of God – Wyndham Lewis
- ☐ Arcadia – Jim Crace

- [ ] Arrow of God – Chinua Achebe
- [ ] An Artist of the Floating World – Kazuo Ishiguro
- [ ] Arcanum 17 – André Breton
- [ ] Around the World in Eighty Days – Jules Verne
- [ ] The Art of Seduction – Robert Greene
- [ ] The Art of War – Sun Tzu
- [ ] The Artamonov Business – Maxim Gorky
- [ ] As a Man Grows Older – Italo Svevo
- [ ] As If I Am Not There – Slavenka Drakulić
- [ ] Ashes and Diamonds – Jerzy Andrzejewski
- [ ] Asphodel – H.D. (Hilda Doolittle)
- [ ] Astradeni – Eugenia Fakinou
- [ ] At Swim-Two-Birds – Flann O'Brien
- [ ] At Swim, Two Boys – Jamie O'Neill
- [ ] At the Mountains of Madness – H.P. Lovecraft
- [ ] Atlas Shrugged – Ayn Rand
- [ ] Atonement – Ian McEwan
- [ ] The Atrocity Exhibition – J.G. Ballard
- [ ] August is a Wicked Month – Edna O'Brien
- [ ] Austerlitz – W.G. Sebald
- [ ] The Autobiography of Alice B. Toklas – Gertrude Stein
- [ ] Auto-da-Fé – Elias Canetti
- [ ] Autumn of the Patriarch – Gabriel García Márquez
- [ ] The Awakening – Kate Chopin

B

- [ ] Babbitt – Sinclair Lewis
- [ ] Back – Henry Green
- [ ] The Back Room – Carmen Martin Gaite
- [ ] Back to Oegstgeest – Jan Wolkers
- [ ] The Ballad for Georg Henig – Viktor Paskov
- [ ] Baltasar and Blimunda – Jose Saramago
- [ ] Barabbas – Par Lagerkvist
- [ ] Bartleby and Co. – Enrique Vila-Matas
- [ ] The Beautiful Mrs. Seidenman – Andrzej Szczypiorski
- [ ] The Beautiful Room is Empty – Edmund White
- [ ] Bebo's Girl – Carlo Cassola
- [ ] Before Night Falls – Reinaldo Arenas
- [ ] The Beggar Maid – Alice Munro
- [ ] Being and Nothingness – Jean-Paul Sartre

- [ ] Bel-Ami – Guy de Maupassant
- [ ] The Bell – Iris Murdoch
- [ ] The Bell Jar – Sylvia Plath
- [ ] Belle du Seigneur – Albert Cohen
- [ ] The Bells of Basel – Louis Aragon
- [ ] Beloved – Toni Morrison
- [ ] Ben-Hur – Lew Wallace
- [ ] A Bend in the River – V.S. Naipaul
- [ ] Berlin Alexanderplatz – Alfred Döblin
- [ ] La Bête Humaine – Émile Zola
- [ ] The Betrothed – Alessandro Manzoni
- [ ] Between the Acts – Virginia Woolf
- [ ] Beyond Good and Evil – Friedrich Nietzsche
- [ ] The Big Sleep – Raymond Chandler
- [ ] Billiards at Half-Past Nine – Heinrich Böll
- [ ] Billy Bathgate – E.L. Doctorow
- [ ] Billy Budd, Foretopman – Herman Melville
- [ ] Billy Liar – Keith Waterhouse
- [ ] The Birds – Tarjei Vesaas
- [ ] The Birds Fall Down – Rebecca West
- [ ] Birdsong – Sebastian Faulks
- [ ] The Bitter Glass – Eilís Dillon
- [ ] Black Box – Amos Oz
- [ ] The Black Dahlia – James Ellroy
- [ ] Black Dogs – Ian McEwan
- [ ] The Black Prince – Iris Murdoch
- [ ] Black Water – Joyce Carol Oates
- [ ] Blaming – Elizabeth Taylor
- [ ] Bleak House – Charles Dickens
- [ ] The Blind Assassin – Margaret Atwood
- [ ] Blind Man With a Pistol – Chester Hines
- [ ] The Blind Owl – Sadegh Hedayat
- [ ] The Blind Side of The Heart – Julia Franck
- [ ] Blindness – Henry Green
- [ ] The Blithedale Romance – Nathaniel Hawthorne
- [ ] Blonde – Joyce Carol Oates
- [ ] Blood and Guts in High School – Kathy Acker
- [ ] Blood Meridian – Cormac McCarthy
- [ ] Blue Noon – Georges Bataille
- [ ] The Bluest Eye – Toni Morrison

- ☐ The Body Artist – Don DeLillo
- ☐ The Bonfire of the Vanities – Tom Wolfe
- ☐ Bonjour Tristesse – Françoise Sagan
- ☐ The Book about Blanche and Marie – Per OlovEnquist
- ☐ The Book of Daniel – E.L. Doctorow
- ☐ The Book of Diquiet – Fernando Pessoa
- ☐ The Book of Evidence – John Banville
- ☐ The Book of Illusions – Paul Auster
- ☐ The Book of Laughter and Forgetting – Milan Kundera
- ☐ Born in Exile – George Gissing
- ☐ Borstal Boy – Brendan Behan
- ☐ Bosnian Chronicle – Ivo Andrić
- ☐ Bouvard and Pécuchet – Gustave Flaubert
- ☐ A Boy's Own Story – Edmund White
- ☐ La Brava – Elmore Leonard
- ☐ Brave New World – Aldous Huxley
- ☐ Breakfast at Tiffany's – Truman Capote
- ☐ Breakfast of Champions – Kurt Vonnegut, Jr.
- ☐ The Breast – Philip Roth
- ☐ Brideshead Revisited – Evelyn Waugh
- ☐ The Bridge on the Drina – Ivo Andrić
- ☐ The Brief Wondrous Life of Oscar Wao – Junot Diaz
- ☐ Brighton Rock – Graham Greene
- ☐ Broad and Aliens is the World – Ciro Alegria
- ☐ Broken April – Ismail Kadare
- ☐ The Brothers Karamazov – Fyodor Dostoevsky
- ☐ Buddenbrooks – Thomas Mann
- ☐ The Buddha of Suburbia – Hanif Kureishi
- ☐ Bunner Sisters – Edith Wharton
- ☐ Burger's Daughter – Nadine Gordimer
- ☐ Burmese Days – George Orwell
- ☐ The Burning Plain – Juan Rulfo
- ☐ The Bus Conductor Hines – James Kelman
- ☐ The Butcher Boy – Patrick McCabe
- ☐ By the Open Sea – August Strindberg

C

- ☐ The Cairo Trilogy – Maguib Mahfouz
- ☐ Cakes and Ale – W. Somerset Maugham
- ☐ Call it Sleep – Henry Roth

- ☐ The Call of the Wild – Jack London
- ☐ Camera Obscura – Hildebrand
- ☐ Camilla – Fanny Burney
- ☐ Cancer Ward – Aleksandr Isayevich Solzhenitsyn
- ☐ Candide – Voltaire
- ☐ Cane – Jean Toomer
- ☐ Cannery Row – John Steinbeck
- ☐ Captain Corelli's Mandolin – Louis de Bernieres
- ☐ Carry Me Down – M.J. Hyland
- ☐ The Case of Comrade Tulayev – Victor Serge
- ☐ The Case of Sergeant Grischa – Arnold Zweig
- ☐ The Case Worker – Gyorgy Konrad
- ☐ Casino Royale – Ian Fleming
- ☐ The Castle – Franz Kafka
- ☐ The Castle of Crossed Destinies – Italo Calvino
- ☐ The Castle of Otranto – Horace Walpole
- ☐ Castle Rackrent – Maria Edgeworth
- ☐ Castle Richmond – Anthony Trollope
- ☐ Cat and Mouse – Günter Grass
- ☐ Cat's Cradle – Kurt Vonnegut
- ☐ Cat's Eye – Margaret Atwood
- ☐ Cataract – Mykhaylo Osadchyl
- ☐ Catch-22 – Joseph Heller
- ☐ The Catcher in the Rye – J.D. Salinger
- ☐ The Cathedral – Oles Honchar
- ☐ Caught – Henry Green
- ☐ Cause for Alarm – Eric Ambler
- ☐ Cecilia – Fanny Burney
- ☐ Celestial Harmonies – Péter Esterházy
- ☐ La Celestina – Fernando de Rojas
- ☐ The Cement Garden – Ian McEwan
- ☐ Chaireas and Kallirhoe – Chariton
- ☐ Chaka the Zulu – Thomas Mofolo
- ☐ The Charterhouse of Parma – Stendhal
- ☐ The Charwoman's Daughter – James Stephens
- ☐ Cheese – Willem Elsschot
- ☐ Chess Story – Stefan Zweig
- ☐ The Child in Time – Ian McEwan
- ☐ The Child of Pleasure – Gabriele D'Annunzio
- ☐ The Childermass – Wyndham Lewis

- ☐ The Children's Book – A.S. Byatt
- ☐ Chocky – John Wyndham
- ☐ Choke – Chuck Palahniuk
- ☐ Christ Stopped at Eboli – Carlo Levi
- ☐ A Christmas Carol – Charles Dickens
- ☐ The Christmas Oratorio – Goran Tunstrom
- ☐ The Cider House Rules – John Irving
- ☐ Cider With Rosie – Laurie Lee
- ☐ Cigarettes – Harry Mathews
- ☐ City of God – E.L. Doctorow
- ☐ City Primeval – Elmore Leonard
- ☐ City Sister Silver – Jàchym Topol
- ☐ Clarissa – Samuel Richardson
- ☐ Claudine's House – Colette
- ☐ The Clay Machine-Gun – Victor Pelevin
- ☐ Clear Light of Day – Anita Desai
- ☐ A Clockwork Orange – Anthony Burgess
- ☐ Closely Watched Trains – Bohumil Hrabal
- ☐ Cloud Atlas – David Mitchell
- ☐ Cloudsplitter – Russell Banks
- ☐ Cocaine Nights – J.G. Ballard
- ☐ Cold Comfort Farm – Stella Gibbons
- ☐ The Collector – John Fowles
- ☐ The Color Purple – Alice Walker
- ☐ The Colour – Rose Tremain
- ☐ Come Back, Dr. Caligari – Donald Bartholme
- ☐ The Comfort of Strangers – Ian McEwan
- ☐ Coming Up for Air – George Orwell
- ☐ The Commandant – Jessica Anderson
- ☐ The Communist Manifesto – Karl Marx and Friedrich Engles
- ☐ Compassion – Benito Perez Galdos
- ☐ The Complete Grimm's Fairy Tales – Jacob and Wilhelm Grimm
- ☐ The Complete Poems of Emily Dickinson – Emily Dickinson
- ☐ Complicity – Iain Banks
- ☐ Concrete – Thomas Bernhard
- ☐ Confederacy of Dunces – John Kennedy Toole
- ☐ Confessions – Jean-Jacques Rousseau
- ☐ The Conquest of New Spain – Bernal Diaz del Castillo
- ☐ Contact – Carl Sagan

- ☐ The Convservationist – Nadine Gordimer
- ☐ Correction – Thomas Bernhard
- ☐ The Corrections – Jonathan Franzen
- ☐ Cost: A Nvel – Roxana Robinson
- ☐ The Count of Monte-Cristo – Alexandre Dumas
- ☐ The Counterfeiters – André Gide
- ☐ The Country Girls – Edna O'Brien
- ☐ Couples, Passerby – Botho Strauss
- ☐ Cranford – Elizabeth Gaskell
- ☐ Crash – J.G. Ballard
- ☐ Crime and Punishment – Fyodor Dostoevsky
- ☐ The Crime of Father Amado – Jose Maria Eca de Quieros
- ☐ Crome Yellow – Aldous Huxley
- ☐ Crossfire – Miyabe Miyuki
- ☐ The Crow Road – Iain Banks
- ☐ Cry, the Beloved Country – Alan Paton
- ☐ The Crying of Lot 49 – Thomas Pynchon
- ☐ Cryptonomicon – Neal Stephenson
- ☐ The Cubs and Other Stories – Mario Vargas Llosa
- ☐ The Curious Incident of the Dog in the Night-Time – Mark Haddon
- ☐ Cutter and Bone – Newton Thornburg

D

- ☐ A Dance to the Music of Time – Anthony Powell
- ☐ Dangerous Liaisons – Pierre Choderlos de Laclos
- ☐ Dangling Man – Saul Bellow
- ☐ Daniel Deronda – George Eliot
- ☐ Dark as the Grave Wherein My Friend is Laid – Malcolm Lowry
- ☐ The Dark Child – Camara Laye
- ☐ The Daughter – Pavlos Matesis
- ☐ David Copperfield – Charles Dickens
- ☐ A Day in Spring – Ciril Kosmac
- ☐ Day of the Dolphin – Robert Merle
- ☐ The Day of the Triffids – John Wyndham
- ☐ A Day Off – Storm Jameson
- ☐ Dead Air – Iain Banks
- ☐ Dead Babies – Martin Amis
- ☐ Dead Souls – Nikolay Gogol

☐ The Deadbeats – Ward Ruyslinck
☐ The Dead Father – Donald Barthelme
☐ Death and the Dervish – Mesa Selimovic
☐ Death Etc – Harold Pinter
☐ Death in Rome – Wolfgang Koeppen
☐ Death in Venice – Thomas Mann
☐ The Death of Artemio Cruz – Carlos Fuentes
☐ The Death of Ivan Ilyich – Leo Tolstoy
☐ The Death of Virgil – Herman Broch
☐ Death Sentence – Maurice Blanchot
☐ Decline and Fall – Evelyn Waugh
☐ Deep River – Shusaku Endo
☐ Deep Rivers – Jose Maria Arguedas
☐ Delta of Venus – Anaïs Nin
☐ Democracy – Joan Didion
☐ The Devil and Miss Prym – Paulo Coelho
☐ The Devil in the Flesh – Raymond Radiguet
☐ The Devil to Pay in the Backlands – Joao Guimaraes Rosa
☐ The Devils – Fyodor Dostoevsky
☐ The Devil's Pool – George Sand
☐ Diary of a Nobody – George & Weedon Grossmith
☐ The Diary of Jane Somers – Doris Lessing
☐ The Diary of a Young Girl – Anne Frank
☐ Dictionary of the Khazars – Milorad Pavić
☐ Dining on Stones – Iain Sinclair
☐ Dirk Gently's Holistic Detective Agency – Douglas Adams
☐ Dirty Havana Trilogy – Pedro Juan Guitierrez
☐ A Disaffection – James Kelman
☐ Dispatches – Michael Herr
☐ Disappearance – David Dabydeen
☐ The Discovery of Heaven – Harry Mulisch
☐ Disgrace – J.M. Coetzee
☐ Disobedience – Alberto Moravia
☐ The Dispossessed – Ursula K. Le Guin
☐ The Divine Comedy – Dante Alighieri
☐ The Diviners – Margaret Laurence
☐ Do Androids Dream of Electric Sheep? – Philip K. Dick
☐ Doctor Faustus – Thomas Mann
☐ Doctor Zhivago – Boris Pasternak
☐ Dog Years – Gunter Grass

- ☐ A Doll's House – Henrik Ibsen
- ☐ Dom Casmurro – Joaquim Maria Machado de Assis
- ☐ Don Juan – Lord Byron
- ☐ Don Quixote – Miguel de Cervantes Saavedra
- ☐ Don't Move – Margaret Mazzantini
- ☐ The Double – José Saramago
- ☐ Down Second Avenue – Ezekiel Mphahlele
- ☐ Down There – Joris-Karl Huysmans
- ☐ Downriver – Iain Sinclair
- ☐ Dracula – Bram Stoker
- ☐ A Dream of Red Mansions – Cao Xueqin
- ☐ The Driver's Seat – Muriel Spark
- ☐ Drop City – T. Coraghessan Boyle
- ☐ The Drowned and the Saved – Primo Levi
- ☐ The Drowned World – J.G. Ballard
- ☐ Drunkard – Émile Zola
- ☐ A Dry White Season – Andre Brink
- ☐ The Dumas Club – Arturo Perez-Reverte
- ☐ Dusklands – J.M. Coetzee

E

- ☐ Eclipse of the Crescent Moon – Geza Gardonyi
- ☐ Effi Briest – Theodore Fontane
- ☐ Elective Affinities – Johann Wolfgang von Goethe
- ☐ The Electric Kool-Aid Acid Test – Tom Wolfe
- ☐ The Elegance of the Hedgehog – Muriel Barbery
- ☐ Elementary Particles – Michel Houellebecq
- ☐ Eline Vere – Louis Couperus
- ☐ Elizabeth Costello – J.M. Coetzee
- ☐ Embers – Sandor Marai
- ☐ The Emigrants – W.G. Sebald
- ☐ Émile; or, On Education – Jean-Jacques Rousseau
- ☐ Emma – Jane Austen
- ☐ Empire of the Sun – J.G. Ballard
- ☐ The Enchanted Wanderer – Nicolai Leskov
- ☐ The End of the Affair – Graham Greene
- ☐ The End of the Road – John Barth
- ☐ The End of the Story – Lydia Davis
- ☐ Enduring Love – Ian McEwan
- ☐ Enemies: A Love Story – Isaac Singer

- [ ] Les Enfants Terribles – Jean Cocteau
- [ ] The Engineer of Human Souls – Josef Skvorecky
- [ ] England Made Me – Graham Greene
- [ ] The English Patient – Michael Ondaatje
- [ ] Enigma of Arrival – V.S. Naipaul
- [ ] The Enormous Room – E.E. Cummings
- [ ] Erewhon – Samuel Butler
- [ ] Essays – Ralph Waldo Emerson
- [ ] Ethan Frome – Edith Wharton
- [ ] Eugene Onegin – Alexander Pushkin
- [ ] Eugénie Grandet – Honoré de Balzac
- [ ] Euphues: The Anatomy of Wit – John Lyly
- [ ] Eva Trout – Elizabeth Bowen
- [ ] Evelina – Fanny Burney
- [ ] Everything is Illuminated – Jonathan Safran Foer
- [ ] Everything That Rises Must Converge – Flannery O'Connor
- [ ] Everything You Need – A.L. Kennedy
- [ ] Excellent Women – Barbara Pym
- [ ] Exercises in Style – Raymond Queneau
- [ ] Extinction – Thomas Bernhard
- [ ] Eyeless in Gaza – Aldous Huxley

F

- [ ] Faceless Killers – Henning Mankell
- [ ] Faces in the Water – Janet Frame
- [ ] Facundo – Domingo Faustino Sarmiento
- [ ] Fado Alexandrino – Antonio Lobo Antunes
- [ ] Faithful and Virtuous Night: Poems – Louise Gluck
- [ ] Fairy Tales – Hans Christian Andersen
- [ ] The Fall of the House of Usher – Edgar Allan Poe
- [ ] Fall on Your Knees – Ann-Marie MacDonald
- [ ] Falling Man – Don DeLillo
- [ ] Family Matters – Rohinton Mistry
- [ ] The Fan Man – William Kotzwinkle
- [ ] Fanny Hill – John Cleland
- [ ] Fantômas – Marcel Allain and Pierre Souvestre
- [ ] Far from the Madding Crowd – Thomas Hardy
- [ ] Farewell My Lovely – Raymond Chandler
- [ ] A Farewell to Arms – Ernest Hemingway

- [ ] Fateless – Imre Kertész
- [ ] Fathers and Sons – Ivan Turgenev
- [ ] Fear and Loathing in Las Vegas – Hunter S. Thompson
- [ ] Fear and Trembling – Amélie Nothomb
- [ ] Fear of Flying – Erica Jong
- [ ] The Feast of the Goat – Mario Vargos Llosa
- [ ] Felicia's Journey – William Trevor
- [ ] The Female Quixote – Charlotte Lennox
- [ ] Ferdydurke – Witold Gombrowicz
- [ ] Ficciones – Jorge Luis Borges
- [ ] Fifth Business – Robertson Davies
- [ ] A Fine Balance – Rohinton Mistry
- [ ] Fingersmith – Sarah Waters
- [ ] Finnegans Wake – James Joyce
- [ ] The First Circle – Aleksandr Isayevich Solzhenitsyn
- [ ] The First Garden – Anne Herbert
- [ ] Flaubert's Parrot – Julian Barnes
- [ ] Flights – Olga Tokarczuk
- [ ] The Floating Opera – John Barth
- [ ] Foe – J.M. Coetzee
- [ ] The Folding Star – Alan Hollinghurst
- [ ] Fool's Gold – Maro Douka
- [ ] Fools of Fortune – William Trevor
- [ ] For Whom the Bell Tolls – Ernest Hemingway
- [ ] The Forbidden Realm – J.J.Slauerhoff
- [ ] The Forest of the Hanged – Liviu Rebreanu
- [ ] Forever a Stranger – Hella Haasse
- [ ] The Forsyte Sage – John Galsworthy
- [ ] Fortunata and Jacinta – Benito Pérez Galdés
- [ ] Foucault's Pendulum – Umberto Eco
- [ ] Foundation – Isaac Asimov
- [ ] The Fox – D.H. Lawrence
- [ ] Frankenstein – Mary Wollstonecraft Shelley
- [ ] Franny and Zooey – J.D. Salinger
- [ ] The French Lieutenant's Woman – John Fowles
- [ ] Froth on the Daydream – Boris Vlan
- [ ] Fruits of the Earth – André Gide
- [ ] Fugitive Pieces – Anne Michaels
- [ ] Fury – Salman Rushdie

G

- ☐ G – John Berger
- ☐ Gabriel's Gift – Hanif Kureishi
- ☐ Gabriela, Clove and Cinnamon – Jorge Amado
- ☐ Garden, Ashes – Danilo Kis
- ☐ The Garden of the Finzi-Continis – Giorgio Bassani
- ☐ The Garden Party – Katherine Mansfield
- ☐ The Garden Where the Brass Band Played – Simon Vestdijk
- ☐ Gargantua and Pantagruel – Françoise Rabelais
- ☐ The Gathering – Anne Enright
- ☐ The German Lesson – Siegfried Lenz
- ☐ Germinal – Émile Zola
- ☐ Get Shorty – Elmore Leonard
- ☐ A Ghost at Noon – Alberto Moravia
- ☐ The Ghost Road – Pat Barker
- ☐ Giles Goat-Boy – John Barth
- ☐ Gimmick! – Joost Zwagerman
- ☐ Giovanni's Room – James Baldwin
- ☐ Girl With Green Eyes – Edna O'Brien
- ☐ The Girls of Slender Means – Muriel Spark
- ☐ Glamorama – Bret Easton Ellis
- ☐ The Glass Bead Game – Herman Hesse
- ☐ The Glass Bees – Ernst Junger
- ☐ The Glass Key – Dashiell Hammett
- ☐ The Glimpses of the Moon – Edith Wharton
- ☐ Go Down, Moses – William Faulkner
- ☐ Go Tell It on the Mountain – James Baldwin
- ☐ Goalie's Anxiety at the Penalty Kick – Peter Handke
- ☐ The Go-Between – L.P. Hartley
- ☐ God Bless You, Mr. Rosewater – Kurt Vonnegut
- ☐ The God of Small Things – Arundhati Roy
- ☐ God's Bits of Wood – Ousmane Sembene
- ☐ The Godfather – Mario Puzo
- ☐ The Golden Ass – Lucius Apuleius
- ☐ The Golden Bowl – Henry James
- ☐ The Golden Notebook – Doris Lessing
- ☐ Gone with the Wind – Margaret Mitchell
- ☐ The Good Earth – Pearl S. Buck
- ☐ Good Morning, Midnight – Jean Rhys
- ☐ The Good Soldier – Ford Madox Ford

☐ The Good Soldier Švejk – Jaroslav Hašek
☐ The Good Terrorist – Doris Lessing
☐ Goodbye to Berlin – Christopher Isherwood
☐ Gormenghast – Mervyn Peake
☐ Gösta Berling's Saga – Selma Lagerlöf
☐ The Graduate – Charles Webb
☐ The Grapes of Wrath – John Steinbeck
☐ The Grass is Singing – Doris Lessing
☐ Gravity's Rainbow – Thomas Pynchon
☐ Great Apes – Will Self
☐ The Great Enigma: New Collected Poems, Tomas Transtromer
☐ Great Expectations – Charles Dickens
☐ The Great Gatsby – F. Scott Fitzgerald
☐ The Great Indian Novel – Shashi Tharoor
☐ The Green Hat – Michael Arlen
☐ Green Henry – Gottfried Keller
☐ The Green Man – Kingsley Amis
☐ Grimus – Salman Rushdie
☐ The Ground Beneath Her Feet – Salman Rushdie
☐ Group Portrait with Lady – Heinrich Böll
☐ Growth of the Soil – Knut Hamsen
☐ The Guide – R.K.Narayan
☐ The Guiltless – Hermann Broch
☐ Gulliver's Travels – Jonathan Swift

H

☐ Hadrian the Seventh – Frederick Rolfe
☐ Half of a Yellow Sun – Chimamanda Ngozi Adichie
☐ Half of Man is Woman – Zhang Xianliang
☐ Halftime – Martin Walser
☐ Hallucinating Foucault – Patricia Duncker
☐ Hamlet – William Shakespeare
☐ The Hamlet – William Faulkner
☐ The Hand of Ethelberta – Thomas Hardy
☐ The Handmaid's Tale – Margaret Atwood
☐ A Handful of Dust – Evelyn Waugh
☐ Hangover Square – Patrick Hamilton
☐ Hard Times – Charles Dickens
☐ Harriet Hume – Rebecca West
☐ The Harvesters – Cesare Pavese

- [ ] Hawksmoor – Peter Ackroyd
- [ ] He Knew He Was Right – Anthony Trollope
- [ ] Heart of Darkness – Joseph Conrad
- [ ] The Heat of the Day – Elizabeth Bowen
- [ ] The Heather Blazing – Colm Tóibín
- [ ] The Heart of Redness – Zakes Mda
- [ ] The Heart of the Matter – Graham Greene
- [ ] A Heart So White – Javier Marias
- [ ] Heartbreak Tango – Manuel Puig
- [ ] Hebdomeros – Giorgio de Chirico
- [ ] Henderson the Rain King – Saul Bellow
- [ ] Henry of Ofterdingen – Novalis
- [ ] Her Privates We – Frederic Manning
- [ ] Here's to You, Jesusa – Elena Poniatowska
- [ ] The Heretic – Miguel Deliber
- [ ] A Hero of Our Times – Mikhail Yurevich Lermontov
- [ ] Herzog – Saul Bellow
- [ ] Hideous Kinky – Esther Freud
- [ ] High Rise – J.G. Ballard
- [ ] The History of the Siege of Lisbon – José Saramago
- [ ] History of Western Philosophy – Bertrand Russell
- [ ] The Hitchhiker's Guide to the Galaxy – Douglas Adams
- [ ] The Hive – Camilo Jose Cela
- [ ] The Hobbit – J.R.R. Tolkien
- [ ] The Holder of the World – Bharati Mukherjee
- [ ] Home – Marilynne Robinson
- [ ] Home and the World – Rabindranath Tagore
- [ ] A Home at the End of the World – Michael Cunningham
- [ ] Homo Faber – Max Frisch
- [ ] The Honorary Consul – Graham Greene
- [ ] The Hothouse – Wolfgang Koeppen
- [ ] The Hound of the Baskervilles – Sir Arthur Conan Doyle
- [ ] The Hour of the Star – Clarice Lispector
- [ ] The Hours – Michael Cunningham
- [ ] The House by the Medlar Tree – Giovanni Verga
- [ ] The House in Paris – Elizabeth Bowen
- [ ] House in the Uplands – Erskine Caldwell
- [ ] House Mother Normal – B.S. Johnson
- [ ] The House of Doctor Dee – Peter Ackroyd
- [ ] The House of Mirth – Edith Wharton

- ☐ The House of the Seven Gables – Nathaniel Hawthorne
- ☐ The House of the Spirits – Isabel Allende
- ☐ The House on the Borderland – William Hope Hodgson
- ☐ The House with the Blind Glass Windows – Herbjorg Wassmo
- ☐ House of Leaves – Mark Z. Danielewski
- ☐ How It Is – Samuel Beckett
- ☐ How Late It Was, How Late – James Kelman
- ☐ How the Dead Live – Will Self
- ☐ How to Win Friends and Influence People – Dale Carnegie
- ☐ Howards End – E.M. Forster
- ☐ The Human Stain – Philip Roth
- ☐ Humboldt's Gift – Saul Bellow
- ☐ Humphrey Clinker – Tobias George Smollett
- ☐ The Hunchback of Notre Dame – Victor Hugo
- ☐ Hunger – Knut Hamsun
- ☐ The Hunger Angel: A Novel – Herta Muller
- ☐ Hyperion – Friedrich Hölderlin

I

- ☐ I Know Why the Caged Bird Sings – Maya Angelou
- ☐ I, Robot – Isaac Asimov
- ☐ I Thought of Daisy – Edmund Wilson
- ☐ I'm Not Scared – Niccolo Ammaniti
- ☐ I'm Not Stiller – Max Frisch
- ☐ The Idiot – Fyodor Dostoevsky
- ☐ If Not Now, When? – Primo Levi
- ☐ If On a Winter's Night a Traveler – Italo Calvino
- ☐ If This Is a Man – Primo Levi
- ☐ Ignorance – Milan Kundera
- ☐ The Iliad - Homer
- ☐ The Immoralist – André Gide
- ☐ Impressions of Africa – Raymond Roussel
- ☐ In a Free State – V.S. Naipaul
- ☐ In a Glass Darkly – Sheridan Le Fanu
- ☐ In Cold Blood – Truman Capote
- ☐ In Parenthesis – David Jones
- ☐ In Search of Klingsor – Jorge Volpi
- ☐ In Sicily – Elio Vittorini
- ☐ In the Forest – Edna O'Brien
- ☐ In the Heart of the Country – J.M. Coetzee

- ☐ In The Heart of the Seas – Shmuel Yosef Agnon
- ☐ In Watermelon Sugar – Richard Brautigan
- ☐ Independent People – Halldór Laxness
- ☐ Indian Summer – Adalbert Stifter
- ☐ Indigo – Marina Warner
- ☐ The Inferno – Henri Barbusse
- ☐ Infinite Jest – David Foster Wallace
- ☐ The Information – Martin Amis
- ☐ The Inheritance of Loss – Kiran Desai
- ☐ Inland – Gerald Murnane
- ☐ Insatiability – Stanislaw Ignacy Witkiewicz
- ☐ Inside Mr. Enderby – Anthony Burgess
- ☐ The Interesting Narrative – Olaudah Equiano
- ☐ Interview With the Vampire – Anne Rice
- ☐ Intimacy – Hanif Kureishi
- ☐ The Invention of Curried Sausage – Uwe Timm
- ☐ Invisible – Paul Auster
- ☐ Invisible Cities – Italo Calvino
- ☐ Invisible Man – Ralph Ellison
- ☐ The Invisible Man – H.G. Wells
- ☐ The Iron Heel – Jack London
- ☐ The Island of Dr. Moreau – H.G. Wells
- ☐ Islands – Dan Sleigh
- ☐ Ivanhoe – Sir Walter Scott

J

- ☐ Jack Maggs – Peter Carey
- ☐ Jacob the Liar – Jurek Becker
- ☐ Jacob's Room – Virginia Woolf
- ☐ Jacques the Fatalist – Denis Diderot
- ☐ Jahrestage – Uwe Johnson
- ☐ Jane Eyre – Charlotte Brontë
- ☐ Jazz – Toni Morrison
- ☐ Jealousy – Alain Robbe-Grillet
- ☐ The Joke – Milan Kundera
- ☐ Joseph and His Brothers – Thomas Mann
- ☐ Joseph Andrews – Henry Fielding
- ☐ Journey to the Alcarria – Camilo Jose Cela
- ☐ Journey to the Centre of the Earth – Jules Verne
- ☐ Journey to the End of the Night – Louis-Ferdinand Céline

- ☐ Jude the Obscure – Thomas Hardy
- ☐ The Judge and His Hangman – Friedrich Dürrenmatt
- ☐ Julie; or, the New Eloise – Jean-Jacques Rousseau
- ☐ July's People – Nadine Gordimer
- ☐ The Jungle – Upton Sinclair
- ☐ Junkie – William Burroughs
- ☐ Just So Stories – Rudyard Kipling
- ☐ Justine – Lawrence Durrell
- ☐ Justine – Marquis de Sade

K

- ☐ Kafka on the Shore – Haruki Murakami
- ☐ Keep the Aspidistra Flying – George Orwell
- ☐ A Kestrel for a Knave – Barry Hines
- ☐ Kidnapped – Robert Louis Stevenson
- ☐ Kieron Smith, Boy – James Kelman
- ☐ The Killer Inside Me – Jim Thompson
- ☐ Kim – Rudyard Kipling
- ☐ The Kindly Ones – Jonathan Littell
- ☐ King Lear of the Steppes – Ivan Turgenev
- ☐ King Solomon's Mines – H. Rider Haggard
- ☐ Kingdom of This World – Alejo Carpentier
- ☐ Kiss of the Spider Woman – Manuel Puig
- ☐ Kitchen – Banana Yashimoto
- ☐ Kokoro – Natsume Soseki
- ☐ The Kreutzer Sonata – Leo Tolstoy
- ☐ Kristin Lavransdatter – Sigrid Undset

L

- ☐ The Labyrinth of Solitude – Octavio Paz
- ☐ Labyrinths – Jorg Luis Borges
- ☐ Lady Chatterley's Lover – D.H. Lawrence
- ☐ Lady Number Thirteen – Jose Carlos Somoza
- ☐ The Lambs of London – Peter Ackroyd
- ☐ Lanark: A Life in Four Books – Alasdair Gray
- ☐ Land – Park Kyong-ni
- ☐ Larva: Midsummer Night's Babel – Julian Rios
- ☐ The Last Chronicle of Barset – Anthony Trollope
- ☐ The Last Days of Humanity – Karl Kraus
- ☐ The Last of Mr. Norris – Christopher Isherwood

- ☐ Last of the Mohicans – James Fenimore Cooper
- ☐ The Last September – Elizabeth Bowen
- ☐ The Last Temptation of Christ – Nikos Kazantzákis
- ☐ The Last World – Christopher Ransmayr
- ☐ The Late-Night News – Petros Markaris
- ☐ The Laws – Connie Palmen
- ☐ Leaden Wings – Zhang Jie
- ☐ Leaves of Grass – Walt Whitman
- ☐ The Left-Handed Woman – Peter Handke
- ☐ Legend – David Gemmell
- ☐ The Leopard – Giuseppe Tomasi di Lampedusa
- ☐ Less Than Zero – Bret Easton Ellis
- ☐ Libra – Don DeLillo
- ☐ Life: A User's Manual – Georges Perec
- ☐ The Life and Adventures of Nicholas Nickleby – Charles Dickens
- ☐ Life and Death of Harriett Frean – May Sinclair
- ☐ The Life and Opinions of the Tomcat Murr – E.T.A. Hoffman
- ☐ The Life and Times of Michael K – J.M. Coetzee
- ☐ Life is a Caravanserai – Emine Özdamar
- ☐ The Life of a Good-for-Nothing – Joseph von Eichendorff
- ☐ Life of Christ – Giovanni Papini
- ☐ The Life of Insects – Victor Pelevin
- ☐ The Life of Lazarillo de Tormes – Anonymous
- ☐ Life of Pi – Yann Martel
- ☐ A Light Comedy – Eduardo Mendoza
- ☐ The Light of Day – Graham Swift
- ☐ Like Life – Lorrie Moore
- ☐ Like Water for Chocolate – Laura Esquivel
- ☐ The Line of Beauty – Alan Hollinghurst
- ☐ The Lion of Flanders – Hendrik Conscience
- ☐ The Little Prince – Antoine de Saint-Exupéry
- ☐ Little Women – Louisa May Alcott
- ☐ Lives of Girls & Women – Alice Munro
- ☐ Living – Henry Green
- ☐ The Living and the Dead – Patrick White
- ☐ Locus Solus – Raymond Roussel
- ☐ Lolita – Vladimir Nabokov
- ☐ London Fields – Martin Amis
- ☐ London Orbital – Iain Sinclair

☐ The Lonely Londoners – Sam Selvon
☐ The Long Dark Teatime of the Soul – Douglas Adams
☐ Long Day's Journey Into Night – Eugene O'Neill
☐ The Long Goodbye – Raymond Chandler
☐ Look Homeward, Angel – Thomas Wolfe
☐ Looking for the Possible Dance – A.L. Kennedy
☐ Lord Jim – Joseph Conrad
☐ Lord of the Flies – William Golding
☐ The Lord of the Rings – J.R.R. Tolkien
☐ The Lost Honor of Katharina Blum – Heinrich Böll
☐ Lost Illusions – Honoré de Balzac
☐ Lost Language of Cranes – David Leavitt
☐ The Lost Steps – Alejo Capentier
☐ Love in a Cold Climate – Nancy Mitford
☐ Love in Excess – Eliza Haywood
☐ Love in the Time of Cholera – Gabriel García Márquez
☐ Love Medicine – Louise Erdich
☐ Love's Work – Gillian Rose
☐ The Lover – Marguerite Duras
☐ Loving – Henry Green
☐ Lucky Jim – Kingsley Amis
☐ The Lusiad – Luis Vaz de Camoes

M

☐ Madame Bovary – Gustave Flaubert
☐ A Maggot – John Fowles
☐ The Magic Mountain – Thomas Mann
☐ The Magician of Lublin – Isaac Bashevis Singer
☐ The Magus – John Fowles
☐ Main Street – Sinclair Lewis
☐ The Making of Americans – Gertrude Stein
☐ Maldoror – Comte de Lautréaumont
☐ Malone Dies – Samuel Beckett
☐ The Maltese Falcon – Dashiell Hammett
☐ A Man Asleep – Georges Perec
☐ The Man of Feeling – Henry Mackenzie
☐ The Man Who Loved Children – Christina Stead
☐ The Man Without Qualities – Robert Musil
☐ The Man with the Golden Arm – Nelson Algren
☐ Man's Fate – Andre Malraux

- [ ] The Mandarins – Simone de Beauvoir
- [ ] Manhattan Transfer – John Dos Passos
- [ ] The Manila Rope – Veijo Meri
- [ ] Manon des Sources – Marcel Pagnol
- [ ] The Manor – Isaac Bashevis Singer
- [ ] The Manors of Ulloa – Emilia Pardo Bazan
- [ ] Mansfield Park – Jane Austen
- [ ] Mao II – Don DeLillo
- [ ] The Marble Faun – Nathaniel Hawthorne
- [ ] Margot and the Angels – Kristien Hemmerechts
- [ ] Marius the Epicurean – Walter Pater
- [ ] Marks of Identity – Juan Goytisolo
- [ ] Martin Chuzzlewit – Charles Dickens
- [ ] Martin Eden – Jack London
- [ ] Martin Fierro – Jose Hernandez
- [ ] Mary Barton – Elizabeth Gaskell
- [ ] Marya – Joyce Carol Oates
- [ ] Mason & Dixon – Thomas Pynchon
- [ ] The Master – Colm Tóibín
- [ ] The Master and Margarita – Mikhail Bulgakov
- [ ] The Master of Ballantrae – Robert Louis Stevenson
- [ ] The Master of Petersburg – J.M. Coetzee
- [ ] Matigari – Ngugi Wa Thiong'o
- [ ] Max Havelaar – Multatuli
- [ ] The Mayor of Casterbridge – Thomas Hardy
- [ ] Measuring the World – Daniel Kehlmann
- [ ] The Melancholy of Resistance – László Krasznahorkai
- [ ] Melmoth the Wanderer – Charles Robert Maturin
- [ ] Memento Mori – Muriel Spark
- [ ] Memoirs of a Geisha – Arthur Golden
- [ ] Memoirs of a Peasant Boy – Xose Neira Vilas
- [ ] Memoirs of Hadrian – Marguerite Yourcenar
- [ ] Memoirs of Martinus Scriblerus – J. Arbuthnot, J. Gay, T. Parnell, A. Pope, J. Swift
- [ ] Memoirs of my Nervous Illness – Daniel P. Schreber
- [ ] Memoirs of Rain – Sunetra Gupta
- [ ] Memory of Fire – Eduardo Galeano
- [ ] Mercier et Camier – Samuel Beckett
- [ ] Metamorphoses – Ovid
- [ ] Michael Kohlhaas – Heinrich von Kleist

172

- ☐ Midaq Alley – Naguib Mahfouz
- ☐ Middlemarch – George Eliot
- ☐ Middlesex – Jeffrey Eugenides
- ☐ The Midnight Examiner – William Kotzwinkle
- ☐ Midnight's Children – Salman Rushdie
- ☐ The Midwich Cuckoos – John Wyndham
- ☐ The Mill on the Floss – George Eliot
- ☐ Miramar – Naguib Mahfouz
- ☐ Les Misérables – Victor Hugo
- ☐ Miss Lonelyhearts – Nathanael West
- ☐ Miss Pettigrew Lives for a Day – Winifred Watson
- ☐ Moby-Dick – Herman Melville
- ☐ A Modest Proposal – Jonathan Swift
- ☐ Moll Flanders – Daniel Defoe
- ☐ Molloy – Samuel Beckett
- ☐ The Monastery – Sir Walter Scott
- ☐ Money: A Suicide Note – Martin Amis
- ☐ Money to Burn – Ricardo Piglia
- ☐ Monica – Saunders Lewis
- ☐ The Monk – M.G. Lewis
- ☐ Monkey: A Journey to the West – Wu Cheng'en
- ☐ The Moon and the Bonfires – Cesare Pavese
- ☐ Moon Palace – Paul Auster
- ☐ The Moonstone – Wilkie Collins
- ☐ The Moor's Last Sigh – Salman Rushdie
- ☐ Morvern Callar – Alan Warner
- ☐ Moscow Stations – Venedikt Yerofeev
- ☐ Mother – Maxim Gorky
- ☐ Mother's Milk – Edward St.Aubyn
- ☐ Mr. Vertigo – Paul Auster
- ☐ Mrs. 'Arris Goes to Paris – Paul Gallico
- ☐ Mrs. Dalloway – Virginia Woolf
- ☐ Murder Must Advertise – Dorothy L. Sayers
- ☐ The Murder of Roger Ackroyd – Agatha Christie
- ☐ Murphy – Samuel Beckett
- ☐ The Museum of Innocence – Orhan Pamuk
- ☐ The Museum of Unconditional Surrender –Dubravka Urgresic
- ☐ The Music of Chance – Paul Auster
- ☐ My Antonia – Willa Cather
- ☐ Myra Breckinridge – Gore Vidal

☐ The Mysteries of Udolpho – Ann Radcliffe

N

☐ Nadja – André Breton
☐ Naked Lunch – William Burroughs
☐ The Name of the Rose – Umberto Eco
☐ The Names – Don DeLillo
☐ The Namesake – Jhumpa Lahiri
☐ Nana – Émile Zola
☐ Native Son – Richard Wright
☐ Nausea – Jean-Paul Sartre
☐ Nervous Conditions – Tsitsi Dangarembga
☐ Neuromancer – William Gibson
☐ Never Give In!: The Best of Winston Churchill's Speeches – Winston Churchill
☐ Never Let Me Go – Kazuo Ishiguro
☐ New Grub Street – George Gissing
☐ New Hampshire – Robert Frost
☐ The New World – Henruy Walda-Sellasse
☐ The New York Trilogy – Paul Auster
☐ News from Nowhere – William Morris
☐ The Newton Letter – John Banville
☐ The Nice and the Good – Iris Murdoch
☐ Nicomachean Ethics – Aristotle
☐ Night and Day – Virginia Woolf
☐ Nights at the Circus – Angela Carter
☐ Nightwood – Djuna Barnes
☐ The Nine Tailors – Dorothy L. Sayers
☐ Nineteen Seventy Seven – David Peace
☐ Nineteen Eighty-Four – George Orwell
☐ No Laughing Matter – Angus Wilson
☐ None but the Brave – Arthur Schnitzler
☐ No One Writes to the Colonel – Gabriel Garcia Marquez
☐ North and South – Elizabeth Gaskell
☐ Northanger Abbey – Jane Austen
☐ The Nose – Nikolay Gogol
☐ Nostromo – Joseph Conrad
☐ The Notebooks of Malte Laurids Brigge – Rainer Maria Rilke
☐ Notes from the Underground – Fyodor Dostoevsky
☐ Novel With Cocaine – M. Ageyev

- [ ] Nowhere Man – Aleksandar Hemon
- [ ] The Nun – Denis Diderot

O

- [ ] Obabakoak – Bernando Atxaga
- [ ] An Obedient Father – Akhil Sharma
- [ ] Oblomovka – Ivan Goncharov
- [ ] The Odyssey – Homer
- [ ] Of Human Bondage – William Somerset Maugham
- [ ] Of Love and Shadows – Isabel Allende
- [ ] Of Mice and Men – John Steinbeck
- [ ] The Old Devils – Kingsley Amis
- [ ] The Old Man and the Sea – Ernest Hemingway
- [ ] Old Masters – Thomas Bernhard
- [ ] Old Possum's Book of Practical Cats – T.S. Eliot
- [ ] The Old Wives' Tale – Arnold Bennett
- [ ] Oliver Twist – Charles Dickens
- [ ] On Beauty – Zadie Smith
- [ ] On Love – Alain de Botton
- [ ] On the Black Hill – Bruce Chatwin
- [ ] On the Edge of Reason – Miroslav Krleza
- [ ] On the Eve – Ivan Turgenev
- [ ] On the Heights of Despair – Emil Cioran
- [ ] On the Road – Jack Kerouac
- [ ] The Once and Future King – T.H. White
- [ ] One Day in the Life of Ivan Denisovich – Aleksandr Isayevich Solzhenitsyn
- [ ] One Flew Over the Cuckoo's Nest – Ken Kesey
- [ ] One Hundred Years of Solitude – Gabriel García Márquez
- [ ] One, None and a Hundred Thousand – Luigi Pirandello
- [ ] Operation Shylock – Philip Roth
- [ ] The Opposing Shore – Julien Gracq
- [ ] The Optimistrist's Daughter – Eudora Welty
- [ ] Oranges Are Not the Only Fruit – Jeanette Winterson
- [ ] Orlando – Virginia Woolf
- [ ] Ormond – Maria Edgeworth
- [ ] Oroonoko – Aphra Behn
- [ ] Oscar and Lucinda – Peter Carey
- [ ] Our Ancestors – Italo Calvino
- [ ] Our Lady of Assassins – Fernando Vallejo

- ☐ Our Mutual Friend – Charles Dickens
- ☐ Out of Africa – Isak Dineson (Karen Blixen)
- ☐ The Outsider – Albert Camus

P

- ☐ Pale Fire – Vladimir Nabokov
- ☐ A Pale View of Hills – Kazuo Ishiguro
- ☐ Pallieter – Felix Timmermans
- ☐ Pamela – Samuel Richardson
- ☐ The Parable of the Blind – Gert Hofmann
- ☐ Parade's End – Ford Madox Ford
- ☐ Paradise – Abdulrazak Gurnah
- ☐ Paradise Lost – John Milton
- ☐ Paradise of the Blind – Duong Thu Huong
- ☐ Party Going – Henry Green
- ☐ A Passage to India – E.M. Forster
- ☐ Passing – Nella Larsen
- ☐ The Passion – Jeanette Winterson
- ☐ The Passion According to G.H. – Clarice Lispector
- ☐ The Passion of New Eve – Angela Carter
- ☐ Pastoralia – George Saunders
- ☐ The Path to the Nest of Spiders – Italo Calvino
- ☐ Patterns of Childhood – Christa Wolf
- ☐ Pavel's Letters – Monika Maron
- ☐ Pereira Declares: A Testimony – Antonio Tabucchi
- ☐ The People of Hemsö – August Strindberg
- ☐ Pepita Jimenez – Juan Valera
- ☐ Le Père Goriot – Honoré de Balzac
- ☐ Peregrine Pickle – Tobias George Smollett
- ☐ Perfume – Patrick Süskind
- ☐ Persuasion – Jane Austen
- ☐ Petals of Blood – Ngugi Wa Thiong'o
- ☐ Pharoah – Boleslaw Prus
- ☐ Phineas Finn – Anthony Trollope
- ☐ The Piano Teacher – Elfriede Jelinek
- ☐ The Picture of Dorian Gray – Oscar Wilde
- ☐ The Pigeon – Patrick Süskind
- ☐ Pierre and Jean – Guy de Maupassant
- ☐ The Pilgrim's Progress – John Bunyan
- ☐ Pilgrimage – Dorothy Richardson

☐ Pippi Longstocking – Astrid Lindgren
☐ The Pit and the Pendulum – Edgar Allan Poe
☐ The Plague – Albert Camus
☐ Platero and I – Juan Ramon Jiminez
☐ Platform – Michael Houellebecq
☐ Play It as It Lays – Joan Didion
☐ The Player of Games – Iain M. Banks
☐ The Plot Against America – Philip Roth
☐ Pluck the Bud and Destroy the Offspring – Kenzaburo Oe
☐ The Plumed Serpent – D.H. Lawrence
☐ Pnin – Vladimir Nabokov
☐ Poetry of Pablo Neruda – Pablo Neruda
☐ The Poisonwood Bible – Barbara Kingsolver
☐ The Poor Mouth – Flann O'Brien
☐ The Port – Antun Soljan
☐ Portnoy's Complaint – Philip Roth
☐ The Portrait of a Lady – Henry James
☐ A Portrait of the Artist as a Young Man – James Joyce
☐ Possessing the Secret of Joy – Alice Walker
☐ Possession – A.S. Byatt
☐ The Posthumous Memoirs of Bras Cubas – Joaquim Maria Machado de Assis
☐ The Postman Always Rings Twice – James M. Cain
☐ The Power and the Glory – Graham Greene
☐ A Prayer for Owen Meany – John Irving
☐ Pricksongs and Descants – Robert Coover
☐ Pride and Prejudice – Jane Austen
☐ The Prime of Miss Jean Brodie – Muriel Spark
☐ The Prince – Niccolò Machiavelli
☐ The Princess of Cleves – Marie-Madelaine Pioche de Lavergne, Comtesse de La Fayette
☐ The Private Memoirs and Confessions of a Justified Sinner – James Hogg
☐ Professor Martens' Departure – Jaan Kross
☐ Professor Unrat – Heinrich Mann
☐ The Professor's House – Willa Cather
☐ Promise at Dawn – Romain Gary
☐ The Prophet – Khalil Gibran
☐ The Public Burning – Robert Coover
☐ The Purloined Letter – Edgar Allan Poe

☐ The Pursuit of Love – Nancy Mitford
☐ Pygmalion – George Bernard Shaw

Q

☐ The Ogre – Michael Tournier
☐ Quartet – Jean Rhys
☐ Quartet in Autumn – Barbara Pym
☐ Queer – William Burroughs
☐ The Quest – Frederik van Eeden
☐ The Quest for Christa T. – Christa Wolf
☐ A Question of Power – Bessie Head
☐ Quicksand – Nella Larsen
☐ The Quiet American – Graham Greene
☐ Quo Vadis – Henryk Sienkiewicz

R

☐ Rabbit is Rich – John Updike
☐ Rabbit Redux – John Updike
☐ Rabbit, Run – John Updike
☐ The Radetzky March – Joseph Roth
☐ The Radiant Way – Margaret Drabble
☐ Ragtime – E.L. Doctorow
☐ The Ragazzi – Pier Paulo Pasolini
☐ The Ragged Trousered Philanthropists – Robert Tressell
☐ The Rainbow – D.H. Lawrence
☐ Rameau's Nephew – Denis Diderot
☐ Rashomon – Akutagawa Ryunosuke
☐ Rasselas – Samuel Johnson
☐ Ratner's Star – Don DeLillo
☐ The Ravishing of Lol V. Stein – Marguerite Duras
☐ The Razor's Edge – William Somerset Maugham
☐ The Reader – Bernhard Schlink
☐ The Real Charlotte – Somerville and Ross
☐ Reasons to Live – Amy Hempel
☐ Rebecca – Daphne du Maurier
☐ The Rebel – Albert Camus
☐ The Recognitions – William Gaddis
☐ The Red and the Black – Stendhal
☐ Red Harvest – Dashiell Hammett
☐ The Red Queen – Margaret Drabble

- ☐ The Red Room – August Strindberg
- ☐ Regeneration – Pat Barker
- ☐ The Regent's Wife – Clarin Leopoldo Alas
- ☐ La Reine Margot – Alexandre Dumas
- ☐ Requiem for a Dream – Hubert Selby Jr
- ☐ The Reluctant Fundamentalist – Mohsin Hamid
- ☐ Remains of the Day – Kazuo Ishiguro
- ☐ Remembering Babylon – David Malouf
- ☐ Remembrance of Things Past – Marcel Proust
- ☐ Republic – Plato
- ☐ Retreat Without Song – Shahan Shahnoor
- ☐ The Return of Philip Latinowicz – Miroslav Krleza
- ☐ The Return of the Soldier – Rebecca West
- ☐ Return of the Native – Thomas Hardy
- ☐ The Revenge for Love – Wyndham Lewis
- ☐ Reveries of a Solitary Walker – Jean-Jacques Rousseau
- ☐ Rickshaw Boy – Lao She
- ☐ The Riddle of the Sands – Erskine Childers
- ☐ The Rings of Saturn – W.G. Sebald
- ☐ Rites of Passage – William Golding
- ☐ Rituals – Cees Nooteboom
- ☐ The River Between – Ngugi wa Thiong'o
- ☐ Rob Roy – Sir Walter Scott
- ☐ The Robber Bride – Margaret Atwood
- ☐ Robinson Crusoe – Daniel Defoe
- ☐ Roderick Random – Tobias George Smollett
- ☐ Romance of the Three Kingdoms – Luo Guanzhong
- ☐ The Romantics – Pankaj Mishra
- ☐ Romeo and Juliet – William Shakespeare
- ☐ A Room with a View – E.M. Forster
- ☐ The Roots of Heaven – Romain Gary
- ☐ Rosshalde – Herman Hesse
- ☐ Roxana – Daniel Defoe

S

- ☐ Sabbath's Theater – Philip Roth
- ☐ The Safety Net – Heinrich Böll
- ☐ Sandokan: The Tigers of Mompracem – Emilio Salgari
- ☐ Santa Evita – Tomas Eloy Martinez
- ☐ The Satanic Verses – Salman Rushdie

- ☐ Saturday – Ian McEwan
- ☐ Saturday Night and Sunday Morning – Alan Sillitoe
- ☐ Savage Detectives – Roberto Bolano
- ☐ The Scarlet Letter – Nathaniel Hawthorne
- ☐ Schindler's Ark – Thomas Keneally
- ☐ Schooling – Heather McGowan
- ☐ A Scots Quair (Sunset Song) – Lewis Grassic Gibbon
- ☐ The Sea – John Banville
- ☐ The Sea of Fertility – Yukio Mishima
- ☐ The Sea, The Sea – Iris Murdoch
- ☐ Seasons of Migrations to the North – Tayeb Salih
- ☐ The Secret Agent – Joseph Conrad
- ☐ The Secret History – Donna Tartt
- ☐ Seize the Day – Saul Bellow
- ☐ Self Condemned – Wyndham Lewis
- ☐ Señor Vivo and the Coca Lord – Louis de Bernieres
- ☐ Sense and Sensibility – Jane Austen
- ☐ Sentimental Education – Gustave Flaubert
- ☐ A Sentimental Journey – Laurence Sterne
- ☐ A Severed Head – Iris Murdoch
- ☐ Sexing the Cherry – Jeanette Winterson
- ☐ The Shadow Line – Joseph Conrad
- ☐ The Shadow Lines – Amitav Ghosh
- ☐ Shame – Salman Rushdie
- ☐ She: A History of Adventure – H. Rider Haggard
- ☐ Shikasta – Doris Lessing
- ☐ Shirley – Charlotte Brontë
- ☐ The Shining – Stephen King
- ☐ The Shipping News – E. Annie Proulx
- ☐ The Shipyard – Juan Carlos Onetti
- ☐ A Short History of Tractors in Ukrainian – Marina Lewycka
- ☐ Shroud – John Banville
- ☐ Siddhartha – Herman Hesse
- ☐ The Siege of Krishnapur – J.G. Farrell
- ☐ Silas Marner – George Eliot
- ☐ Silence – Shusaku Endo
- ☐ Silent Cry – Kenzaburo Oe
- ☐ Silk – Alessandro Baricco
- ☐ Simon and the Oaks – Marianne Fredriksson
- ☐ The Singapore Grip – J.G. Farrell

- ☐ Sister Carrie – Theodore Dreiser
- ☐ Slaughterhouse-five – Kurt Vonnegut, Jr.
- ☐ Slow Man – J.M. Coetzee
- ☐ Small Island – Andrea Levy
- ☐ Small Remedies – Shashi Deshpande
- ☐ Smell of Sadness – Alfred Kossmann
- ☐ Smilla's Sense of Snow – Peter Høeg
- ☐ Smiley's People – John Le Carré
- ☐ Snow – Orhan Pamuk
- ☐ So Long a Letter – Mariama Ba
- ☐ Solaris – Stanislaw Lem
- ☐ Soldiers of Salamis – Javer Cercas
- ☐ Some Experiences of an Irish R.M. – Edith Somerville and Martin Ross
- ☐ Some Prefer Nettles – Junichiro Tanizaki
- ☐ Sometimes a Great Notion – Ken Kesey
- ☐ Song of Solomon – Toni Morrison
- ☐ Sons and Lovers – D.H. Lawrence
- ☐ The Sorrow of Belgium – Hugo Claus
- ☐ The Sorrows of Young Werther – Johann Wolfgang von Goethe
- ☐ Soul Mountain – Xingjian gao
- ☐ The Sound and the Fury – William Faulkner
- ☐ The Sound of Waves – Yukio Mishima
- ☐ Southern Seas – Manuel Vasquez Montalban
- ☐ Spring Flowers, Spring Frost – Ismail Kadare
- ☐ Spring Torrents – Ivan Turgenev
- ☐ Sputnik Sweetheart – Haruki Murakami
- ☐ The Spy Who Came in from the Cold – John Le Carré
- ☐ The Stechlin – Theodore Fontane
- ☐ Steppenwolf – Herman Hesse
- ☐ The Stone Diaries – Carol Shields
- ☐ Stone Junction – Jim Dodge
- ☐ The Storm of Steel – Ernst Junger
- ☐ The Story of Lucy Gault – William Trevor
- ☐ The Story of O – Pauline Réage
- ☐ Story of the Eye – Georges Bataille
- ☐ Strait is the Gate – André Gide
- ☐ The Strange Case of Dr. Jekyll and Mr. Hyde – Robert Louis Stevenson
- ☐ Stranger in a Strange Land – Robert Heinlein

- [ ] The Street of Crocodiles – Bruno Schulz
- [ ] The Successor – Ismail Kadare
- [ ] A Suitable Boy – Vikram Seth
- [ ] Suite Francaise – Irene Nemirovsky
- [ ] Sula – Toni Morrison
- [ ] Summer – Edith Wharton
- [ ] The Summer Book – Tove Jansson
- [ ] Summer in Baden-Baden – Leonid Tsypkin
- [ ] Summer Will Show – Sylvia Townsend Warner
- [ ] The Sun Also Rises – Ernest Hemingway
- [ ] Super-Cannes – J.G. Ballard
- [ ] Surfacing – Margaret Atwood
- [ ] The Swarm – Frank Schatzing
- [ ] The Swimming-Pool Library – Alan Hollinghurst
- [ ] Swiss Family Robinson – Johann David Wyss

T

- [ ] The Taebek Mountains – Jo Jung-rae
- [ ] A Tale of a Tub – Jonathan Swift
- [ ] The Tale of Genji – Murasaki Shikibu
- [ ] A Tale of Love and Darkness – Amos Oz
- [ ] The Tale of the Bamboo Cutter – Anonymous
- [ ] A Tale of Two Cities – Charles Dickens
- [ ] A Tale of Two Gardens – Octavio Paz Lozano
- [ ] The Talented Mr. Ripley – Patricia Highsmith
- [ ] The Talk of the Town – Ardal O'Hanlon
- [ ] Tarka the Otter – Henry Williamson
- [ ] Tarr – Wyndham Lewis
- [ ] The Tartar Steppe – Dino Buzzati
- [ ] Tarzan of the Apes – Edgar Rice Burroughs
- [ ] The Temple of My Familiar – Alice Walker
- [ ] The Temptation of Saint Anthony – Gustave Flaubert
- [ ] The Tenant of Wildfell Hall – Anne Brontë
- [ ] Tender is the Night – F. Scott Fitzgerald
- [ ] Tent of Miracles – Jorge Amado
- [ ] Tess of the D'Urbervilles – Thomas Hardy
- [ ] Testament of Youth – Vera Brittain
- [ ] Thais – Anatole France
- [ ] Thank You, Jeeves – P.G. Wodehouse
- [ ] That They May Face the Rising Sun – John McGahern

☐ Their Eyes Were Watching God – Zora Neale Hurston
☐ Them – Joyce Carol Oates
☐ Thérèse Raquin – Émile Zola
☐ They Shoot Horses, Don't They? – Horace McCoy
☐ The Thin Man – Dashiell Hammett
☐ Things – Georges Perec
☐ Things Fall Apart – Chinua Achebe
☐ The Things They Carried – Tim O'Brien
☐ The Thinking Reed – Rebecca West
☐ The Third Man – Graham Greene
☐ The Third Policeman – Flann O'Brien
☐ The Third Wedding – Costas Taktsis
☐ The Thirty-Nine Steps – John Buchan
☐ Thomas of Reading – Thomas Deloney
☐ The Thousand and One Nights – Anonymous
☐ A Thousand Cranes – Yasunari Kawabata
☐ Three Lives – Gertrude Stein
☐ The Three Musketeers – Alexandre Dumas
☐ The Three Trapped Tigers – Guillermo Cabrera Infante
☐ Threepenny Novel – Bertolt Brecht
☐ Through the Looking Glass, and What Alice Found There – Lewis Carroll
☐ Thursbitch – Alan Garner
☐ Timbuktu – Paul Auster
☐ The Time of Indifference – Alberto Moravia
☐ Time of Silence – Luis Martin-Santos
☐ The Time of the Hero -Mario Vargas Llosa
☐ The Time Machine – H.G. Wells
☐ Time's Arrow – Martin Amis
☐ The Tin Drum – Günter Grass
☐ The Tin Flute – Gabrielle Roy
☐ Tinker Tailor Soldier Spy – John Le Carré
☐ Tipping the Velvet – Sarah Waters
☐ Tirant lo Blanc – Joanot Martorell
☐ Titus Groan – Mervyn Peake
☐ To Each His Own – Leonardo Sciascia
☐ To Have and Have Not – Ernest Hemingway
☐ To Kill a Mockingbird – Harper Lee
☐ To the Lighthouse – Virginia Woolf
☐ To the North – Elizabeth Bowen

- ☐ Tom Jones – Henry Fielding
- ☐ Tono-Bungay – H.G. Wells
- ☐ A Town Like Alice – Nevil Shute
- ☐ The Trial – Franz Kafka
- ☐ Trainspotting – Irvine Welsh
- ☐ Transit – Anna Seghers
- ☐ The Travels of Persiles and Sigismunda – Miguel de Cervantes Saavedra
- ☐ Trawl – B.S. Johnson
- ☐ Treasure Island – Robert Louis Stevenson
- ☐ The Tree of Man – Patrick White
- ☐ The Trick is to Keep Breathing – Janice Galloway
- ☐ The Triple Mirror of the Self – Zulfikar Ghose
- ☐ Tristram Shandy – Laurence Sterne
- ☐ Tropic of Cancer – Henry Miller
- ☐ Tropic of Capricorn – Henry Miller
- ☐ Troubles – J.G. Farrell
- ☐ Troubling Love – Elena Ferrante
- ☐ The Trusting and the Maimed – James Plunkett
- ☐ The Turn of the Screw – Henry James
- ☐ The Twilight Years – Sawako Ariyoshi
- ☐ The Twins – Tessa de Loo
- ☐ Typical – Padgett Powell

U

- ☐ Ulysses – James Joyce
- ☐ The Unbearable Lightness of Being – Milan Kundera
- ☐ Uncle Petros and Goldbach's Conjecture – Apostolos Doxiadis
- ☐ Uncle Silas – Sheridan Le Fanu
- ☐ Uncle Tom's Cabin; or, Life Among the Lonely – Harriet Beecher Stowe
- ☐ The Unconsoled – Kazuo Ishiguro
- ☐ Under Fire – Henri Barbusse
- ☐ Under Satan's Sun – Georges Bernanos
- ☐ Under the Net – Iris Murdoch
- ☐ Under the Skin – Michel Faber
- ☐ Under the Volcano – Malcolm Lowry
- ☐ Under the Yoke – Ivan Vazov
- ☐ The Underdogs – Mariano Azuela
- ☐ Underworld – Don DeLillo

- ☐ The Unfortunate Traveller – Thomas Nashe
- ☐ The Unknown Soldier – Vaino Linna
- ☐ Unless – Carol Shields
- ☐ The Unnamable – Samuel Beckett
- ☐ Untouchable – Mulk Raj Anand
- ☐ The Untouchable – John Banville
- ☐ U.S.A. – John Dos Passos

V

- ☐ V. – Thomas Pynchon
- ☐ Vanishing Point – David Markson
- ☐ Vanity Fair – William Makepeace Thackeray
- ☐ Vathek – William Beckford
- ☐ Venus in Furs – Leopld von Sacher-Masoch
- ☐ Vernon God Little – DBC Pierre
- ☐ Veronika Decides to Die – Paulo Coelho
- ☐ Vertigo – W.G. Sebald
- ☐ The Vicar of Wakefield – Oliver Goldsmith
- ☐ The Vice-Consul – Marguerite Duras
- ☐ The Viceroys – Federico De Roberto
- ☐ The Victim – Saul Bellow
- ☐ View with a Grain of Sand – Wislawa Szymborska
- ☐ Vile Bodies – Evelyn Waugh
- ☐ Villette – Charlotte Brontë
- ☐ Vineland – Thomas Pynchon
- ☐ The Violent Bear It Away – Flannery O'Connor
- ☐ Vipers' Tangle – Francois Mauriac
- ☐ The Virgin in the Garden – A.S. Byatt
- ☐ Virgin Soil – Ivan Turgenev
- ☐ The Virgin Suicides – Jeffrey Eugenides
- ☐ A Void/Avoid – Georges Perec
- ☐ Voss – Patrick White
- ☐ The Voyage Out – Virginia Woolf

W

- ☐ W, or the Memory of Childhood – Georges Perec
- ☐ Waiting for the Barbarians – J.M. Coetzee
- ☐ Waiting for the Dark, Waiting for the Light – Ivan Klima
- ☐ Walden – Henry David Thoreau
- ☐ War and Peace – Leo Tolstoy

☐ The War at the End of the World – Mario Vargas Llosa
☐ The War of the Worlds – H.G. Wells
☐ War with the Newts – Karel Capek
☐ The Wars – Timothy Findley
☐ The Wasp Factory – Iain Banks
☐ Watchmen – Alan Moore & David Gibbons
☐ The Water-Babies – Charles Kingsley
☐ The Water Margin – Shi Nai'an and Luo Guanzhong
☐ Waterland – Graham Swift
☐ Watt – Samuel Beckett
☐ The Waves – Virginia Woolf
☐ The Way for the Gas, Ladies and Gentlemen – Tadeusz Borowski
☐ The Way of All Flesh – Samuel Butler
☐ We – Yevgeny Zamyatin
☐ The Well of Loneliness – Radclyffe Hall
☐ What a Carve Up! – Jonathan Coe
☐ What I Loved – Siri Hustvedt
☐ What Maisie Knew – Henry James
☐ Whatever – Michel Houellebecq
☐ Where Angels Fear to Tread – E.M. Forster
☐ White Noise – Don DeLillo
☐ White Teeth – Zadie Smith
☐ The White Tiger – Aravind Adiga
☐ Wide Sargasso Sea – Jean Rhys
☐ The Wild Boys – William Burroughs
☐ Wild Harbour – Ian MacPherson
☐ Wild Swans – Jung Chang
☐ Willard and His Bowling Trophies – Richard Brautigan
☐ Wilhelm Meister's Apprenticeship – Johann Wolfgang von Goethe
☐ The Wind in the Willows – Kenneth Grahame
☐ The Wind-Up Bird Chronicle – Haruki Murakami
☐ The Wings of the Dove – Henry James
☐ Wise Blood – Flannery O'Connor
☐ Wise Children – Angela Carter
☐ The Witness – Juan Jose Saer
☐ Wittgenstein's Mistress – David Markson
☐ Wittgenstein's Nephew – Thomas Bernhard
☐ The Wizard of Oz – L. Frank Baum

- ☐ Woman at Point Zero – Nawal El Saadawai
- ☐ Women in Love – D.H. Lawrence
- ☐ The Woman in White – Wilkie Collins
- ☐ A Woman's Life – Guy de Maupassant
- ☐ Women in Love – D.H. Lawrence
- ☐ The Wonderful "O" – James Thurber
- ☐ The Woodlanders – Thomas Hardy
- ☐ The World According to Garp – John Irving
- ☐ A World for Julius – Alfredo Bryce Echenique
- ☐ A World of Love – Elizabeth Bowen
- ☐ World's End – T. Coraghessan Boyle
- ☐ Worstward Ho – Samuel Beckett
- ☐ Written on the Body – Jeanette Winterson
- ☐ Wuthering Heights – Emily Brontë

X

Y

- ☐ The Year of the Death of Ricardo Reis – José Saramago
- ☐ The Year of the Hare – Arto Paasilinna
- ☐ The Years – Virginia Woolf
- ☐ The Yellow Wallpaper – Charlotte Perkins Gilman
- ☐ Yes – Thomas Bernhard
- ☐ The Young Man – Botho Strauss
- ☐ Young Törless – Robert Musil
- ☐ Your Face Tomorrow – Javier Marias
- ☐ Youth – J.M. Coetzee

Z

- ☐ Z – Vassilis Vassilikos
- ☐ Zeno's Conscience – Italo Svevo
- ☐ Zorba the Greek – Nikos Kazantzákis

THE ANIMAL LOVER BUCKET LIST

- ☐ Swim with manatees
- ☐ Hold a real big snake around your neck
- ☐ Hold a koala
- ☐ Dive with crocodiles
- ☐ Swim with dolphins
- ☐ Swim with sea turtles
- ☐ Ride an ostrich
- ☐ High five and hold a monkey/chimpanzee
- ☐ Milk a cow
- ☐ Pet a tiger up close
- ☐ Hold a tarantula
- ☐ Ride a horse
- ☐ Play with alpacas
- ☐ Swim with or feed stingrays
- ☐ Shear a sheep
- ☐ Play with seals
- ☐ Hold an iguana
- ☐ Hold a crocodile
- ☐ Have my own Dog
- ☐ Interact with sloths
- ☐ Interact with lions (and/or hold a lion cub)
- ☐ Play with meerkats in the wild
- ☐ Play with lemurs in the wild
- ☐ Kiss a frog/toad
- ☐ See the following animals in the wild:
    - ☐ Giant Panda
    - ☐ Bear
    - ☐ Snake

- ☐ Kangaroo
- ☐ Elephant
- ☐ Lion
- ☐ Giraffe
- ☐ Hyena
- ☐ Bison
- ☐ Blue Whale
- ☐ Platypus
- ☐ Rhino
- ☐ Hippo
- ☐ Polar Bear
- ☐ Gorilla
- ☐ Moose
- ☐ Cheetah
- ☐ Penguin
- ☐ Interact with deer
- ☐ "Find Nemo" (AKA dive with clown fish)
- ☐ Rehabilitate wild animals
- ☐ Be a Sea World marine mammal keeper for a day
- ☐ Bottle-feed a lamb
- ☐ Take honey from a beehive
- ☐ Release baby turtles into the ocean
- ☐ Have a parrot and teach it to "talk"
- ☐ Have a cat
- ☐ Play with kangaroos

- ☐ Ride in a horse-drawn carriage
- ☐ Catch a firefly
- ☐ Cuddle an orangutan
- ☐ Pet a Kinkajou
- ☐ Milk a poisonous snake
- ☐ Swim with a school of fish
- ☐ Ride a camel
- ☐ Ride a camel in the desert
- ☐ Help at an animal shelter
- ☐ Compete in a Frog Jumping Contest
- ☐ Complete a Horse Jumping Obstacle
- ☐ Feed a Crocodile
- ☐ Feed a Koala Bear
- ☐ Feed an Ostrich
- ☐ Herd Cattle
- ☐ Hold a Monkey
- ☐ Horseback Ride on the Beach
- ☐ Kiss a Sea Lion
- ☐ Have a pond in your backyard
- ☐ Hold a shark
- ☐ Whale Watching
- ☐ Watch a caterpillar turn into a butterfly

ABSOLUTE MUST BUCKET LIST

- [ ] Adopt a pet
- [ ] Buy a house
- [ ] Graduate college
- [ ] Be a bridesmaid/groomsman
- [ ] Get engaged
- [ ] Get married
- [ ] Go on a picnic
- [ ] Get a passport
- [ ] Sing karaoke
- [ ] Learn a musical instrument
- [ ] Go to a sex store
- [ ] Invest in a vibrator
- [ ] Fall in love
- [ ] Get your heartbroken
- [ ] Drive a convertible with the top down
- [ ] Sit on a jury
- [ ] See a lunar eclipse
- [ ] Sleep under the stars
- [ ] Go on a road trip
- [ ] Donate blood
- [ ] Ride in a limo
- [ ] Vote in an election
- [ ] Blind date
- [ ] Double date
- [ ] Create a family tree
- [ ] Go skinny dipping
- [ ] Act in a play
- [ ] Discover your life's purpose
- [ ] Do something newsworthy
- [ ] Have your picture painted
- [ ] Take part in a focus group
- [ ] Coin a phrase
- [ ] Get your astrology chart made
- [ ] Get an action figure made of yourself
- [ ] Find a four-leaf clover
- [ ] Go Black Friday shopping
- [ ] Jump out of a cake
- [ ] Witness a solar eclipse
- [ ] Cover the bed in rose petals
- [ ] Spend time with a person from another generation
- [ ] Stay up all night talking
- [ ] Complete a cross-stitch piece
- [ ] Complete a "Paint by numbers"
- [ ] Create a bumper sticker
- [ ] Create a flower arrangement
- [ ] Create your own personal stationary
- [ ] Get your handwriting analyzed
- [ ] Knit a scarf
- [ ] Make a candle
- [ ] Make a coloring book
- [ ] Make a scrapbook
- [ ] Make a tie-dye shirt
- [ ] Make mosaic art
- [ ] Make soap
- [ ] Make stained glass

- ☐ Paint something at a ceramic store
- ☐ Refinish a piece of furniture
- ☐ Sew something you can wear
- ☐ Take pictures in a photo booth
- ☐ Wrap a present perfectly
- ☐ Apply to be on a reality show
- ☐ Be in a commercial
- ☐ Be on the cover of a magazine
- ☐ Buy the best seat in the house
- ☐ Close the club
- ☐ Contact someone with my own name
- ☐ Create a video and upload it to the internet
- ☐ Crowd surf
- ☐ Design a room I love
- ☐ Do the hula
- ☐ Get a caricature drawing by a street artist
- ☐ Get comped/upgraded something
- ☐ Be street performer
- ☐ Go to a paint party
- ☐ Have 15 minutes of fame
- ☐ Host a game night
- ☐ Perform a magic trick
- ☐ Play a pinball machine
- ☐ Play a song on a harmonica
- ☐ Play Bingo at a Bingo hall
- ☐ Read a book before the movie
- ☐ Ride a mechanical bull
- ☐ See a 3D movie
- ☐ See a ballet
- ☐ Set a Guinness book of world record
- ☐ Sit front row at a basketball game
- ☐ Take a new route to work
- ☐ Touch a famous piece of art
- ☐ Walk the red carpet
- ☐ Watch a documentary
- ☐ Watch all the Oscar winning best pictures
- ☐ Watch all the golden globe winning best pictures
- ☐ Watch the space shuttle launch
- ☐ Wear a sumo wrestling suit
- ☐ Yodel
- ☐ Buy a cute outfit at a second-hand store
- ☐ Create a perfect updo
- ☐ Duplicate an outfit from a magazine
- ☐ Sleep on satin sheets
- ☐ Be on a jumbotron at a stadium
- ☐ Build a sand castle
- ☐ Chop firewood
- ☐ Coin a word
- ☐ Do a boudoir photo shoot
- ☐ Drive on the other side of the road

- ☐ Haggle at an open market
- ☐ Have a collection
- ☐ Have a stranger buy a drink for you
- ☐ Have a White Christmas
- ☐ Investigate an Urban Legend
- ☐ Join a book club
- ☐ Make a model car
- ☐ New Year's Eve Kiss
- ☐ Own an original piece of artwork
- ☐ Photobomb someone
- ☐ Read a book on the New York Time's Best Seller list
- ☐ Research the origins of your surname
- ☐ Share your most embarrassing moment
- ☐ Slide down a firehouse pole
- ☐ Stay awake for 24 hours
- ☐ Surprise someone
- ☐ Take an old-time photo
- ☐ Take an underwater selfie
- ☐ Use a chainsaw
- ☐ Use a paddle to bid at an auction
- ☐ Whistle with a blade of grass
- ☐ Whistle with two fingers
- ☐ Win a stuffed animal at a carnival
- ☐ Be an organ donor on my license
- ☐ Be present at a birth
- ☐ Do 24-hour of silence
- ☐ Experience a new religion
- ☐ Find the meaning of your name
- ☐ Create a small library filled with high quality books
- ☐ Have a "man-cave"
- ☐ Make an "identical" photo from your childhood now that you're grown up
- ☐ Chop down a tree with an ax
- ☐ Take a photo of yourself holding a photo of yourself holding a photo of yourself #photoception (then repeat every 5-10 years for the rest of your life)
- ☐ Kiss in the rain
- ☐ Name a star
- ☐ Have a meaningful conversation with a stranger
- ☐ Play matchmaker
- ☐ Meet the President
- ☐ Kiss a stranger
- ☐ Kiss on top of a Ferris wheel
- ☐ Meet a world leader
- ☐ See the Pope
- ☐ Hire a Mariachi band and serenade someone
- ☐ Paint a self-portrait
- ☐ Touch a rock from the moon or meteorite

THE LEARNING CURVE BUCKET LIST

- ☐ Make a balloon animal
- ☐ Video editing skills
- ☐ Get rid of bad habits and develop positives ones
- ☐ Sign language (at least 100 signs) and the alphabet
- ☐ Play chess
- ☐ Juggle
- ☐ Say "hello" in 50 languages
- ☐ Master a difficult skill with my left hand
- ☐ Learn a new English "academic" word every day for a year
- ☐ Have basic fluency in 10 languages – and high fluency in 5
  - ☐
  - ☐
  - ☐
  - ☐
  - ☐
  - ☐
  - ☐
  - ☐
  - ☐
  - ☐
- ☐ Make an origami animal (e.g., paper crane)
- ☐ Negotiate

- ☐ Web development (e.g., this, and more websites)
- ☐ CPR
- ☐ Tie a tie
- ☐ Use chopsticks
- ☐ Become decent with Adobe Photoshop
- ☐ Throw a Boomerang
- ☐ Learn a new software program
- ☐ Conversational Spanish
- ☐ The Heimlich Maneuver
- ☐ Master a new language
- ☐ Say "Thank You" in 10 Languages
- ☐ Braid hair
- ☐ How to speed read
- ☐ Fly a plane
- ☐ Blow glass
- ☐ Play a bagpipe
- ☐ Start a fire without matches/lighter
- ☐ Fly a seaplane
- ☐ Take an IQ test and get into the Mensa Society
- ☐ Learn a line dance
- ☐ Master a video game
- ☐ Pick a lock
- ☐ Learn Military time

CLASSES TO TAKE
BUCKET LIST

- ☐ Pole Dancing
- ☐ Fencing Class
- ☐ Self Defense
- ☐ Spin
- ☐ Yoga
- ☐ Laughing yoga
- ☐ Bikram Yoga
- ☐ Goat Yoga
- ☐ Anti-Gravity Yoga
- ☐ Dance lessons for
    - ☐ Salsa
    - ☐ Tango
    - ☐ Ballroom
    - ☐ Samba
    - ☐ Hip-Hop
    - ☐ Zumba
    - ☐ Tap Dance
- ☐ Etiquette
- ☐ Photography
- ☐ Cooking
- ☐ Improv
- ☐ Belly Dance
- ☐ Sculpting
- ☐ Painting
- ☐ Art
- ☐ Creative Writing
- ☐ Auto Mechanics
- ☐ Pilates
- ☐ Zero Gravity Pilates
- ☐ Bar Method Ballet
- ☐ Burlesque
- ☐ Pottery
- ☐ Create something useful in a wood-working workshop
- ☐ Attend a Sausage-Making class
- ☐ Take a Falconry Class

ADVENTUROUS BUCKET LIST

- ☐ Go off-roading
- ☐ Race a go kart
- ☐ Ride a longboard
- ☐ Ride in a cyclo
- ☐ Ride in a glass elevator
- ☐ Ride a jetski
- ☐ Ride a water scooter
- ☐ Ride a unicycle
- ☐ Ride on a tandem bike
- ☐ Ride a bike
- ☐ Ride an electric bike
- ☐ Do a wheelie on a bike
- ☐ Ride in a dune buggy
- ☐ Ride in a gondola
- ☐ Ride in a songthaew
- ☐ Ride on a subway
- ☐ Ride on a train
- ☐ Test drive/buy/rent a sleek sportscar
- ☐ Toboggan
- ☐ Tube down a river
- ☐ Cruise in a classic car
- ☐ Cruise in a low rider
- ☐ Cruise on a clipper ship
- ☐ Drive a race car
- ☐ Drive a speed boat
- ☐ Drive a tractor
- ☐ Drive a Zamboni
- ☐ Drive an ATV
- ☐ Get a scuba diving license
- ☐ Scuba dive
- ☐ Scuba dive/snorkel with sharks
- ☐ Skydive
- ☐ Fly in a vertical wind tunnel (indoor skydiving)
- ☐ Do the world's highest bungee jump
- ☐ Climb a vertical mountain/wall – at least 20 m
- ☐ Fly a helicopter
- ☐ Do a tough kayak river rafting course
- ☐ Drive a hovercraft
- ☐ Jump from a tall bridge
- ☐ Ride a snowmobile
- ☐ Try zorbing (water and dry version)
- ☐ Kayak through dark bat caves
- ☐ Helmet dive
- ☐ Go on a cave safari
- ☐ Go ice fishing
- ☐ Go deep sea fishing
- ☐ Go flyfishing
- ☐ Kiting, both water and snow
- ☐ Ziplining
- ☐ Flyboarding
- ☐ Go hunting
- ☐ Ride a segway
- ☐ Ride in a segway race
- ☐ Try flywake
- ☐ Walk across hot coals (firewalking)
- ☐ Shoot a shotgun
- ☐ Shoot a handgun
- ☐ Shoot a machine gun
- ☐ Shoot a rocket launcher

- ☐ Shoot a sniper
- ☐ Shoot an LMG
- ☐ Canoeing
- ☐ Windsurf
- ☐ Underwater scooter
- ☐ Go tufting
- ☐ Rappel down a waterfall
- ☐ Throw an axe
- ☐ Do a triathlon
- ☐ Win a game of 8-ball
- ☐ Win a game of ping pong
- ☐ Do a color run
- ☐ Do a handstand
- ☐ Do a themed run
- ☐ Run a Tough Mudder
- ☐ Participate in a 5k race
- ☐ Finish a 10k
- ☐ Finish a half marathon
- ☐ Finish a marathon
- ☐ Try American football
- ☐ Hit the archery bulls-eye
- ☐ Join a bowling league
- ☐ Jump at a trampoline house
- ☐ Kayak
- ☐ Ride bikes on the beach
- ☐ Go heli-skiing
- ☐ Go snowshoeing
- ☐ Bowl
- ☐ Bowl a strike
- ☐ Bowl a turkey (3 strikes in a row)
- ☐ Bowl a 200+ game
- ☐ Climb an indoor rock wall
- ☐ Complete a ropes course
- ☐ Dive off the high diving board
- ☐ Barefoot waterski
- ☐ Walk on stilts
- ☐ Karate
- ☐ Karate chop & break a wood board
- ☐ Perfect a karate kick
- ☐ Ski a black diamond trail
- ☐ Go roller blading
- ☐ Go roller skating
- ☐ Run a nine-minute mile
- ☐ Skateboard on a ramp
- ☐ Skeet shoot
- ☐ Spar with a professional boxer
- ☐ Spin a basketball on my finger
- ☐ Survive at paintball
- ☐ Make a free throw shot
- ☐ Make a hole in one
- ☐ Mud wrestle
- ☐ Play a game of croquet
- ☐ Play a game of pool bowling
- ☐ Play a round of golf
- ☐ Play a tennis match
- ☐ Play badminton
- ☐ Play racquetball
- ☐ Complete a real big maze
- ☐ Water ski
- ☐ Snowboard
- ☐ Paddle board

- [ ] Ice skate
- [ ] Curl
- [ ] Fence
- [ ] Tai chi
- [ ] Parasailing
- [ ] Rock climbing
- [ ] Snorkeling
- [ ] Backflip
- [ ] Sailing
- [ ] Hiking
- [ ] Join a volleyball or softball league
- [ ] Fast for 48 hours
- [ ] Bungee jump
- [ ] Paragliding
- [ ] Rappel off a building
- [ ] Bog snorkeling
- [ ] Cave tubing
- [ ] Snorkel in a shipwreck
- [ ] Boogie boarding
- [ ] Go dirt biking
- [ ] Driving range (golf)
- [ ] Do a rail successfully on a wakeboard
- [ ] Play real life foosball
- [ ] Get flown off from a water air-bed (blob jumping)
- [ ] Kick a field goal
- [ ] Climb a mountain
- [ ] Drive a motorcycle
- [ ] Catch fish with bare hands
- [ ] Shrimping
- [ ] Clamming
- [ ] Cross country on a bicycle
- [ ] Bobsled
- [ ] Rope swing into water
- [ ] Catch a lobster
- [ ] Get stuck on a Velcro wall
- [ ] Pan for gold
- [ ] Go on an expedition
- [ ] Go crabbing
- [ ] Play bubble soccer
- [ ] Participate in iron man
- [ ] Surf
- [ ] Charter a yacht
- [ ] Play a round of foot billiard
- [ ] Complete an escape room
- [ ] Go cliff jumping
- [ ] Go spelunking
- [ ] Do skeleton racing
- [ ] Ice climb
- [ ] Drive a sports car in over 100m per hour
- [ ] Insanity ride
- [ ] Wing walking
- [ ] Do a wipeout obstacle course
- [ ] Fly on a trapeze
- [ ] Take a ride on a harley
- [ ] Swim in an infinity pool
- [ ] Fly in a blimp
- [ ] Participate in a regatta
- [ ] Ride a gyrocopter
- [ ] Complete a large labyrinth
- [ ] Experience virtual reality
- [ ] Participate in a large international poker tournament
- [ ] Find a treasure with a metal detector
- [ ] Find a pearl in an oyster
- [ ] Create an ice sculpture

- ☐ Participate in geocaching
- ☐ Paint a mural
- ☐ Eat fire
- ☐ Bamboo rafting
- ☐ Fat biking
- ☐ Kite surf
- ☐ Navigate a personal underground sub
- ☐ Ride in a hot air balloon
- ☐ Ride in a luge
- ☐ Skijoring
- ☐ Whitewater rafting
- ☐ Climb to the top of a tree
- ☐ Destroy stuff in a rage room
- ☐ Experience weightlessness
- ☐ Leave mark in graffiti
- ☐ Play Twister with paint
- ☐ Play hide and seek in Ikea

BE A KID AGAIN BUCKET LIST

- ☐ Fly a Kite
- ☐ Make a snow angel
- ☐ Swing on a swing set
- ☐ Build a snowman
- ☐ Bury yourself in the sand
- ☐ Go sledding
- ☐ Roll down a hill
- ☐ Go to the batting cages
- ☐ Play miniature golf
- ☐ Ride every ride at an amusement park
- ☐ Laser tag
- ☐ Tell scary stories in a haunted house
- ☐ Join a choir
- ☐ Write a fan letter to your all-time favorite hero or heroine
- ☐ Write to a pen pal
- ☐ Spend the night in a treehouse
- ☐ Play on a Slip-n-Slide
- ☐ Race an RC car
- ☐ Ride on one of the largest rollercoasters
- ☐ Ride a scary rollercoaster
- ☐ Run through sprinklers
- ☐ Roll in a huge pile of leaves
- ☐ Go to Six Flags theme park

THE ADULTING BUCKET LIST

- ☐ Host a dinner party
- ☐ Travel for the weekend to see an old friend or family member
- ☐ Buy dinner for yourself at a street vendor and find a park bench to sit, eat and people watch
- ☐ Rent a fancy car and go on a weekend trip somewhere new
- ☐ Spend a random night in the city and get a hotel. Order room service in a robe like a boss
- ☐ Take yourself out for a glass of champagne at a restaurant with a good view
- ☐ Take yourself out on a dinner date
- ☐ Throw a tea party
- ☐ Read a book in one day
- ☐ Quit your job
- ☐ Sit at a bar by yourself and drink a martini
- ☐ Tell a stranger they're beautiful
- ☐ Find a really hard recipe and attempt it
- ☐ Go to your local farmer's market
- ☐ Grow a garden
- ☐ Throw a huge party and invite every one of your friends
- ☐ Get to know your neighbors
- ☐ Throw a themed party
- ☐ Attend a random free seminar
- ☐ Do a couple's costume for Halloween

FINANCIAL LEGACY
BUCKET LIST

- ☐ Start a company
- ☐ Start a social organization/foundation
- ☐ Get a Bachelor's degree
- ☐ Get a Master's degree
- ☐ Get a Doctorate degree
- ☐ Graduate with a stellar academic record
- ☐ Buy my personal domain
- ☐ Have a personal website up and running
- ☐ Be someone's mentor
- ☐ Have an industry mentor
- ☐ Invent something
- ☐ Be part of a startup founding team
- ☐ Obtain a patent
- ☐ Build a substantial business network and nurture it well
- ☐ Have a full-time internship at a big international company
- ☐ Be on a radio show and/or podcast
- ☐ Be an independent consultant on things you're good at
- ☐ Get (inter)national coverage for one of your startups
- ☐ Give the Commencement Speech at a major university
- ☐ Turn a hobby you love into a profitable business
- ☐ Do work that makes you say to yourself, "I would do this for free"
- ☐ Give a lecture at a university
- ☐ Have a job that travels
- ☐ Help others help the world
- ☐ Become a millionaire
- ☐ Become a multi-millionaire
- ☐ Give a Ted Talk
- ☐ Ask for a raise
- ☐ Be the Boss
- ☐ Set up a passive income machine
- ☐ Become 100% debt free
- ☐ Become a successful investor in the stock market
- ☐ Invest in real estate
- ☐ Have diversified income sources

- ☐ Pay back student loans
- ☐ Invest in several startups
- ☐ Teach a Class
- ☐ Design an app
- ☐ Buy property abroad
- ☐ Be a leader in your field
- ☐ Be a member of an exclusive club
- ☐ Earn six figures per year
- ☐ Find a career you love
- ☐ Flip a house
- ☐ Get paid to travel
- ☐ Have three months of bills in savings
- ☐ Have a housecleaner
- ☐ Have a positive net worth
- ☐ Have an IRA
- ☐ Have your own business cards
- ☐ Hire a personal shopper
- ☐ Have a Fico Credit Score over 800
- ☐ Make a piece of jewelry
- ☐ Make a will
- ☐ Own a successful business
- ☐ Own Tiffany Jewelry
- ☐ Sell something on the internet
- ☐ Set up an emergency fund
- ☐ Be asked for my autograph
- ☐ Be on the New York Times Bestsellers List
- ☐ Get a standing ovation
- ☐ Get Ordained
- ☐ Google search your name and have at least one page of stuff
- ☐ Be a guest speaker
- ☐ Win an award for making a difference
- ☐ Give a keynote speech
- ☐ Hold a motivational speech
- ☐ Do public speaking for an audience greater than 1,000
- ☐ Interview ten inspirational people
- ☐ Have a house or cabin by a lake
- ☐ Make some art and successfully sell it
- ☐ Be on a morning TV show as a guest
- ☐ Go to an auction at Christie's or Sotheby's

- ☐ Keep a $100 bill in your wallet and let it act as your "money magnet."
- ☐ Design your own t-shirt
- ☐ Enter art in an exhibit

SELF-CARE BUCKET LIST

- ☐ Go to a yoga retreat
- ☐ Spend the entire day alone
- ☐ Spend a week at a silent retreat
- ☐ Unplug for a week
- ☐ Send flowers to yourself
- ☐ Participate in a sweat lodge purification ceremony
- ☐ Get a colonic
- ☐ Meditate
- ☐ Get a facial
- ☐ Get laser hair removal
- ☐ Buy at least one designer handbag
- ☐ Get a massage
- ☐ Get a mani-pedi
- ☐ Go to a Korean spa
- ☐ Make a home spa day: bubble bath, candles, facial mask and wine
- ☐ Invest in a little black dress and sexy stilettos
- ☐ Get teeth whitened
- ☐ Get a spray tan
- ☐ Try an infrared sauna or heat wrap
- ☐ Dye your hair a daring color
- ☐ Learn to take a compliment
- ☐ Write down your personal mission statement
- ☐ Forgive your parents
- ☐ Overcome your fear of failure
- ☐ Conquer your biggest fear
- ☐ Reflect on your greatest weakness, and realize it's your greatest strength
- ☐ Attend a Tony Robbins event
- ☐ Attend a meditation course
- ☐ Don't drink alcohol for a year
- ☐ Keep a daily gratitude journal
- ☐ Acupuncture
- ☐ Achieve my ideal weight or be at peace with your body
- ☐ Take a bath in a natural hot spring
- ☐ Get a seaweed wrap
- ☐ Get a waxed
- ☐ Do a Cleanse

- ☐ Find my signature scent
- ☐ Get a fish pedicure
- ☐ Get a foot massage
- ☐ Go on a clothes shopping spree
- ☐ Have a professional photo shoot
- ☐ Have palm read
- ☐ Learn your best pose for photographs
- ☐ Own a pair of designer shoes
- ☐ Relax in a sensory deprivation tank
- ☐ Spend the day at a resort spa
- ☐ Take a mud bath
- ☐ Try brow threading
- ☐ Try cupping therapy
- ☐ Wear a wig for a day
- ☐ Wear colored contacts
- ☐ Go completely tech-free for a week
- ☐ Go on a spa retreat

PHILANTHROPIST
BUCKET LIST

- ☐ Put change into someone's expired Meter
- ☐ Give away a day salary 5 times in a week to a non-profit organization
- ☐ Pay for a random person's groceries
- ☐ Volunteer for a social organization in Asia or Africa (one that actually helps)
- ☐ Pay for the person behind me in a drive-thru
- ☐ Visit and help at a hospice
- ☐ Help out at a soup kitchen
- ☐ Order and pay for a pizza and send it to friends without them knowing and without taking credit for it
- ☐ Win a live charity auction (on something)
- ☐ Volunteer at Mother's Day Classic
- ☐ Put an anonymous blank envelope containing $100 into the mailbox of a family/person I know to be struggling
- ☐ Get in touch with old teachers/role models from the past and tell them just how much their positive influence meant to me
- ☐ Bring candy and stuff to do to hospitalized children (and entertain)
- ☐ Donate my old electronics to schools or nonprofit organizations that support lower-income families who need working equipment
- ☐ Put up post it notes like: "you are beautiful" etc. on public toilet mirrors
- ☐ When in full-time job, donate x% of my income monthly/annually to a charity
- ☐ Start micro-volunteering (e.g., http://helpfromhome.org/) or Sparked
- ☐ Leave encouraging notes in self-help books (or any other books) for others to find
- ☐ Anonymously grant a wish on someone's Amazon wishlist
- ☐ Cut coupons and leave them by the appropriate items in a grocery store for others to use
- ☐ Anonymously send someone flowers

- ☐ 20+ donations in a year
- ☐ Tell someone everything you love about them.
- ☐ Make a list of 101 things you love about your mom, dad, brother and girlfriend.
- ☐ Create a SocialVibe account and earn money for nonprofits by looking at ads (or something similar)
- ☐ Raise at least $10k for a charity
- ☐ Bring your old magazines to a hospital waiting room to make patients' waits a little less nerve racking.
- ☐ Join a bone marrow registry
- ☐ Continuously lend on Kiva (microloans)
- ☐ Make a list of the things you are grateful for or the things that you love
- ☐ Donate books to the library
- ☐ Forward junk mail to raise money for the "Lunch Box" or something similar
- ☐ Donate a laptop to a student who needs one
- ☐ Be a "genie" and grant three wishes for nonprofits. Many have "wish lists" of items they are currently looking for.
- ☐ Participate in Earth Hour
- ☐ Build a house with Habitat for Humanity
- ☐ Donate grains of rice
- ☐ Donate clothing
- ☐ Entertain the elderly at a nursing home
- ☐ Help an endangered animal
- ☐ Help someone with their bucket list
- ☐ Be a great and trustworthy babysitter for friends and family
- ☐ Sponsor a child's wish through the "Make-a-Wish Foundation"
- ☐ Teach English in a foreign country
- ☐ Plant a community garden
- ☐ Join a disaster relief effort
- ☐ Start a charity
- ☐ Include a charitable foundation in your will
- ☐ Help a homeless person get a fresh start
- ☐ Perform a random act of kindness every day, for a year
- ☐ Teach an elementary class
- ☐ Take kids to a shopping spree
- ☐ Host a couchsurfer
- ☐ Host a homeless
- ☐ Leave cookies on a stranger's doorstep

- ☐ Leave flowers on someone's doorstep
- ☐ Make a large anonymous donation to a non-profit
- ☐ Make a stranger's day
- ☐ Make someone laugh during their chemotherapy treatment
- ☐ Pay for someone else's flight ticket so they can come and visit
- ☐ Pay off a stranger's Christmas lay-away gifts for their children
- ☐ Perform a kind deed to at least 10 people with no expectations
- ☐ Sponsor a child
- ☐ Spoil my loved one for Valentine's Day
- ☐ Text a random mobile number and wish them a good day
- ☐ Send mom a dozen roses for no reason
- ☐ Send your parents on vacation
- ☐ Carve your family's names into a tree
- ☐ Carve your love and your name into a tree
- ☐ Do a cute scavenger hunt for the one you love
- ☐ Give "free hugs" in a public place
- ☐ Send a care package to a soldier
- ☐ Volunteer at an orphanage
- ☐ Foster a puppy
- ☐ Do a charity walk
- ☐ Donate toys at the holidays
- ☐ Do 100 hours of volunteer work
- ☐ Plant a tree

THE LITTLE THINGS
BUCKET LIST

- ☐ Gamble in a casino
- ☐ Go to a drive-in movie theater
- ☐ Get hypnotized
- ☐ Jump in a pool/ocean fully-clothed
- ☐ Take a picture every day for a year
- ☐ Meet someone famous
- ☐ Attend a murder mystery dinner
- ☐ Attend a masquerade ball
- ☐ Watch the sunrise
- ☐ Ride a bike where there are breathtaking views
- ☐ Go on a Ferris wheel and take an epic selfie at the very top
- ☐ Tell the bartender, "Surprise me"
- ☐ Watch the best rated movie from the year you were born, and then the worst
- ☐ Go out without underwear
- ☐ Sing the absolute loudest you can in the shower
- ☐ Try to get on a game show and or be a game show contestant
- ☐ Find any free concert. Don't look at what music is playing, just go
- ☐ Watch the sunrise and sunset in the same day
- ☐ Be an extra in a movie or TV show
- ☐ Send a message in a bottle
- ☐ Bury a time capsule for someone to find years to come
- ☐ Go on a submarine ride
- ☐ Take part in an audience for a TV show
- ☐ Completely finish the New York Times Crossword Puzzle
- ☐ Read a book a week for a year
- ☐ Solve a Rubik's Cube
- ☐ Decide something extremely important by a coin flip
- ☐ Say yes to everything for a day
- ☐ Have a drone
- ☐ Have a 3D printer
- ☐ Finish a 1000+ jigsaw puzzle

- ☐ Complete a 3D jigsaw puzzled
- ☐ Have your tarot cards read
- ☐ Watch a meteor shower
- ☐ Walk on a glass ceiling
- ☐ Experience midnight sun
- ☐ Lay in a field of flowers
- ☐ Take a romantic photoshoot
- ☐ Place a self-made painting in the house
- ☐ Create a homemade board game
- ☐ Make a Droste effect photo

CRAZY TOWN BUCKET LIST

☐ Give someone a tattoo
☐ Do an epic wake-up prank, film it and upload it
☐ Cover a car in post-it notes
☐ Be in a flash mob
☐ Ask a street musician to play your favorite song and dance with a stranger
☐ Get dressed in something you'd never wear and go out. Let your crazy clothes give you a new identity for the night.
☐ Introduce yourself to people at a bar with an alias name and an alias life
☐ Tell the barista at Starbucks your name is Beyoncé
☐ Try often to fake a (funny) name at Starbucks
☐ Buy a custom cake that says something embarrassing. Some suggestions: "Sorry, You're Pregnant." Or "I Had Sex with Your Brother."
☐ Wear a costume to a non-costume party, Elle Woods-style.
☐ Grab some friends and do an ultimate dare night
☐ Make a complete and utter fool of yourself
☐ Stay out all night dancing, go to work and never have gone home
☐ Put your name down to be a passenger of the first tourist shuttle to the moon
☐ Answer a personal ad
☐ Make one huge bet in roulette
☐ Dress up as Mario Cart characters and go go-karting
☐ Perform a ridiculously romantic stunt
☐ Pillow fight flash-mob
☐ Destroy a guitar
☐ Go to a movie dressed as something that has nothing to do with the movie (i.e. Lord of the Rings dressed as a M&M.)
☐ Phrases to Say
    ☐ In a taxi: "Follow that car"
    ☐ In a bar: "A martini, shaken not stirred."
    ☐ In a restaurant: "I'll have what she's having."
    ☐ On a boat: "I'm king of the world."
☐ Win and yell Bingo (or yell Bingo without having it)
☐ Start a slow clap at a major event
☐ Duct tape someone to a wall

- ☐ Fill a room full of balloons
- ☐ Mail a secret to PostSecret
- ☐ Walk up to a small child that resembles you and tell them that you are them from the future
- ☐ Bet at dog races
- ☐ Bet on horse races

WRITE WHATEVER YOUR LITTLE HEART DESIRES

- ☐ Write a physical thank you letter to a company that treated you well
- ☐ Write a letter to your future self and open it after 10 years
- ☐ Write a haiku
- ☐ Write a novel in one month
- ☐ Write a song
- ☐ Write a love note with lipstick on the bathroom mirror
- ☐ Write a letter in calligraphy
- ☐ Write a cookbook
- ☐ Write a book and publish it
- ☐ Write a children's book
- ☐ Write down your family's history
- ☐ Write a self-help book
- ☐ Write an e-book
- ☐ Write your memoir
- ☐ Write and launch an email series
- ☐ Write a will
- ☐ Write your name in wet cement
- ☐ Write a love letter
- ☐ Write a poem
- ☐ Have a blog about something your passionate about
- ☐ Have a blog that makes a difference to someone's lives.
- ☐ Get your blog publicized in various magazines/websites
- ☐ Build a blog with 1,000+ subscribers
- ☐ Write and compose an album
- ☐ Publish an article in a newspaper or magazine
- ☐ Publish a paper in a journal
- ☐ Add something useful to Wikipedia

BOARD GAMES GALORE

- ☐ Dominos
- ☐ Twister
- ☐ Backgammon
- ☐ Battleship
- ☐ Checkers
- ☐ Chess
- ☐ Connect Four
- ☐ Guess Who?
- ☐ Monopoly
- ☐ Scrabble
- ☐ Clue
- ☐ Doom
- ☐ Jenga
- ☐ Risk
- ☐ Taboo
- ☐ Cards Against Humanity
- ☐ Uno
- ☐ Trouble
- ☐ Balderdash
- ☐ Candy Land
- ☐ Chinese Checkers
- ☐ Dungeons & Dragons
- ☐ Life
- ☐ Girl Talk
- ☐ Labyrinth
- ☐ Ouija
- ☐ Pictionary
- ☐ Scattergories
- ☐ Scene It?
- ☐ Sequence
- ☐ Chutes and Ladders
- ☐ Time's Up!
- ☐ Trivial Pursuit
- ☐ Upwords
- ☐ Yahtzee
- ☐ Mouse Trap

- ☐ Boggle
- ☐ Mad Gab
- ☐ Apples to Apples
- ☐ Megachess

CARD GAMES GALORE

- ☐ Rummy
- ☐ Hearts
- ☐ Patience
- ☐ Bridge
- ☐ Baccarat
- ☐ Around the World
- ☐ Crazy Eights
- ☐ Five-Card Draw
- ☐ Skip-Bo
- ☐ Gin Rummy
- ☐ Spades
- ☐ War
- ☐ 500
- ☐ Skat
- ☐ Texas Hold 'em
- ☐ Deuces Wild
- ☐ Blackjack
- ☐ Poker
- ☐ Mississippi Stud
- ☐ 500 rummy
- ☐ Cribbage
- ☐ 400
- ☐ Casino War
- ☐ Klondike
- ☐ Durak
- ☐ Shithead
- ☐ Sixty-Two
- ☐ Solitaire
- ☐ Spider Solitaire
- ☐ Oh Hell
- ☐ Freecell
- ☐ Go Fish
- ☐ Jabberwocky
- ☐ Magic the Gathering
- ☐ Nines
- ☐ Old Maid
- ☐ Ombre
- ☐ Pyramid
- ☐ Pyramid Solitaire
- ☐ Speed
- ☐ Spoons
- ☐ Tarot
- ☐ Vegas Rummy